Journal

of

Soviet and Post-Soviet Politics and Society

Vol. 10, No. 1 (2024)

Special Section

Teaching IR in Wartime

JSPPS 10:1 (2024)

GENERAL EDITOR AND ISSUE EDITOR-IN-CHIEF:

Julie Fedor, University of Melbourne

GUEST EDITORS:

Kateryna Zarembo, New Europe Center (Ukraine)
Michèle Knodt, Jean Monnet Centre of Excellence "EU in Global Dialogue"
Maksym Yakovlyev, National University of Kyiv-Mohyla Academy

JSPPS Editorial Team

Julie Fedor, *University of Melbourne* (General Editor)
Andreas Umland, *National University of Kyiv-Mohyla Academy* (Consulting Editor)

JSPPS Advisory Board

Timofey Agarin, Queen's University, Belfast
Mikhail Alexseev, San Diego State University, CA
Catherine Andreyev, University of Oxford
Anne Applebaum, The Legatum Institute, London
Anders Åslund, Peterson Inst. for International Economics
Margarita Balmaceda, Seton Hall University, NJ
Harley Balzer, Georgetown University, DC
Timm Beichelt, European University Viadrina, Frankfurt (Oder)
Mark R. Beissinger, Princeton University, NJ
Thomas Bohn, Justus Liebig University, Giessen
Giovanna Brogi, University of Milan
Paul Chaisty, University of Oxford
Vitaly Chernetsky, University of Kansas, Lawrence
Ariel Cohen, Institute for the Analysis of Global Security, MD
Timothy J. Colton, Harvard University, MA
Peter J.S. Duncan, University College London
John B. Dunlop, Stanford University, CA
Gerald M. Easter, Boston College, MA
Mark Edele, University of Melbourne
Alexander Etkind, Central European University
M. Steven Fish, University of California at Berkeley
Gasan Gusejnov, Freie Universität Berlin
Nikolas K. Gvosdev, U.S. Naval War College, RI
Michael Hagemeister, Ruhr University, Bochum
Stephen E. Hanson, College of William & Mary, VA
Olexiy Haran, Kyiv-Mohyla Academy
Nicolas Hayoz, University of Fribourg
Andreas Heinemann-Grüder, University of Bonn
Stephen Hutchings, University of Manchester, UK
Stefani Hoffman, The Hebrew University of Jerusalem
Wilfried Jilge, University of Basel
Markku Kangaspuro, University of Helsinki
Adrian Karatnycky, Atlantic Council, New York
Andrei Kazantsev-Vaisman, Bar-Ilan University, Ramat Gan
Jeffrey Kopstein, University of Toronto
Hrant Kostanyan, Centre for European Policy Studies

Paul Kubicek, Oakland University, MI
Walter Laqueur, Georgetown University, DC
Marlene Laruelle, George Washington University, DC
Carol Leonard, University of Oxford
Leonid Luks, The Catholic University of Eichstaett-Ingolstadt
Luke March, University of Edinburgh
Mykhailo Minakov, Kyiv-Mohyla Academy
Olga Onuch, University of Manchester
Mitchell Orenstein, Northeastern University, MA
Nikolay Petrov, Stiftung Wissenschaft und Politik
Andriy Portnov, European University Viadrina
Serhii Plokhii, Harvard University, MA
Alina Polyakova, Atlantic Council, DC
Maria Popova, McGill University, Montreal
Alex Pravda, University of Oxford
Mykola Riabchuk, Ukrainian Academy of Sciences, Kyiv
Felix Riefer, Lew Kopelew Forum at Cologne (Book Reviews Editor)
Per Anders Rudling, Lund University
Ellen Rutten, University of Amsterdam
Jutta Scherrer, École des Hautes Études en Sciences Sociales
Dieter Segert, University of Vienna
Anton Shekhovtsov, The Legatum Institute, London
Oxana Shevel, Tufts University, MA
Stephen Shulman, Southern Illinois University, Carbondale
Valerie Sperling, Clark University, MA
Susan Stewart, SWP, Berlin
Lisa M. Sundstrom, University of British Columbia
Mark Tauger, West Virginia University, Morgantown
Vera Tolz-Zilitinkevic, University of Manchester
Amir Weiner, Stanford University
Sarah Whitmore, Oxford Brookes University, UK
Andrew Wilson, University College London
Christian Wipperfürth, DGAP, Berlin
Andreas Wittkowsky, ZIF, Berlin
Jan Zielonka, University of Oxford

Bibliographic information published by the Deutsche Nationalbibliothek
The Deutsche Nationalbibliothek lists this publication in the Deutsche Nationalbibliografie; detailed bibliographic data are available on the Internet at http://dnb.dnb.de.

Bibliografische Information der Deutschen Nationalbibliothek
Die Deutsche Nationalbibliothek verzeichnet diese Publikation in der Deutschen Nationalbibliografie; detaillierte bibliografische Daten sind im Internet über http://dnb.d-nb.de abrufbar.

Cover picture: Kharkivoda.gov.ua, via Wikimedia Commons, licensed under CC BY 4.0, https://creativecommons.org/licenses/by/4.0,

Journal of Soviet and Post-Soviet Politics and Society
Vol. 10, No. 1 (2024)

Stuttgart: *ibidem*-Verlag / *ibidem* Press

Erscheinungsweise: halbjährlich / Frequency: biannual

ISSN 2364-5334

Ordering Information:
PRINT: Subscription (two copies per year): € 58.00 / year (+ S&H: € 6.00 / year within Germany, € 10.00 / year international). The subscription can be canceled at any time.

Single copy or back issue: € 34.00 / copy (+ S&H: € 3.00 within Germany, € 4.50 international).

E-BOOK: Individual copy or back issue: € 19.99 / copy. Available via amazon.com or google.books.

For further information please visit www.jspps.eu

ISBN (Print) 978-3-8382-1693-5
ISBN (E-Book [PDF]) 978-3-8382-7693-9
© *ibidem*-Verlag / *ibidem* Press
Hannover • Stuttgart, Germany 2025

Leuschnerstraße 40
30457 Hannover
info@ibidem.eu

Alle Rechte vorbehalten

Das Werk einschließlich aller seiner Teile ist urheberrechtlich geschützt. Jede Verwertung außerhalb der engen Grenzen des Urheberrechtsgesetzes ist ohne Zustimmung des Verlages unzulässig und strafbar. Dies gilt insbesondere für Vervielfältigungen, Übersetzungen, Mikroverfilmungen und elektronische Speicherformen sowie die Einspeicherung und Verarbeitung in elektronischen Systemen.

All rights reserved

No part of this publication may be reproduced, stored in or introduced into a retrieval system, or transmitted, in any form, or by any means (electronic, mechanical, photocopying, recording or otherwise) without the prior written permission of the publisher.
Any person who commits any unauthorized act in relation to this publication may be liable to criminal prosecution and civil claims for damages.

Contents

SPECIAL SECTION: TEACHING IR IN WARTIME

GUEST EDITORS:
KATERYNA ZAREMBO, MICHÈLE KNODT and MAKSYM YAKOVLYEV

Teaching the Russian War against Ukraine: Ukraine as a Microcosm of the Paradigm Shift from International Relations to Planetary Politics
IAN MANNERS 1

Will the Russian War against Ukraine Bring Changes to the Teaching of International Relations?
OLENA KHYLKO 33

Teaching International Political Economy in Times of War
THOMAS FETZER 65

From Shock to Adaptation through National Unity and Action: Third-year Undergraduate Students of Kyiv-Mohyla Academy Reflect on the First Eighty Days of Russia's War against Ukraine
GALYNA SOLOVEI 83

ARTICLES

Narratives about Baikonur: City and Cosmodrome
KULSHAT MEDEUOVA and ULBOLSYN SANDYBAYEVA 107

From Decentralization to Warfare Resistance: Building a Cohesive Ukraine
OLEKSANDRA DEINEKO and AADNE AASLAND 141

Epic Indigenization: Literature and Nation on the Soviet-Finnish Borders under Stalinism
DIEGO BENNING WANG 173

ABOUT THE GUEST EDITORS 207

ABOUT THE CONTRIBUTORS... 209

Teaching the Russian War Against Ukraine: Ukraine as a Microcosm of the Paradigm Shift from International Relations to Planetary Politics[1]

Ian Manners

Abstract: *The impact of the Russian war against Ukraine should have far-reaching repercussions on the teaching of International Relations (IR) and European Union (EU) studies. In this article, it is argued that Ukrainian resistance to the invasion must be part of an important shift in thinking about IR and the EU within holistic planetary politics. First, the terminologies and technologies of teaching IR and EU studies, Ukraine and Russia, EU enlargement and the "post-Soviet space" after the end of the Cold War are introduced. Second, the conventional teaching of IR and EU studies in Western Europe, 1991–2022 is analyzed by looking at what was included and excluded in the study of these disciplines. Third, the transformation of teaching IR and EU studies after the invasion and counter-offensive of 2022–2024 is examined by focusing on the rapid process of re-education and rethinking of teaching on Ukraine and Russia in IR and EU studies courses. Finally, it is concluded that a paradigm shift to teaching planetary politics is necessitated by the Russian war against Ukraine and other 21st century crises.*

The 30-year period of Ukrainian independence after the collapse of the Soviet Union had not featured much, if at all, in the teaching of International Relations (IR) in western European universities.

---

[1] I am very grateful to Kateryna Zarembo, Michèle Knodt, Maksym Yakovlyev, Thomas Fetzer, Mridula Ghosh, Olena Khylko, Galyna Solovei, Nina Krickel-Choi, Simon Stattin, Ted Svensson, and Anders Uhlin for their thoughtful reflections and critical comments.

The 2013–2014 Maidan Revolution and 2014 Russian Annexation of Crimea and the Donbas featured as interesting events in IR, while the 2016 EU–Ukraine Free Trade Area and 2017 Association Agreement were also interesting to European Union (EU) studies. But neither Ukraine nor these events were widely taught in western European IR or EU studies prior to the Russian invasion on the 24 February 2022. This article analyzes the impact of the Russian war against Ukraine on the teaching of IR and EU studies in Europe. It argues that Ukrainian resistance to the invasion is part of an important shift in thinking about IR and the EU in empirical and theoretical terms, as well as accelerating a changed pedagogic paradigm to teaching IR and EU studies within holistic planetary politics.

The article does this in five steps by drawing on personal experiences of teaching, research publications, and textbooks from the period 1991–2024. First, the article introduces the terminologies and technologies of teaching IR and EU studies, Ukraine and Russia, EU enlargement and the "post-Soviet space" after the end of the Cold War. Second, the article analyzes the conventional teaching of IR and EU studies in Western Europe, 1991–2022, by looking at what was included and excluded in the study of these disciplines. Third, the article examines the transformation of teaching IR and EU studies after the invasion and counter-offensive of 2022–2024 focusing on the rapid process of re-education and rethinking of teaching on Ukraine and Russia in IR and EU studies courses. Fourth, the article concludes by thinking ahead to the necessary paradigm shift to teaching planetary politics that the Russian war against Ukraine and other 21st century crises demand. This paradigm shift centers the planet as a whole and decenters western and Eurocentric IR and EU studies, ensuring that peripheralized, marginalized, or colonized subjects such as postcolonial Africa, Asia, or post-Soviet Eastern Europe, as well as ecology, stateless peoples, and planetary justice, are properly part of constituting 21st century planetary politics. Thus, the article argues the need to understand Ukraine as a microcosm of symbiotic planetary politics, an example of the wider planetary organic crisis of five symbiotic dimensions of economy, society, ecology, conflict, and polity.

The personal experiences of teaching, research publication, and textbooks come from teaching IR and EU studies at the University of Bristol, Swansea University, University of Kent, Brussels School of International Studies, Malmö University, Roskilde University, University of Copenhagen, and Lund University from 1991 to 2024. During this period, I have taught IR and EU studies at both undergraduate and postgraduate levels almost every year for three decades and have seen trends and fashions come and go. But during this period these two disciplines have become more confident about teaching disciplinary history and theory as the core, much to the expense of peripheral, marginal, or colonized subjects such as Ukraine. This article addresses this problem by asking questions about the new teaching challenges driven by the Russian invasion of Ukraine.

1. Introduction: Teaching the Russian War Against Ukraine

> Americans and Europeans were guided through the new century by a tale about "the end of history," by what I will call the *politics of inevitability*, a sense that the future is just more of the present, that the laws of progress are known, that there are not alternatives, and therefore nothing really to be done.... Americans and Europeans kept telling themselves their tales of inevitability for a quarter of a century after the end of communism, and so raised a millennial generation without history.... The fates of Russia, Ukraine, and Belarus after 1991 showed well enough that the fall of one system did not create a blank slate on which nature generated markets and markets generated rights (Snyder 2018: 7).

The terminologies and technologies of teaching IR and EU studies in western European universities evolved rapidly with the end of the Cold War and the birth of the "New Europe" following Timothy Snyder's "politics of inevitability." Narrating the interim period 1991–2022 in terms of teaching IR is impossible; every teaching experience was and is so different, Europe west and Europe east, global north and global south. But there are two features which

Timothy Snyder, one of the leading scholars of international relations in and between Russia, Europe, and America, uses to describe this period: the *politics of inevitability* and the *politics of eternity*. The *politics of inevitability* since the 1980s is the assumption that There-Is-No-Alternative to neoliberalism, defined as the privatization of public life, including the deregulation and privatization of nationalized industries, financial services, welfare state, and government (Manners 2018: 1225). While these neoliberal assumptions survived the Global Financial Crisis (GFC) of 2007–2008 and the Eurozone Sovereign Debt crisis of 2009–2012, the COVID-19 pandemic and the return of the *politics of eternity* challenge hyper-globalization. In contrast, the *politics of eternity* "places one nation at the center of a cyclical story of victimhood" where "eternity politicians manufacture crisis and manipulate the resultant emotion" (Snyder 2018: 8). The past 18 years of democratic decline since 2005 have seen the rise of the *politics of eternity* and eternity politicians across the world (Freedom House 2024).

Using personal reflections on teaching based on syllabi and textbooks provides one route to the experiences of teaching IR and EU studies prior to and after the Russian invasion of Ukraine. Having taught courses in IR and EU studies in seven different departments across at least three different countries brings some comparative experience and overview of teaching. These personal reflections will be strengthened by using and developing Felix Berenskötter's (2018) review of "How textbooks cover theories" to assess to what extent and how transatlantic IR textbooks cover theories and issues in contemporary IR. A second route to understanding the changes of teaching IR in wartime is to examine the intellectual context in which teaching takes place through a series of longitudinal research publication trends generated using Clarivate Web of Science Social Science Citation Index (SSCI). While SSCI generates a number of analytical problems, it does help provide an overview of the incidence of certain research terms in IR during 1990-2023.[2] In the next section 2 the research terms include

---

2   The SSCI produces path-dependent citation patterns emphasizing US-institutional bias.

"Ukraine," "Crimea," "Donbas(s)" and "environmental," "climate change," and "green". In section 3 the research terms include "geopolitics," "multipolar," and "neoimperial/neocolonial." In the concluding section 4 the research terms include "ecology," "climate crisis/emergency," and "planetary politics." These analyses show how the core of IR and EU studies focuses on certain subjects, such as geopolitics, in contrast to the peripheralized margins of Ukraine and the climate crisis. Where possible these terms will also be used to examine the textbooks.

The article then provides both a personal experience of an international university professor during the Russian war against Ukraine, but also tries to narrate the terminologies and technologies of teaching IR and EU studies. The analysis of syllabi and textbooks illustrates the changing technologies of teaching IR and EU studies. The analysis of both (pre-)wartime terms and planetary political terms illustrates the changing terminologies of teaching IR and EU studies. The combination of these analyses leads to the argument that Ukrainian resistance to the Russian invasion is part of an important shift in thinking about IR and the EU in empirical and theoretical terms accelerating the need for a change in pedagogic paradigm to teaching IR and EU studies.

2. International Relations of the 20th Century

The General Assembly,
Reaffirming the paramount importance of the Charter of the United Nations in
the promotion of the rule of law among nations,
1. *Affirms* its commitment to the sovereignty, political independence, unity
and territorial integrity of Ukraine within its internationally recognized borders;
2. *Calls upon* all States to desist and refrain from actions aimed at the
partial or total disruption of the national unity and territorial integrity of Ukraine,
including any attempts to modify Ukraine's borders through the threat or use of
force or other unlawful means;
(UN General Assembly Resolution 68/262 2014)

In general, the teaching of IR over the past 100 years has focused on the conservative state-centric concerns of the 20th century, placing the League of Nations and the United Nations (UN) at the center of study. The February to March 2014 Russian occupation and annexation of Ukrainian Crimea and Donbas led to the 7 March 2014 UN GA resolution 68/262 on the "Territorial integrity of Ukraine" (above). One hundred members voted to defend the principles of the UN charter and international peace. Ninety-three members declined to defend the UN and international peace. While the failure of so many members to defend UN principles was not unique, this vote and subsequent UN GA votes in 2022 marked the end of 20th century IR.

Early post-Cold War courses and textbooks were marked by a simultaneous loosening of the intellectual straitjacket and the desire to repack the period into existing intellectual frames. The earliest IR textbooks to capture the post-Cold War shift in thinking included Burchill and Linklater (1996), Brown (1997), and Baylis and Smith (1997), while the earliest EU textbooks included Nugent (1994), Wallace and Wallace (1996), McCormick (1999), and Bretherton and Vogler (1999). None of these textbooks considered Ukraine to any extent, except as a brief historical footnote in the dissolution of the Soviet Union. Instead, IR and EU courses mixed together the "classical" story of IR state-centrism with the "new" story of IR borderless-liberalism. The neo-liberal aspects of IR such as globalization and corporatization focused on the "globalization of world politics" (Baylis, Smith, and Owens 2022) and "supraterritoriality" (Scholte 2000) which left Ukraine and its sovereignty, democracy, and politics to the markets of the *politics of inevitability*. The neo-statist aspects of IR such as nationalism and egoism focused on "how states think" (Mearsheimer and Rosato 2023) and "rationality in foreign policy" (Stein 2016) which left Ukraine and its sovereignty, security, and politics to the power games of the *politics of eternity*.

During 2000–2004 I taught a master's course on "European Union Enlargement" which included topics on Belarus, Moldova, Ukraine, and on Armenia, Azerbaijan, and Georgia (Manners 1999, 2010). But in general during this period there were a number of aspects of Ukraine that we did not teach, such as the 1000-year old origins of European Kyivan Rus or Ukraine as a founding member of the UN in 1945, and there were a number that we mistaught, such as the acquiescence of Ukraine in the Soviet Union and the idea of post-Cold War Eastern Europe as a "post-Soviet space." As Charts 1 and 2 (below) demonstrate, IR research on Ukraine, Crimea, and Donbas broadly reflected this absence of teaching and textbook consideration during the period 1990–2014, but also the belated inclusion of these topics since the Russian occupation and invasion of Ukraine.

Chart 1. SSCI references to "International Relations," "Ukraine", "Crimea", and "Donbas(s)," 1990-2023, expressed absolutely.

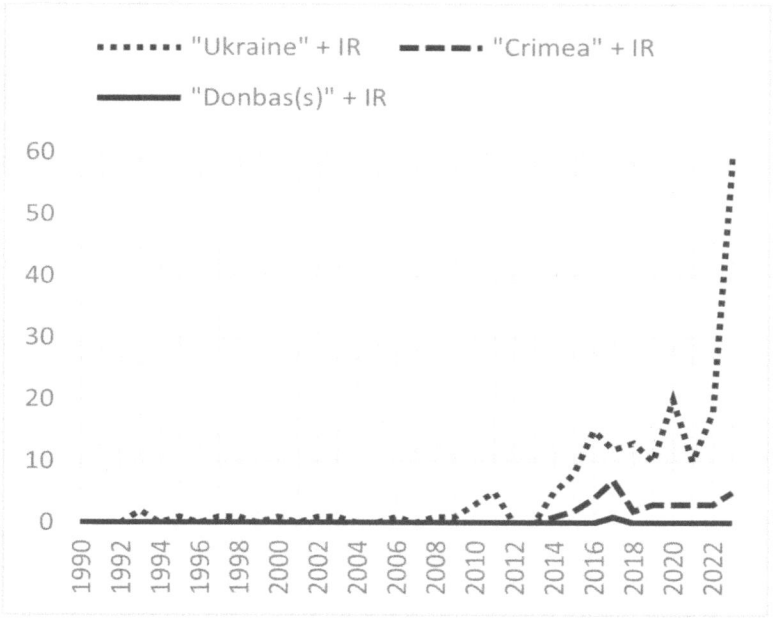

Chart 2. SSCI references to "International Relations", "Ukraine," "Crimea," and "Donbas(s)," 1990–2023, expressed in percentages.

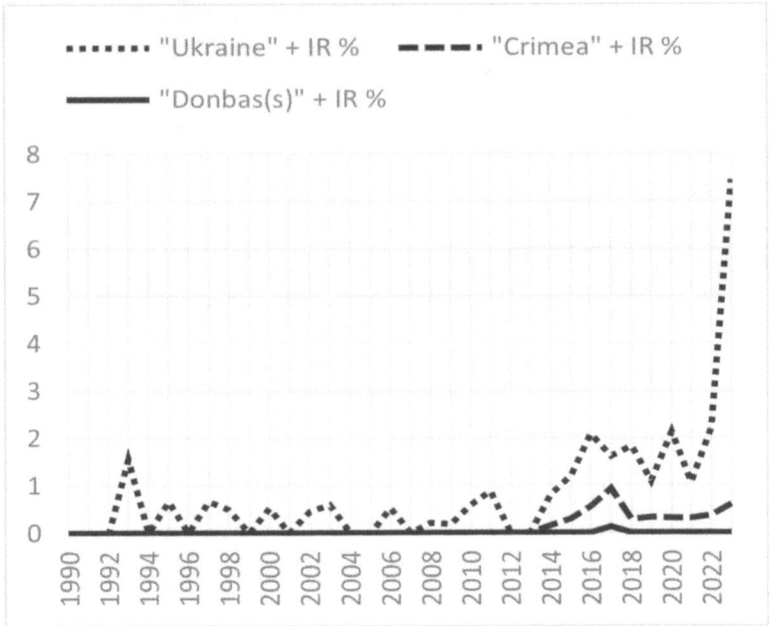

Chart 1 shows the comparative incidence of the phrases "International Relations" plus "Ukraine," "Crimea," and "Donbas(s)" from 1990 to 2023 in the SSCI. A few references to Ukraine occurred during the 1990s and have increased steadily since the 2014 Russian occupation of Crimea and Donbas. Articles referring to Crimea increased after 2014, but Donbas references are effectively zero. Chart 2 shows the comparative incidence of the phrases "International Relations" plus "Ukraine," "Crimea," and "Donbas(s)" as a percentage of the incidence of the phrase "International Relations," 1990 to 2023, in the SSCI. This chart makes it possible to see whether references to Ukraine, Crimea, and Donbas are more or less common as a proportion of published articles over time. The chart shows that there was an interest in research articles between 1991 Ukrainian independence, 2004–2005 Orange Revolution, and 2013–2014 Maidan Revolution under 1% of overall IR articles. The 2014 Russian occupation and the 2022 Russian invasion led to a growth to over 7% of IR articles in 2023. Articles referring to "Crimea" peaked in 2017 (1% of IR articles) and "Donbas(s)" peaked in 2020 following the Russian occupation of these Ukrainian regions.

Overall, the IR research community had very little interest in Ukraine, Crimea, and Donbas in the 25 years from 1990 to 2014. But Ukraine is hardly unique in this respect. To think more holistically about blind spots in IR teaching and research, the article will compare Ukraine with the broad issue of environmental climate change. Russia's status as both a "petrostate" and one of the world's worst fossil fuel polluters enables it to invade Ukraine and use "ecocide" as a weapon, hence the comparison facilitates the discussion of planetary politics. Similar to charts 1 and 2, charts 3 and 4 (below) compare the absolute and relative references to environmental, climate change, and green in IR research.

Charts 3 and 4. SSCI references to "International Relations," "Green,"[3] "Environmental," and "Climate Change," 1990-2023, expressed absolutely and in percentages.

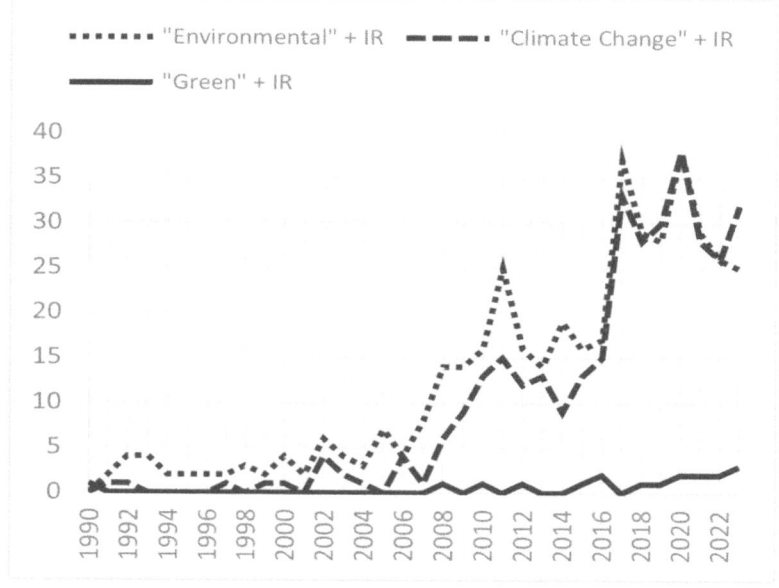

---

3   "Green" = ("greening" OR "green economy" OR "green theory" OR "green growth" OR "green politics" OR "green world").

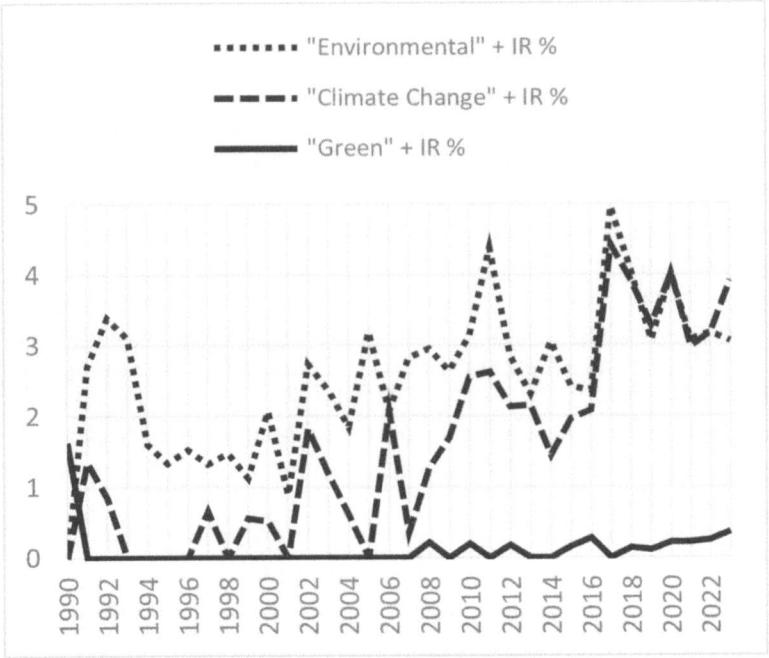

Chart 3 (top) shows the relative occurrence of the phrases "International Relations" plus "Environmental," "Climate Change," and "Green" in SSCI articles from 1990 to 2023. Articles on "environmental" IR increased steadily from 1991 to 2011, surged in 2017 and 2020, before declining in 2023. Articles on "Climate Change" and IR grew slowly between 2007 and 2017 articles, surged in 2020, before declining in 2022. Articles on "Green" IR emerge slowly over the past decade but are not significant. The average of 25–40 environmental and climate change articles per year during 2017–2023 is about half the 60 articles on Ukraine and IR in 2023.

Chart 4 (bottom) shows the relative occurrence of the phrases "International Relations" plus "Environmental," "Climate Change," and "Green" as a percentage of the incidence of the phrase "International Relations" in the SSCI 1990 to 2023. Articles on "environmental" IR were erratically higher in 1992, 2011, and 2017. In contrast, articles on "climate change" increased above 3% after the 2015 Paris Agreement. In general, there was almost zero percentage interest in "green" IR during the period. Whereas IR interest in Ukraine rose to nearly 8% of SSCI articles published in 2023, IR interest in environmental and climate change remain at about 3–4% of published IR articles. In other words, insignificant.

In contrast to the lack of IR interest in Ukraine, textbooks and courses since the late 1990s have generally had one chapter or one lecture on environmental politics. For example, Matthew Paterson's chapters on "green politics" in Burchill and Linklater (1996) and Devatak and True (2022), Robyn Eckersley's (latterly with Olaf Corry) chapter on "green theory" in Dunne, Kurki, Kušić, and Smith (2024), John Vogler's chapter on "environmental issues" in Baylis, Smith, and Owens (2022), or Cynthia Weber's (2021) chapter on "Environmentalism." Uniquely amongst IR textbooks, Simon Dalby's chapter on "nature" and Carl Death's chapter on the "planet" represent two chapters in Edkins and Zehfuss (2018). However, in my experience no widely-used textbook or widely-taught course has ever taken the ecological and climate emergencies seriously by starting a textbook with a framing chapter on the centrality of the environment or ecology as part of a holistic analysis of planetary politics. In this way, the lack of concern for teaching Ukrainian and planetary politics in IR are interwoven—Ukraine can be considered a microcosm in the paradigmatic shift from IR to planetary politics. Just as the peripheralized, marginalized, and colonized subject of Ukraine has not been adequately taught in the IR and EU studies of western European universities, neither has ecological unsustainability. Clearly other subjects such as the postcolonial world or the non-human world could, and should, be part of genuinely planetary politics.

3. Geopolitics of the 19th Century

> The sides underline that Russia and China, as world powers and permanent members of the United Nations Security Council, intend to firmly adhere to moral principles and accept their responsibility, strongly advocate the international system with the central coordinating role of the United Nations in international affairs, defend the world order based on international law, including the purposes and principles of the Charter of the United Nations, advance multipolarity and promote the democratization of international relations, together create an even more prospering,

stable, and just world, jointly build international relations of a new type (Putin and Xi 2022).

The transformation of teaching, including the elevation of "geopolitics," during the Russian invasion and Ukrainian counter-offensive, 2022–2024, has focused on the rapid process of re-education and rethinking of teaching on Ukraine and Russia in IR and EU studies courses. The joint Russia–China Joint Statement on International Relations of 4 February 2022 claimed that the two countries intended to firmly adhere to the moral principles, central coordinating role, and international law of the UN. However, the illegal Russian annexation and human rights abuses in Crimea and parts of Eastern Ukraine since 2014, and Chinese human rights abuses against Uyghurs and other minorities in Xinjiang since 2014, demonstrate the failure to adhere to the moral principles and international law of the UN and the Universal Declaration of Human Rights. Just 20 days later the Russian invasion of Ukraine and the support of China ridiculed Putin and Xi's joint declaration. During 5 votes in the UN General Assembly on 2 March 2022, 24 March 2022, 7 April 2022, 12 October 2022, and 23 February 2023 Russia consistently disregarded and broke the purposes and principles of the Charter of the UN, supported by 4 other autocracies (Belarus, Eritrea, North Korea, and Syria). China led a group of 30+ other, largely autocratic countries, to abstain from supporting the UN and Ukraine during these votes. In contrast, the purposes and principles of the UN and Ukraine were upheld by the support of 140+ largely democratic countries during these votes. Thus, while the failure of so many members to defend the principles of the UN and the territorial integrity of Ukraine marked the end of 20th Century IR in 2014, the events of 2022 indicated that many countries were intent on returning to the geopolitics of the 19th century, prior to the establishment of the UN.

During 2021 to 2023 I taught and convened the required first-semester undergraduate/bachelor's course in "International Politics" for approximately 150 Swedish students at Lund University. The course uses the 20th century conventions of introducing theories and issues, and is taught with a combination of a simple Swedish textbook (Gustavson and Tallberg 2021) and a more advanced English textbook (Baylis, Smith, and Owens 2022). After the February 2022 invasion we were able to adapt the course by adding a new secondary book, Mark Galeotti (2022) *Putin's Wars: From Chechnya to Ukraine* to the book review section of the course, as well as introducing the war into the parts of the course on international conflict and international cooperation. These adaptations are clearly similar to so many IR courses and textbooks across western Europe—existing paradigms and purveyors of IR knowledge remain hegemonic despite the radical transformations of 21st century IR.

Charts 5 and 6. SSCI references to "International Relations", "Geopolitics,"[4] "Multipolar,"[5] and "Neoimperial/Neocolonial,"[6] 1990-2023, expressed absolutely and in percentages.

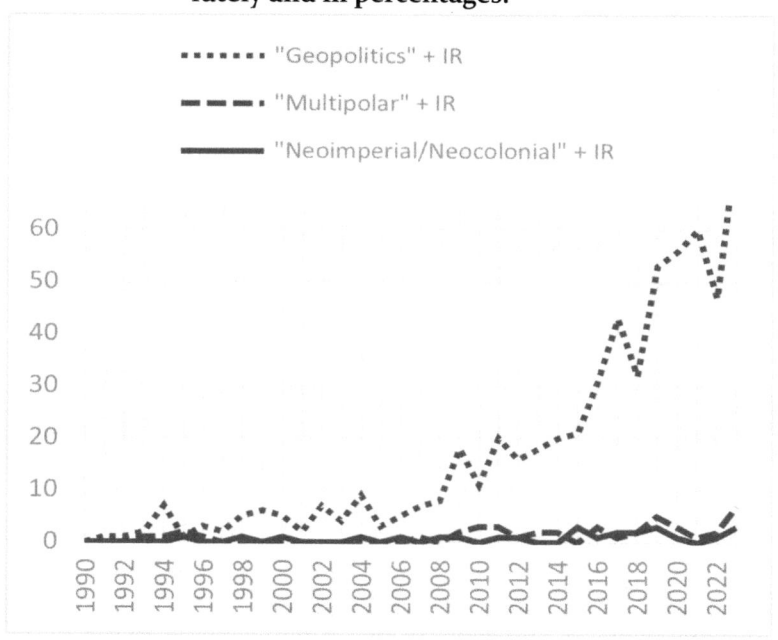

---

4   "Geopolitics" = ("geopolitics" OR "geopolitical").
5   "Multipolar" = ("multipolar" OR "multi-polar").
6   "Neo-imperial" = ("neo-imperial" OR "neoimperial" OR "neo-imperialism" OR "neoimperialism").
    "Neo-colonial" = ("neo-colonial" OR "neocolonial" OR "neo-colonialism" OR "neocolonialism").

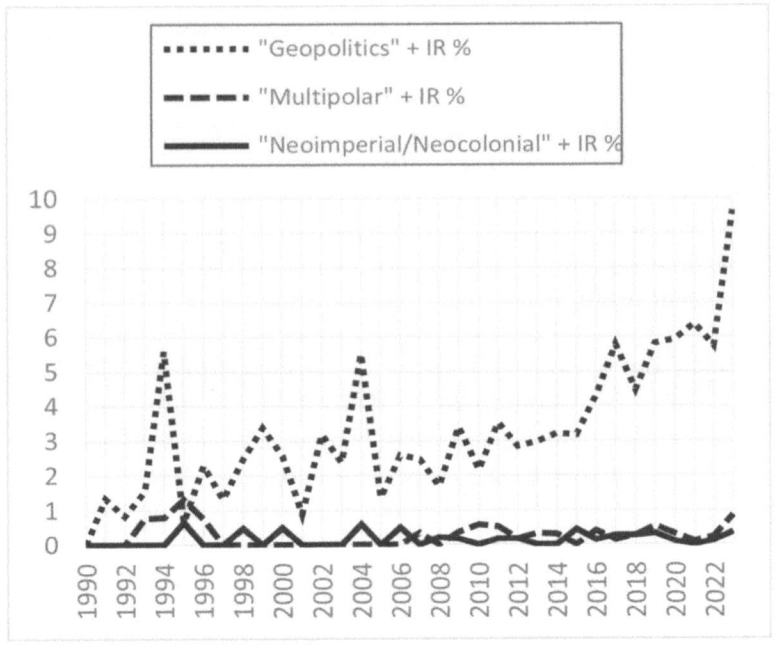

Chart 5 (top) shows the increasing amount of research referring to "International Relations" plus "Geopolitics", during 1990 to 2023, with a more subtle increase in research referring to "Multipolar," and "Neoimperial/Neocolonial." Research referring to "geopolitics" has increased from zero articles in 1990 until 80 articles in 2023. The USA's war on terror, Chinese foreign policy, and the Russian invasion of Ukraine appear to be driving this development. These developments are also reflected in the gradual but more subtle increases in articles referring to "multipolar" and "neoimperial/neocolonial" to describe the rise of the BRICS since the 2007 GFC. Comparing chart 5 with chart 1 suggests that while there was a gradual increase in references to geopolitics from 2008 to 2015, the rapid increase in articles referring to geopolitics corresponds to the Russian occupation and invasion of Ukraine from 2014 to 2023. Chart 6 (bottom) shows the relative use of the phrases "International Relations" plus "Geopolitics," "Multipolar," and "Neoimperial/Neocolonial" as a percentage of the incidence of the phrase "International Relations," 1990 to 2023. The chart shows how references to geopolitics, and to a lesser extent multipolar, were relatively higher after the end of the Cold War (until 2004), then rising again after 2015. The relative patterns for geopolitics, post-2014, is obviously similar to those for Ukraine in charts 1 and 2.

These SSCI results and the survey of recently updated IR textbooks indicate two worrying trends in response to the Russian invasion. Firstly, recently updated IR textbooks, such as Viotti and Kauppi (2023: 229) and Dunne, Kurki, Kušić, and Smith (2024), treat the Russian invasion of Ukraine as a case study in "realism" (Williams 2024: 68). While Baylis, Smith, and Owens (2022) provides a fairer analysis of the invasion in terms of globalization, new world dis-order, rising powers, global security, European integration, global trade and finance, the overall trend is that the Russian invasion can be understood and analyzed in terms of existing IR frameworks. Secondly, as the increasing amount of IR research referring to geopolitics demonstrates, the invasion is widely seen in conventional IR as part of a geopolitical struggle between global powers USA and EU vs. Russia and China.

In contrast to these 19th century views of geopolitics, the Russian invasion of Ukraine suggests five lessons for teaching a more 21st century IR that overcomes the "persistence of Cold War binaries" (Pishchikova 2023). First, the Russian invasion must be understood as an act of neoimperialism and neocolonialism, rather than being "westsplained" as realist geopolitics (Kurylo 2023; Hendl Burlyuk, O'Sullivan, and Arystanbek 2024). Russian neoimperialism to reimpose the imperial Russian empire of 1721–1917 or the Soviet empire of 1917–1991 is the driving force under Vladimir Putin, including the military interventions in Moldova 1990–1992, Chechnya 1994–1996 and 1999–2009, Georgia 2008, Ukraine 2014 and 2022 (Kuzio 2009; Snyder 2018; Oksamytna 2023). Neocolonialism involves self-identifying ethnic Russians in these countries acting as the colonial rulers of occupied territories such as Transnistria, Chechnya, Abkhazia, South Ossetia, Crimea, and Donbas, which in 2022 led to the "postcolonial moment in Russia's war against Ukraine" (Mälksoo 2023 in Burlyuk and Musliu 2023: 609; also Berglund and Bolkvadze 2024).

Second, the support for the Russian invasion and opposition to the purposes and principles of the UN charter must be understood within the context of a "multipolar" view of emergent international order with the "great powers" of USA, China, Russia, and India as dominant powers. The absurdity of such a limited view of multipolarity in IR is that these four powers currently make up approximately 42% of the world's population and will diminish to approximately 26% of the world's population by 2100 (Vollset et al. 2020). A more accurate reading of this changing world order is that in general democracies support, and autocracies oppose, the UN and international rule of law. The UN GA votes on occupation and invasion of Ukraine demonstrate this reading, with Russia supported by the closed autocracies of Belarus, Cuba, North Korea, and Syria (plus China, Laos, Mali, Nicaragua, Uzbekistan, and Vietnam on one-off votes). In contrast, the UN and Ukraine are supported by 140 states, that are over 75% democracies (V-Dem Institute 2024). In this context, the need for support for the UN and the international rule of law in the opposition to Russian imperialism was made clearly by Kenyan UN Ambassador Martin Kimani in a speech to the UN Security Council on 21 February 2022:

> Rather than form nations that looked ever backward into history with a dangerous nostalgia, we chose to look forward to a greatness none of our many nations and peoples had ever known. We chose to follow the rules of the OAU and the United Nations Charter not because our borders satisfied us but because we wanted something greater forged in peace.... We further strongly condemn the trend—in the last few decades—of powerful states, including members of this Security Council, breaching International Law with little regard. Multilateralism lies on its deathbed tonight. It has been assaulted, as it has been by other powerful states in the recent past.... Let me conclude by reaffirming Kenya's respect for the territorial integrity of Ukraine within its internationally recognized borders (Kimani 2022; Yakovlyev 2022).

Third, the Russian invasion must be seen as part of a wider campaign of disinformation, grey zone and hybrid warfare involving the state-funded private military company Wagner Group, Patriot Media Group, Internet Research Agency, Russian Institute for Strategic Studies, Russia Today/RT, Sputnik news agency, and a myriad of state-backed disinformation operations (Khylko 2023;

Kormych and Malyarenko 2023; Krainikova and Prokopenko 2023; Solovei 2023). This disinformation and influence campaign began with Putin's appointment in 1999 and stretches across Europe to the USA, and from the Middle East to Africa. In Europe the campaign has been most successful in undermining democracy in the UK, with highly placed individuals within politics and widespread interference in the 2014 Scottish independence and 2016 EU membership referenda (Digital, Culture, Media and Sport Committee 2019; Mueller 2019; Intelligence and Security Committee 2020). In addition, the campaign has supported and shaped far-right parties across the EU with "trojan horse" parties such as UKIP, French National Front/Rally, Alternative for Germany, Italian Northern League, Netherlands Party for Freedom, and Sweden Democrats all serving the interests of Russia (Anton 2022; Oksanen 2015, 2022; Polyakova *et al.* 2016, 2017, 2018; Shekhovtsov 2023).

Fourth, tragically the Russian invasion of Ukraine involves four mass atrocity crimes: genocide, war crimes, crimes against humanity, and ethnic cleansing. In March 2022 the International Criminal Court (ICC) opened an investigation into the Situation in Ukraine, including war crimes and crimes against humanity or genocide (ICC 2022). Crimes against humanity are the most widespread atrocity, defined as acts "committed as part of a widespread or systematic attack directed against any civilian population" (article 7, ICC 1998: 3–5). In October 2023 the UN Independent International Commission of Inquiry (UN IICI) on Ukraine documented evidence of "indiscriminate attacks by Russian armed forces, which have led to deaths and injuries of civilians and the destruction and damage of civilian objects" (UN IICI 2023: 2). Russian war crimes are equally prevalent, defined as "violations of international humanitarian law (treaty or customary law) that incur individual criminal responsibility under international law.... war crimes must always take place in the context of an armed conflict, either international or non-international" (Geneva Conventions 1949; article 8, ICC 1998: 5–10). The UN ICI (2023) collected evidence showing that "Russian authorities have committed the war crimes of willful killing, torture, rape and other sexual violence, and the deportation of children to the Russian Federation." In

March 2023 the ICC (2023) issued arrest warrants against Vladimir Putin and Maria Alekseyevna Lvova-Belova over allegations of involvement in the war crime of child abductions during the invasion of Ukraine.

Fifth, in complete contrast to teaching and scholarship on the "post-Soviet space," the Ukrainian response to the Russian invasion has demonstrated loudly and clearly across the world the determination and agency of Ukrainians to control their own destiny (Kudlenko 2023; Poberezhna, Burlyuk, and van Heelsum 2024). Following the Maidan Revolution the Association Agreement between the EU and Ukraine, including a Deep and Comprehensive Free Trade Area, was agreed in 2014 leading to the 2019 amendment of the Constitution of Ukraine aiming to join the EU and NATO. After the Russian invasion, the process of Ukrainian EU membership was accelerated with an application to join in February 2022, leading to the European Council opening accession negotiations in December 2023 (Rabinovych and Pintsch 2024; Noutcheva and Zarembo 2024). Ukraine is not alone in seeking a more secure destiny within European organizations with Denmark joining the EU's CSDP in 2022, Finland and Sweden joining NATO in 2023 and 2024, and at the same time Ukraine, Georgia, Bosnia and Herzegovina have all sought greater security within NATO (Wiesner and Knodt 2024; Zarembo 2024).

These five lessons of Russian neoimperialism and neocolonialism, opposition to the purposes and principles of the UN charter, disinformation and manipulation, Russian mass atrocity crimes, and finally Ukrainian independence and agency all demonstrate the importance of shifting IR teaching away from 19th century geopolitics and four-power multipolarism, and towards 21st century planetary politics that escapes the binary paradigm of the past 75 years.

4. Conclusion: Ukraine as a Microcosm of Planetary Politics in the 21st Century

> Chernobyl perhaps marks the start of the wider public awareness of the fragility of the human environment. But even without a Chernobyl or a

greenhouse effect, the result of a great lessening of the fear of nuclear war was always likely to be that mankind, the well-off section of it, anyway, would start to concentrate its anxieties on the health of the planet (Woollacott "Planet Politics" 1989).

The necessary paradigm shift to teaching the Russian war against Ukraine and other crises demands new thinking about planetary politics in the 21st century. As Martin Woollacott presciently observed in 1989, the events in Ukrainian Chornobyl marked the start of a wider awareness of the fragility of the human environment, the greenhouse effect, and the health of the planet he called "planet politics." It is only through understanding and coming to terms with the paradigm shift from international relations to planetary politics over the past 35 years that it is possible to contribute in a meaningful way to teaching the Russian invasion of Ukraine as a microcosm of planetary politics (Manners 2002: 10; 2008: 37). Fourteen years after Woollacott's labeling of the era of planetary politics, Karen Litfin (2003: 481) argued that "planetary politics ... are characterized by truly planetary relations of causality that can only be understood and addressed holistically." Planetary politics means that economic, social, ecological, conflictual and political relations and crises cannot be considered independently—they are symbiotic (Manners 2023, 2024a).

 The Russian invasion of Ukraine is a microcosm of the wider planetary organic crisis of five symbiotic dimensions of economy, society, ecology, conflict, and polity (Manners 2020, 2024b). Stephen Gill and Solomon Benatar (2020: 171) argue that the planetary organic crisis involves "interacting and deepening structural crises of economy/development, society, ecology, politics, culture and ethics—in ways that are unsustainable." The invasion of Ukraine represents a microcosm of these crises and politics because of the way in economic (in)equality, social (in)justice, ecological (un)sustainability, conflict (in)security, and political (ir)resilience are symbiotic in understand both the driving forces and the prospects for Ukraine.

 Economically, the Ukrainian and Russian economies both experienced negative growth during the period 1989–1997, but during 1998–2008 the Ukrainian economy outperformed the Russian economy. The GFC had a negative effect on both economies, but the Ukrainian economic downturn in 2014–2015 was particularly bad. The Russian invasion has a destructive effect on the Russian economy, but worse on the Ukrainian economy. However, in terms of economic (in)equality the economies are quite different with Ukraine having a 0.45 gini income inequality index, broadly comparable to that of the EU, while Russia has an index of 0.60—one of the worst in the global north (Alvaredo et al. 2022). The extent to which Russian wealth and inequality is being "sucked up" to wealthy oligarchs surrounding Putin is seen in the dominating role of Russia's ultra wealthy 1% taking 25% of the national income share, while the Russian super wealthy 10% take 50% of the national income share. In comparison, Ukraine is broadly in line with EU averages, with the top 1% taking 10–12% of national income share and the top 10% taking 35% of national income share.

Socially, the Social Progress Index (SPI) ranks the EU an average of 44th position out of 170 countries with an index score of 84 on 3 dimensions of basic human needs, foundations of wellbeing, and opportunity (Social Progress Imperative 2024). Ukraine ranks 59th on the SPI with an index score of 70 (up from 66 in 2011), similar to other EU applicants Albania, North Macedonia, Bosnia and Herzegovina. Russia ranks 76th on the SPI with an index score of 67 (down from 68 in 2017), with a fall in opportunity, most significantly a collapse in rights and voice, since 2011. Changing demographics will be one of the greatest challenges to social justice this century, with the EU 27 population falling from approximately 448 million today to roughly 308 million by 2100, or to approximately 340 million if the EU enlarges to 36 by 2100 (Vollset et al. 2020). Both Russia and Ukraine have low fertility rates, lowered by the invasion and war, that will lead Russian population to drop from approx. 146 million today to approx. 106 million by 2100, and Ukrainian population to drop from approx. 41 million today to approx. 18 million by 2100.

Ecologically, the invasion of Ukraine has involved "ecocide" with nuclear power stations such as Chornobyl and Zaporizhzhia put at risk, while munitions and landmines contaminate and condemn fields and forests, dams such as Kakhovka are destroyed, and rivers such as the Desna poisoned (Yavorska et al. 2024; Shahini et al. 2024). As the world's major exporter of natural gas and second largest exporter of oil in 2022 Russia is both a "petrostate" (making up 30–50% of state budget) and one of the world's worst fossil fuel polluters. Adriana Petryna (2023: 15) argues that the Russian invasion of Ukraine centers a range of planetary challenges, including the need for "de-occupation as planetary politics," and shows how "genocide legitimizes both anti-human and anti-planetary violence." As charts 7 and 8 illustrate below, the study of eco-centric "ecology," rather than anthropocentric environment in IR only emerged since the 2010 Nagoya Protocol to the Convention on Biological Diversity and the 2015 Paris Agreement. In contrast, the realization of the "climate crisis" and "planetary politics" in IR are far more recent phenomena from 2020 onwards, possibly driven by the COVID-19 pandemic.

Charts 7 and 8. SSCI references to "International Relations," "Ecology,"[7] "Climate Crisis,"[8] and "Planetary Politics,"[9] 1990–2023.

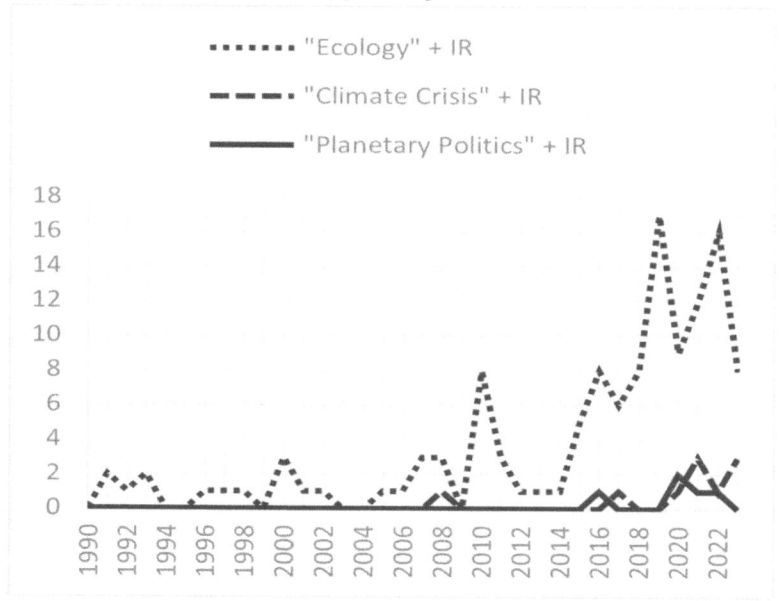

---

7   "Ecology" = "Ecology" OR "Ecological."
8   "Climate Crisis" = "Climate Crisis" OR "Climate Emergency."
9   "Planetary Politics" = "Planet Politics" OR "Planetary Politics."

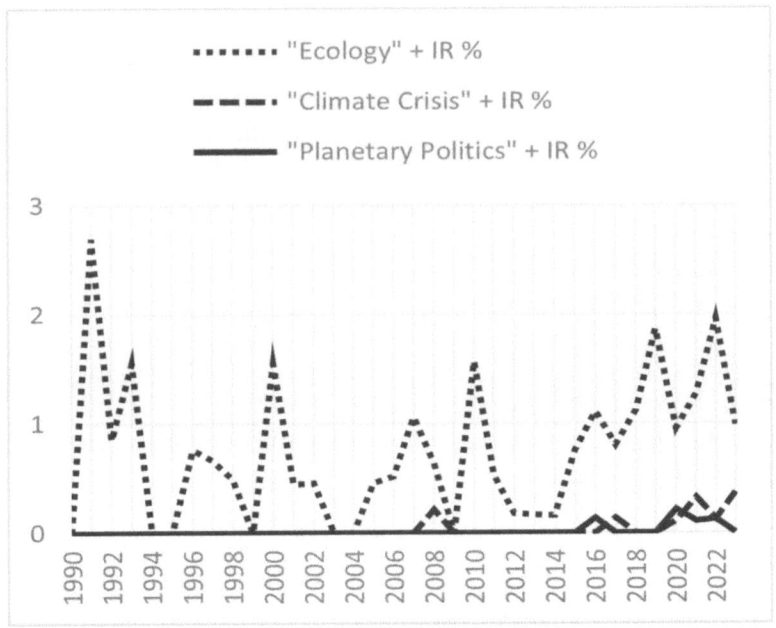

Chart 7 (top) shows the slowly increasing amount of research referring to "Ecology" in IR scholarship from 2009 until 2022. However, the amount of ecological IR research is tiny compared to the previous charts, perhaps reflecting psychological climate disavowal (Thierry, Horn, Von Hellermann, and Gardner 2023). In comparison, IR research on the climate crisis/emergency has only begun to emerge since the IPCC AR5 in 2014 and the Paris Agreement in 2015 demonstrated the failure to address the crisis/emergency. The anthropocentrism and egocentrism of contemporary IR scholarship remained hegemonic during the period, with planetary political attempts to escape the paradigm by Karen Litfin (2003), Paul Gilroy (2004), Gayatri Spivak (2003), and Achille Mbembe (2022) barely registering in IR. However, compared to the 400 plus references to environmental IR and 300 plus references to climate change since 2007, the 125 references to ecological IR lie 16 years behind in terms of research and publication.

Chart 8 (bottom) shows the relative use of the phrases "International Relations" plus "Ecology," "Climate Crisis/Emergency," and "Planetary Politics" as a percentage of the incidence of the phrase "International Relations," 1990 to 2023. The chart shows how references to ecology have been sporadic since the end of the Cold War. While this pattern is somewhat similar to climate change IR research, the relative levels of research references is about half for ecological research.

In terms of conflict, the Russian invasion of Ukraine is a microcosm of the increasing impunity with which neoimperial great powers take actions in multipolar politics. Prior to 2010 inter-state conflicts had been slowly falling in number across the world (there was only an interstate conflict between Eritrea and Djibouti during 2004–2010). Since 2010 inter-state conflicts in the Middle East, South Asia, Caucasus, and Ukraine have thrown the world back into arms racing, with risks of regional conflict in the Sahel, Palestine, Yemen/Iran/Saudi Arabia, Kashmir, the Black Sea, the Baltic, and Taiwan. As Ukrainian scholars of the invasion have made clear, understanding the conflict needs far greater knowledge than westplaining the grabbing up of territories like a game of *Risk* (Burlyuk and Musliu 2023: 607; Tyushka 2023: 652). As the discussions of economy, society, and ecology suggest, in unequal, unjust, and unsustainable countries such as Russia the population and civil society are just too weak and fractured to form the foundation of a viable society and oppose the ruling kleptocracy. In this context, neoimperialism and neocolonialism with impunity are the foundation for the governing oligarchy, as Ukrainian scholars are only too familiar.

Finally, the general culmination of economic inequality, social injustice, ecological unsustainability, and conflict insecurity lead to the observation that both freedom and democracy are under threat across the world. The Russian invasion of Ukraine represents a microcosm of this wider pattern with Russian inequality, injustice, and unsustainability facilitating its aggression and impunity, as part of the Russian decline of freedom and democracy. According to Freedom House (2024) the world has now seen 18 years of decline in global freedom, with Russia being at its most free in 1991, remaining "partly free" from 1991–2003, and dropping to "not free" from 2004 to 2024. Similar evidence is presented by the V-Dem Institute (2024), with autocratization continuing to be the dominant trend of the past 15 years. According to V-Dem, Russia was in the "autocratic grey zone" from 1992-1999, then became an "electoral autocracy" from 1999 onwards where it is currently ranked 159th on the liberal democracy index (out of 179 countries). Thus, the long-term decline in Russian freedom and democracy since 1991 has led to it becoming a "not free" "electoral autocracy" since Putin came to power in 1999.

In contrast, according to Freedom House, Ukraine was "partly free" from 1991-2003, became "free" after the 2005 Orange Revolution from 2005-2010, returned to "partly free" under Viktor Yanukovych in 2010 and has kept this status ever since. V-Dem Institute data demonstrates how Ukraine was a form of autocracy between 1991–1993, 1998–2005, 2010-2018, 2022–2023, and was a form of democracy between 1994–1997, 2006–2009, 2019–2021, and is currently ranked 109th on the liberal democracy index. What these two sources of data demonstrate is that Russia is an irresilient autocracy without the capacity to recover from elected dictatorship since 1999, while Ukraine is a more resilient polity with the ability to spring back from autocracy to democracy as it has done in 1994 (first parliamentary and presidential elections), 2006 (Orange Revolution and election of President Yushchenko), and 2019 (election of President Zelenskyy). Thus, the irresilience and decline of Russian democracy helps fuel its invasion of Ukraine, whilst the resilience of Ukrainian democracy helps it resist the Russian invasion.

These five dimensions of planetary politics illustrate how Ukraine is a microcosm of larger events but leave plenty of space for Ukrainian determination and agency. The teaching of the Russian invasion and war against Ukraine must help students and teachers alike to understand the symbiotic relationships between inequality, injustice, unsustainability, insecurity, and resilience in the planetary politics of the 21st century. The article argued that the greatest challenge of teaching IR in the context of the Russian war against Ukraine is that western IR is stuck in a 20th century paradigm of thinking. The article then set out how incorporating the war into a first semester introductory course on international politics initially involved adapting the course to the empirical events, such as lectures on conflict and cooperation. But the war has led to five lessons for rethinking the teaching of neoimperialism and neocolonialism, opposition to the purposes and principles of the UN charter, disinformation and manipulation, Russian mass atrocity crimes, and Ukrainian independence and agency. While the article did not discuss teaching methods and technology, it did demonstrate the need to shift paradigms of thinking about teaching and address the need for Ukrainian knowledge about the war. In this respect the article used the rich and wide range of Ukrainian scholarship and literature to discuss this knowledge, as the bibliography demonstrates. Finally, although the article did not address the emotional and psychological impact of the war on students and staff, it is clear from personal experience that the planetary organic crisis is having an increasingly negative effect on the mental health of all, including the effects of the rise of far-right autocrats and their neoimperialism, the invasion of Ukraine and the conflict in Gaza, and the ecological and climate catastrophe.

References

Alvaredo, Facundo, Atkinson, Anthony, Piketty, Thomas, and Saez, Emmanuel. (2022) *World Inequality Database*. Paris: World Inequality Lab. http://wid.world/data.

Anton, Wiebke. (2022) *"Russia" in the European Parliament: Voting Patterns, Discourse-Coalitions and Self-Other Representations*. Munich: Ludwig-Maximilians-University.

Baylis, John, and Smith, Steve. (eds.) (1997) *The Globalization of World Politics: An Introduction to International Relations*. Oxford: Oxford University Press.

Baylis, John, Smith, Steve, and Owens, Patricia. (eds.) (2022) *The Globalization of World Politics: An Introduction to International Relations*, 9th ed. Oxford: Oxford University Press.

Berenskötter, Felix. (2018) "E pluribus unum? How textbooks cover theories," in Gofas, Andreas, Hamati-Ataya, Inanna, and Onuf, Nicholas (eds.) *Sage Handbook of History, Philosophy and Sociology of International Relations*. London: Sage, 446–68.

Berglund, Christofer, and Bolkvadze, Ketevan. (2024) "Sons of the Soil or Servants of the Empire? Profiling the Guardians of Separatism in Abkhazia and South Ossetia," *Problems of Post-Communism* 71(1): 37-48.

Bretherton, Charlotte, and Vogler, John. (1999) *The European Union as a Global Actor*. London: Routledge.
Brown, Chris. (1997) *Understanding International Relations*. Basingstoke: Macmillan.
Burchill, Scott, and Linklater, Andrew. (eds.) (1996) *Theories of International Relations*. Basingstoke: Macmillan.
Burlyuk, Olga, and Musliu, Vjosa. (2023) "The Responsibility to Remain Silent? On the Politics of Knowledge Production, Expertise and (Self-) Reflection in Russia's War against Ukraine," *Journal of International Relations and Development* 26(4): 605–18.
Devetak, Richard, and True, Jacqui. (2022) *Theories of International Relations*, 6th ed. London: Bloomsbury.
Digital, Culture, Media and Sport Committee. (2019) *Disinformation and "Fake News,"* House of Commons (2017–19, HC 1791), 18 February.
Dunne, Tim, Kurki, Milja, Kušić, Katarina, and Smith, Steve. (eds.) (2024) *International Relations Theories: Discipline and Diversity*, 6th ed. Oxford: Oxford University Press.
Edkins, Jenny, and Zehfuss, Maja. (eds.) (2018) *Global Politics: A New Introduction*, 3rd ed. London: Routledge.
Freedom House. (2024) *Freedom in the World 2024: The Mounting Damage of Flawed Elections and Armed Conflict*. Washington DC: Freedom House.
Galeotti, Mark. (2022) *Putin's Wars: From Chechnya to Ukraine*. Oxford: Osprey Publishing.
Geneva Conventions. (1949) Four Geneva Conventions and three Protocols on the treatment of soldiers, prisoners of war and non-combatants during wartime, 1949, 1977, and 2005. Switzerland: International Committee of the Red Cross.
Gill, Stephen, and Benatar, Solomon. (2020) "Reflections on the Political Economy of Planetary Health," *Review of International Political Economy* 27(1): 167–90.
Gilroy, Paul. (2004) *After Empire: Melancholia or Convivial Culture?* Abingdon: Routledge.
Gustavsson, Jakob, and Tallberg, Jonas. (eds.) (2021) *Internationella relationer*. Lund: Studentlitteratur.
Hendl, Tereza, Burlyuk, Olga, O'Sullivan, Mila, and Arystanbek, Aizada. (2024) "(En)Countering Epistemic Imperialism: A Critique of 'Westsplaining' and Coloniality in Dominant Debates on Russia's Invasion of Ukraine," *Contemporary Security Policy* 45(2): 171–209.
Intelligence and Security Committee. (2020) *Russia Report*, House of Commons (2017-2019, HC 632) 21 July.

International Criminal Court. (1998) *Rome Statute adopted by the United Nations Diplomatic Conference of Plenipotentiaries on the Establishment of an International Criminal Court*, 17 July.

International Criminal Court. (2022) "Situation in Ukraine," ICC-01/22, 2 March. https://www.icc-cpi.int/situations/ukraine.

International Criminal Court. (2023) "Situation in Ukraine: ICC judges issue arrest warrants against Vladimir Vladimirovich Putin and Maria Alekseyevna Lvova-Belova," Press Release: 17 March. https://www.icc-cpi.int/news/situation-ukraine-icc-judges-issue-arrest-warrants-against-vladimir-vladimirovich-putin-and.

Khylko, Olena. (2023) "Resilience-Building in Grey Security Zone Countries," *Scientific Collection "InterConf+"* 34(159): 37–48.

Kimani, Martin. (2022) "Statement during the UN SC Meeting on the Situation in Ukraine," Permanent Mission of the Republic of Kenya, 21 February.

Kormych, Borys, and Malyarenko, Tetyana. (2023) "From Gray Zone to Conventional Warfare: The Russia-Ukraine Conflict in the Black Sea," *Small Wars & Insurgencies* 34(7): 1235–70.

Krainikova, Tetiana, and Prokopenko, Serhii. (2023) "Waves of Disinformation in the Hybrid Russian-Ukrainian War," *Current Issues of Mass Communication* 33: 12–25.

Kudlenko, Anastasiia. (2023) "Roots of Ukrainian Resilience and the Agency of Ukrainian Society Before and After Russia's Full-Scale Invasion," *Contemporary Security Policy* 44(4): 513–29.

Kurylo, Bohdana. (2023) "The Ukrainian Subject, Hierarchies of Knowledge Production and the Everyday: An Autoethnographic Narrative," *Journal of International Relations and Development* 26(4): 685–97.

Kuzio, Taras. (2009) "Strident, Ambiguous and Duplicitous: Ukraine and the 2008 Russia-Georgia War," *Demokratizatsiya* 17(4): 350–72.

Litfin, Karen. (2003) "Planetary Politics," in Agnew, John, Mitchell, Katharyne, and Toal, Gerard. (eds.) *A Companion to Political Geography*. Oxford: Blackwell, 470–82.

McCormick, John. (1999) *Understanding the European Union: A Concise Introduction*. Basingstoke: Macmillan.

Mälksoo, Maria. (2023) "The Postcolonial Moment in Russia's War against Ukraine," *Journal of Genocide Research* 25(3-4): 471–81.

Manners, Ian. (1999) "The European Union and Moldova Beyond the PCA," in Bruton, Leilah (ed.) *The Republic of Moldova: Time for a New EU Strategy?* Brussels: Stiftung Wissenschaft und Politik, 57–77.

Manners, Ian. (2002) *European [security] Union: from existential threat to ontological security*, COPRI working paper 5 (Copenhagen: Copenhagen Peace Research Institute). https://portal.research.lu.se/

files/108768568/Ian_Manners_2002_European_security_Union_from_existential_threat_to_ontological_security_COPRI_5.pdf.

Manners, Ian. (2009) "The Normative Power of the European Union in a Globalised World," in Laïdi, Zaki (ed.) *EU Foreign Policy in a Globalized World: Normative Power and Social Preferences*. London: Routledge, 23–37.

Manners, Ian. (2010) "As You Like It: European Union Normative Power in the European Neighbourhood Policy," in Whitman, Richard, and Wolff, Stefan (eds.) *The European Neighbourhood Policy in Perspective: Context, Implementation and Impact*. Basingstoke: Palgrave Macmillan, 29–50.

Manners, Ian. (2018) "Political Psychology of European Integration: The (Re)production of Identity and Difference in the Brexit Debate," *Political Psychology* 39(6): 1213–32.

Manners, Ian. (2020) "European Communion and Planetary Organic Crisis," in Brack, Nathalie, and Gürkan, Seda (eds.) *Theorising the Crises of the European Union*. London: Routledge, 159–82.

Manners, Ian. (2023) "Planetary Politics in the Twenty-Second Century." in Horn, Laura, Mert, Ayşem, and Müller, Franziska. (eds.) *The Palgrave Handbook of Global Politics in the 22nd Century*. Cham: Springer International Publishing, 271–90.

Manners, Ian. (2024a) "Arrival of Normative Power in Planetary Politics," *Journal of Common Market Studies* 62(3): 825–44.

Manners, Ian. (2024b) "Normative Power in the Planetary Organic Crisis," *Cooperation and Conflict* 59. https://doi.org/10.1177/00108367241244954.

Mbembe, Achille. (2022) "How to Develop a Planetary Consciousness," *Noema Magazine*, 11 January. https://www.noemamag.com/how-to-develop-a-planetary-consciousness/.

Mearsheimer, John, and Rosato, Sebastian. (2023) *How States Think: The Rationality of Foreign Policy*. New Haven, CT: Yale University Press.

Mueller, Robert. (2019) *Report on The Investigation into Russian Interference in the 2016 Presidential Election*. Washington: US Department of Justice, 18 April.

Noutcheva, Gergana, and Zarembo, Kateryna. (2024) "Normative Power at its Unlikeliest: EU Democratic Norms and Security Service Reform in Ukraine," *Cooperation and Conflict* 59. https://doi.org/10.1177/00108367241244978

Nugent, Neil. (1994) *The Government and Politics of the European Union*, 3rd ed. Basingstoke: Macmillan.

Oksamytna, Kseniya. (2023) "Imperialism, Supremacy, and the Russian Invasion of Ukraine," *Contemporary Security Policy* 44(4): 497–512.

Oksanen, Patrik. (2015) "Russia-index: 11 new EU-sceptic parties added," 10 January. https://eublogg.wordpress.com/2015/01/10/russia-index-11-new-eu-sceptic-parties-added/.

Oksanen, Patrik. (2022) "SD:s rysslandsröster i Europaparlamentet sticker ut," Säkerhetsrådet, Frivärld, 7 September. https://frivarld.se/sakerhetsradet/sds-rysslandsroster-sticker-ut-i-europaparlamentet/.

Petryna, Adriana. (2023) "De-Occupation as Planetary Politics: On the Russian War in Ukraine," *American Ethnologist* 50(1): 10–18.

Poberezhna, Anastasiia, Burlyuk, Olga, and van Heelsum, Anja. (2024) "A Superhero Army, a Courageous People and an Enchanted Land: Wartime Political Myths and Ontological Security in the 2022 Russian Invasion of Ukraine," *Czech Journal of International Relations* 59(1): 59–92.

Polyakova, Alina, Laruelle, Marlene, Meister, Stefan, and Barnett, Neil. (2016) *The Kremlin's Trojan Horses: Russian Influence in France, Germany, and the United Kingdom.* Washington DC: Atlantic Council.

Polyakova, Alina, Kounalakis, Markos, Klapsis, Antonis, Germani, Luigi Sergio, Iacoboni, Jacopo, de Borja Lasheras, Francisco, and de Pedro, Nicolás. (2017) *The Kremlin's Trojan Horses 2.0: Russian influences in Greece, Italy, and Spain.* Washington DC: Atlantic Council.

Polyakova, Alina, Splidsboel-Hansen, Flemming, van Der Noordaa, Robert, Bogen, Øystein, Sundbom, Henrik. (2018) *The Kremlin's Trojan Horses 3.0: Russian influences in Denmark, the Netherlands, Norway, and Sweden.* Washington DC: Atlantic Council.

Pishchikova, Katerina. (2023) "What Ukraine Teaches Us About International Relations and Vice Versa," *Interdisciplinary Political Studies* 9(2): 97–107.

Putin, Vladimir, and Xi, Jinping. (2022) "Joint Statement of the Russian Federation and the People's Republic of China on the International Relations Entering a New Era and the Global Sustainable Development," Beijing, 4 February.

Rabinovych, Maryna, and Pintsch, Anne. (2024) "From the 2014 Annexation of Crimea to the 2022 Russian War on Ukraine: Path Dependence and Socialization in the EU–Ukraine Relations," *Journal of Common Market Studies.* https://doi.org/10.1111/jcms.13572.

Scholte, Jan Aarte. (2000) *Globalization: A Critical Introduction.* Basingstoke: Macmillan.

Shahini, Ermir, Shebanina, Olena, Kormyshkin, Iurii, Drobitko, Antonina, and Chernyavskaya, Natalya. (2024) "Environmental Consequences for the World of Russia's war against Ukraine," *International Journal of Environmental Studies* 81(1): 463–74.

Shekhovtsov, Anton. (2023) *Russian Political Warfare: Essays on Kremlin Propaganda in Europe and the Neighbourhood, 2020-2023*. Stuttgart: *ibidem* Press.

Snyder, Timothy. (2018) *The Road to Unfreedom: Russia, Europe, America*. New York: Tim Duggan Books.

Social Progress Imperative. (2024) *2024 Social Progress Index*. Washington, DC: Social Progress Imperative. www.socialprogress.org

Solovei, Galyna. (2023) "Russian Myths of 'One People' and 'NATO's Attack on Russia' in the Legitimization of the Russo-Ukrainian War," in Catalan-Matamoros, Daniel (ed.) *Disinformation and Fact-Checking in Contemporary Society*. Madrid: Dykinson, 101–16.

Spivak, Gayatri. (2003) *Death of a Discipline*. New York: Columbia University Press.

Stein, Janice Gross. (2008) "Foreign Policy Decision-Making: Rational, Psychological, and Neurological Methods," in Smith, Steve, Hadfield, Amelia, and Dunne, Timothy (eds.) *Foreign Policy: Theories, Actors, Cases*, 3rd edn. Oxford: Oxford University Press, 130–46.

Thierry, Aaron, Horn, Laura, von Hellermann, Pauline, and Gardner, Charlie. (2023) "'No Research on a Dead Planet': Preserving the Socio-Ecological Conditions for Academia," *Frontiers in Education* 8. https://doi.org/10.3389/feduc.2023.1237076.

Tyushka, Andriy. (2023) "In 'Crisis' We Trust? On (Un)Intentional Knowledge Distortion and the Exigency of Terminological Clarity in Academic and Political Discourses on Russia's War against Ukraine," *Journal of International Relations and Development* 26(4): 643–59.

United Nations General Assembly Resolution. (2014) Resolution 68/262, "Territorial Integrity of Ukraine," adopted by the sixty-eighth session of the United Nations General Assembly, 27 March.

United Nations Independent International Commission of Inquiry. (2023) Inquiry on Ukraine pursuant to Human Rights Council resolution 52/32, A/78/540. Geneva: UN Human Rights Council.

V-Dem Institute. (2024) *Democracy Report 2024: Democracy Winning and Losing at the Ballot*. Gothenburg: V-Dem Institute.

Viotti, Paul, and Kauppi, Mark. (2023) *International Relations Theory*, 7th ed. Harlow: Pearson.

Vollset, Stein Emil, *et al.* (2020) "Fertility, Mortality, Migration, and Population Scenarios for 195 Countries and Territories from 2017 to 2100: A Forecasting Analysis for the Global Burden of Disease Study," *The Lancet* 396(10258): 1285–306.

Wallace, Helen, and Wallace, William. (eds.) (1996) *Policy-Making in the European Union*, 3rd ed. Oxford: Oxford University Press.

Weber, Cynthia. (2021) *International Relations Theory: A Critical Introduction*, 5th ed. Abingdon: Routledge.

Wiesner, Claudia, and Knodt, Michèle. (eds.) (2024) *The War Against Ukraine and the EU: Facing New Realities.* Cham: Springer Nature.

Williams, Michael. (2024) "Classical Realism," in Dunne, Tim, Kurki, Milja, Kušić, Katarina, and Smith, Steve. (eds.) *International Relations Theories: Discipline and Diversity*, 6th ed. Oxford: Oxford University Press, 55–71.

Woollacott, Martin. (1989) "The Year Ahead: Planet Politics—Why 1989 Could and Should be a Year of Miracles," *The Guardian*, 2 January.

Yakovlyev, Maksym. (2022) "European Imperialism and Colonialism in Africa: Conceptual Lessons for Understanding the Former Soviet Union and Present-Day Russia," *African Journal of Economics, Politics and Social Studies* 1(1): 31–39.

Yavorska, Victoria, Oleksii Buriachenko, Liudmyla Vasechko, Valerii Shapoval, Oleksii Vasechko, and Roman Yedeliev (2024) "Examining the International Political and Legal Accountability of States for Genocide, Ecocide, and Weapons of Mass Destruction: Current Norms, Practices, and Political Implications," *Multidisciplinary Science Journal* 6, 2024ss0739. https://doi.org/10.31893/multiscience.2024ss0739.

Zarembo, Kateryna (2024) "Still Normative Power Europe? The Perception of the EU in Ukraine Amidst the Russian War of Aggression," in Claudia Wiesner and Michèle Knodt (eds.) *The War Against Ukraine and the EU: Facing New Realities.* Cham: Springer Nature, 189–206.

Will the Russian War against Ukraine Bring Changes to the Teaching of International Relations?[1]

Olena Khylko

Abstract: This paper addresses the epistemic injustice in the teaching of IR at Western universities revealed through the analysis of post-2022 syllabi and curricula. It aims to analyze how the Russian war against Ukraine may affect the ongoing discourse on the decolonization of IR in which Western academia is criticized for perpetuating exclusionary hierarchical constructs centered on the policies and practices of great powers and institutions. Meanwhile, the role of small powers in regions which have not been traditionally considered as colonized in a classical sense, has been marginalized in mainstream IR theory. Analysis of post-2022 IR studies curricula and syllabi on IR theory and Postcolonial studies reveals the unreadiness of Western academia to question the explanatory value of the mainstream IR theories. The ongoing process of decolonizing IR still lacks recognition of Eastern European postcolonial cases and experiences, including the case of Russia–Ukraine relations. University courses focused on Russian politics and with reading lists that feature Russian scholars while excluding their Ukrainian counterparts, will continue the practices of normalizing Russia's aggression, silencing Ukrainian voices, and failing to examine the reasons for Ukrainian actions and responsive practices. These conclusions suggest the need to develop tools for overcoming the existing epistemic inter-coloniality embedded in the teaching of IR,

---

[1] The author is grateful to the team of editors for their efforts. The author is grateful for the support of this research by European Union, NextGenerationEU.

whereby Ukrainians are deprived of agency as knowledge generators and Ukraine's right to a decent place in postcolonial studies is denied.

Introduction

While recent decades have seen a drive to decolonize IR studies in the academy, this movement still has its own blind spots. Efforts to decolonize IR to this day remain overly focused on emancipation from Western-centrism, leaving the legacy of Russian influence on IR studies unnoticed along with silencing the role of Eastern Europe in knowledge production. The role of small powers from regions not traditionally considered as colonized has been marginalized in mainstream IR theory, which comprises the ontological and epistemological cornerstones for understanding IR. From this angle, this essay aims to take a closer look at changes that might be brought to the teaching of IR studies and IR theory stemming from the experience obtained from the war and Ukraine's resilience. I examine and compare the IR curricula and syllabi at a selection of leading Western schools from the period preceding and following the Russian invasion of 2022. I start with an assessment of how the war tested the validity of the mainstream theories dominating IR studies. I then proceed to show the place of Ukraine and the Eastern European region more broadly in the dichotomy of theorizing IR and Area Studies. Finally, I analyze the trends in the syllabi of IR theory and adjacent courses and substantiate the rationale for embedding the empirical potential of the war into postcolonial theoretical approaches, the attractiveness of which lies in a rich potential for alternative explanations in IR (Mälksoo 2021: 6).

    Despite the declared "end of IR theory" (Dunne, Hansen, Wight 2013), IR theory continue to maintain rich potential for explaining the relationship between actors and organizations in the world political process. They empower IR studies by making them "theory-led, theory-literate and theory-concerned" (Dunne, Hansen, Wight 2013). IR theory, being a part of IR studies' intellectual structure (Waever and Tickner 2013) or a "sort of codification of political practice" (Buzan 2018: 394), performs explanatory and constitutive functions (Smith 1995: 27–28) which fulfil the crucial role of a more time-independent intellectual education and enable reflection on changing challenges (Guzzini 2001: 99).

IR theory has traditionally focused on the explanatory potential of the mainstream theories elaborated by the western, predominantly Anglo-American, scholarship. As early as in 1993 Alfredo C. Robles, Jr. (526–27) wrote that "parochialism still holds sway in the teaching of IR," emphasizing that 80 percent of all references in US academic IR literature were to US scholars. Shaken by the decolonization discourse (Davis A. et al. 2020; Hassan and Sajjad 2022; Tucker 2018), teachers of IR theory courses have been, albeit very slowly and reluctantly, starting to include in their syllabi the works of non-Western scholars—rather at the level of Advanced/Critical/Postcolonial courses on IR theory than introductory courses to IR. Still, even these modest attempts to make IR studies truly global (Acharya 2014) tend overwhelmingly to reflect ignorance of the explanatory potential of Eastern European empirical material for enriching and complementing IR theories.

This epistemic injustice is addressed by this paper, which suggests that Eastern European post- and neocolonial experience should be included into courses or modules on postcolonial theories in IR. This will contribute to re-centring IR and furthering a shift to greater pluralization (Tickner 2013; Acharya and Buzan 2017) by leveraging up non-core or local knowledge and making it more meaningful for IR studies (Kaczmarska 2020). It aims to contribute to restorative and inclusionary epistemic justice (Hutchings 2023), revealing the silencing of voices outside Eurocentrism (Zondi 2016) and showing the added value of the region's states and Ukraine's experience, in particular, for IR studies teaching. Such inclusion could activate the capacity for an integrative pluralism (Dunne 2013: 406) which equips a theory with added value and with organizational tools to distinguish what is important and what is not and to specify the relations between the factors deemed to be important (Dunne 2013: 410).

Deficiencies of the Mainstream IR Theories Revealed by Russia's War against Ukraine

The scope and declared goals of Russian military intervention in Ukraine in February 2022 as well as Ukraine's determined resistance has raised questions about the deficiencies of the mainstream International Relations theoretical paradigms (Dutkiewicz and Smolenski 2023) when it comes to comprehending regional (inter)dependencies, interactions, motivations for behavior and decision-making by local actors, as well as predicting hazardous scenarios that go beyond conventional paradigms and mindsets. This section will indicate several significant vulnerabilities in the dominant IR theories which need to be addressed and compensated by other approaches or theories.

Proponents of the realist paradigm—with its penchant for "great power narcissism" (Hagström 2021) and corresponding marginalization of the agency of small and medium powers—claim the West holds responsibility for Russia's aggression against Ukraine (Mearsheimer 2014; Walt 2022) and insist that it was the promise of NATO membership to Kyiv given at the 2008 Bucharest Summit that provoked Moscow (Mearsheimer 2014). However, this stance elides the fact that Vladimir Putin's revisionist speech at 2007 Munich Security Conference took place before the Bucharest summit—an important aspect highlighted by Joseph Nye (2022b). Moreover, already in 2000, long before the Bucharest Summit, the updated text of the Foreign Policy Concept of the Russian Federation indicated Moscow's dissatisfaction with the existing world order, claiming that "calculations related to the formation of new equal, mutually beneficial, partnership relations between Russia and the outside world did not materialise" (2000). Among the main foreign policy goals listed in the Concept is that of strengthening Russia's positions "as a great power and as one of the influential centres of the modern world" *(ibid.)*—a goal for which Russia needed Ukraine in order to get "a critical mass," as Putin believed (Trenin 2013). Given Russia's intention to strengthen its geopolitical posture, keeping Ukraine in the "gray zone" without appropriate security guarantees could hardly be considered as a reliable option, even from the point of view of realists (Khylko 2017).

Realists' downplaying of the effect domestic politics produce on foreign policy decisions, and their belief that "the pressures of [international] competition weigh more heavily than ideological preferences or internal political pressures" (Waltz 1986: 329), criticized by opponents (Snyder 2013; Shultz 2013) who stressed the significance of parochial interests of elites and institutional factors, hampered analysis of the specificity of both the Russian authoritarian political regime and domestic changes in Ukraine. The latter were brought about partially in connection with approximation of Ukrainian law with that of the EU and partially by depriving Russia of its agents of influence seeking permanent destabilization in Ukraine.

Neoliberals, in their turn, have believed for decades that democratization of Russia could be a precondition for a transformative process that would render conflicts inexpedient (Bouchet 2015; Gat 2005). They assumed that economic interdependence in a highly globalized world made wars too expensive, which should deter countries from taking an aggressive stance (Copeland 1996). Following this logic, it would be highly disadvantageous for Russia to start a war, as its economic well-being depended heavily on trade with the European Union, which was a key buyer of its energy resources, and the development of the Russian economy was strongly dependent on Western technologies. But the full-scale invasion of Ukraine has shown that rational economic considerations do not always prevail over other motivations. As Joseph Nye notes, "while economic interdependence can raise the costs of war, it clearly does not prevent it" (2022a).

The preoccupation of realists with Cold War great power rivalry and the pursuit of power maximization hampered their insightfulness in analyzing specifics and motivations of Russia's policies in the Eastern European region and specifically in Ukraine. At the same time, neoliberals overestimated the ability of interdependence to bring competitors closer together and overlooked the importance of other reasons shaping the policies of regional actors. For both realists and neoliberals, Eastern Europe, apart from Russia, "has generally appeared as an object of projecting power and visions of governance rather than a subject in its own right in the field of making, and making sense of, international relations," as Maria Mälksoo notes (2021: 871).

Constructivists provide fertile ground for comprehending certain motivations for Russia's behavior that are beyond the paradigms of realism and liberalism. As Alexander Wendt argued already in 1992, power politics is not a naturally predefined mode of interaction between states, but a socially constructed reality that the states continue to reproduce (1992). Based on constructivism's ideas, researchers contend that rational choice models are insufficient for exhaustive explanations of the behavior of Russia, whose perception of interest and security is interlinked with its "alternative identities," built around notions of Russia "as a supranational entity or region, understood in cultural civilisationist terms, or in geoeconomic terms—or both at the same time" (Kazharski 2019: 190).

Still, despite the valuable insights into Russia's behavior provided by constructivist notions of interests being shaped by identities, the ruthlessness of Russian full-scale invasion of Ukraine in 2022, as well as the resoluteness of Ukraine's resistance, provide encouragement for expanding the range of IR paradigms to understand these events and the preconditions that led to them. In this regard, the ongoing discussions on the need for decolonization of IR (Davis A. et al. 2020; Hassan and Sajjad 2022; Tucker 2018) have inspired renewed attempts to apply a postcolonial lens to the study of the Eastern European region in general and the Russia–Ukraine war in particular. Unlike the 1990s and 2000s, when the study of postcolonialism in Russia–Ukraine relations was mainly focused on cultural issues (e.g., see Pavlyshyn 1993), this time the postcolonial lens is proposed to be applied to the entire complex of interactions. This intention was additionally stimulated when Yale University Professor Timothy Snyder clearly stated that the Russian war in Ukraine was "a colonial war" and that "Ukraine is a post-colonial country" (2022). The postcolonial and imperial nature constituted by Russia's war against Ukraine was also stressed by other—Ukrainian and Western—scholars (Burlyuk and Musliu 2023: 606). This marks a significant shift in academic discourse, as Ukraine has long been "among the most flagrantly neglected cases of Soviet colonialism due to the allegedly insufficient applicability of the label 'postcolonial' to the former Soviet/Russian imperial space" (Mälksoo 2023: 473).

Paradoxically at first glance, the strengthening of neo-colonialist tendencies in the politics of the Russian Federation in the 2010s, intensified the academic discourse representing Russia itself as an object of Western colonization, a "European colony" and "subaltern empire" that invaded Ukraine driven by "defensive logic," feeling "threatened by what it perceives is an expansion of the Western empire" (Morozov 2015: 135, 167). Tamar Koplatadze argues that this tendency is largely rooted in the peculiar theoretical discourse on Russia's subaltern and internally colonized identity vis-à-vis the West, and that "within this narrative, the Russian Empire and the Soviet Union are regarded as non-colonial powers since the Russian population allegedly suffered more under Russo-Soviet rule than non-Russian nationalities in the annexed territories" (2022). Vera Tolz and Stephen Hutchings note that narratives of Western colonialism and victimization of Russia, echoing the nineteenth-century Slavophiles and early-twentieth-century Eurasianists, have become widespread not only in Russia itself, but also among Western left-wing groups and wider non-Western audiences (2023). Andrey Makarychev and Ryhor Nizhnikau argue that "Russia actively utilizes the Western academic rules for its own benefit," mimicking the major vocabularies and redeploying dominant narratives to support the Kremlin propaganda "through Russia-sympathetic scholars" (2023). Inscribed in IR syllabi (e.g, Georgetown University 2020) the respective sources contribute to further marginalization of Ukraine and victimization of Russia.

At the same time, the application of postcolonial approaches from a Ukrainian perspective remains less visible, in what Bohdana Kurylo reads as a "refusal to recognise the Ukrainian subject as a legitimate knowledge generator and an agent of its own liberation from Russian colonialism" (2023). Victoria Donovan stresses that Western decolonial discourse "in fact reproduce(s) the same hierarchies of authority and power," continuing to speak "on behalf of" the marginalized others, including Ukrainians (2023: 169). Vitaly Chernetsky notes that Ukraine's subaltern and marginalized position is "also reflected in the similarly subaltern and marginalized position of Ukrainian studies vis- à-vis Russian studies in the West" (2003: 36–37).

This fits in the general trend of objectifying the countries of Eastern Europe in IR studies (Davies N. 2022; Dudko 2023) and "Western epistemic practices of marginalization and silencing of the CEE Subaltern/Other" sometimes referred to as "Westsplaining" (O'Sullivan and Krulišová 2023). Aliaksei Kazharski points out that the Western discourse on Central and Eastern Europe suffers from "distortions caused by its deep Russo-centrism" and the "assumption that powerful players can and should talk to Moscow over the heads of Central and Eastern European countries" (2022). Such epistemic imperialism leads to the domination of the outsider narratives about what Ukraine is, "often wholly skipping the knowledge produced in Ukraine, by Ukrainians, or by those who study Ukraine specifically," stresses Maria Sonevytsky (2022: 22). Míla O'Sullivan and Kateřina Krulišová point out that, inter alia, the "Western practices of exclusion of those directly impacted by Russian imperial aggression" and "speaking over Ukraine" contributed to misunderstandings about the imperial nature of the Russian invasion (2023).

For the purposes of teaching IR, we consider postcolonialism to hold valuable potential for providing alternative interpretations rooted in justice and the adoption of alternative norms (Wilkens 2017); challenging rationalist notions of power as a tool constraining self-determination (Fanon 1963: 146; Bhabha 1994: 20); and explaining sophisticated connections between memory, historical experiences, and politics, offering insights into the motivations behind resistance and patterns of transformation as vehicles for emancipation. Moreover, it exposes the legacies of colonial rule and imperial administration that inform contemporary global politics (Küçük 2022: 157). Given its ethical underpinnings, postcolonialism offers a promising lens for analyzing the actions of small and medium powers, often marginalized by realists. The study of colonial practices is essential for understanding how these practices have influenced societal responses to domination and shaped various forms of resistance.

Marginalizing Ukraine and the Eastern European Region in IR studies

The assumed superiority and centrality of the West in IR studies (Sanjay Seth 2021; Acharya and Buzan 2007; Mälksoo 2021) has determined how IR teaching is organized. A discussion about decolonizing IR and enriching the field with non-Western experience was initiated by Hoffmann (Hoffmann 1977) and has gone on for almost fifty years, aiming to deconstruct the modern architecture of knowledge (Tlostanova and Mignolo 2012). Yet, as Arlene Tickner writes, "twenty-five years after Stanley Hoffmann's critical depiction of IR as an American social science, the basic contours of IR have changed surprisingly little. IR textbooks continue to be written by American authors and rely upon 'Americano-centric' representations of global politics in which the United States is normally at the core of world events" (Tickner 2013: 297).

A decolonial approach to IR begins with acknowledging that "entrenched and deeply rooted social and political hierarchies based on exclusionary practices shape both geopolitics and the production of knowledge" (Adamson 2020: 131; Tickner and Wæver 2009; Acharya 2014). Decoloniality, in its turn, "de-normalized the normative, problematized default positions, debunks the a-perspectival, destabilizes the structure, and [offers] a programme to rehabilitate epistemic formations that continue to be repressed under coloniality" (Gallien 2020: 28).

Thus, reasoning for relegating Ukraine as well as the entire Eastern European region (excluding Russia) to a peripheral knowledge represented as lacking its own epistemological value owing to being perceived as a subordinate and complementary source of knowledge (Wolff 1994; Todorova 1997; Said 1979) is deeply rooted in IR studies and teaching, especially in the colonial architecture of IR knowledge, but also in a dichotomy of IR theorizing and Area Studies. Another reason for this "low-profile" epistemological interest is rooted in the liminality of Ukraine and the Eastern European region on the academic mental map. Ukraine and the region are neither "West" nor "non-West," neither "Global North" nor "Global South" (Acharya and Buzan 2010). The term "Global East" was invented to compensate for the lack of attribution and recognition to those who do not belong anywhere. Being placed in this category, the region experienced "dual exclusion"—while it was sidelined in current debates about the revalidation of Southern knowledge, it was also not included in imaginaries of a "Global North" (Muller 2020: 738). Mälksoo proves more broadly how Eastern European studies' status as a peripheral knowledge in IR is manifested by the underrepresentation of Eastern European scholars in most influential academic institutions and journals as well as by practices whereby the states of the region are represented as "mute objects, utilised simply for testing the validity of theoretical elaborations advanced by scholars in the West" (Malksoo 2021: 19).

In 2014, Acharya, appealing to the Global IR establishment, among other dimensions of this phenomenon named "commitment to pluralistic universalism," "redefining existing IR theories and methods and building new ones from societies hitherto ignored as sources of IR knowledge, integrating the study of regions and regionalisms into the central concerns of IR," and "recognizing a broader conception of agency" (Acharya 2014). This paper addresses the validity of Acharya's claims and investigates whether and how the teaching of IR reflected these appeals to improve what does not work in IR studies. It contributes to a discussion about "abundant westernization of the field but about its pluralization with the inclusion of what was not initially there" (Dunne 2013: 406).

This research argues that while Ukraine and the East European region are still "defining their place in the international division of academic labour" (Guzzini 2001: 108), their experience can contribute to teaching IR theories in a number of ways. This complicated search for placing Ukraine and Eastern Europe in the existing knowledge hierarchy stems from a binary dichotomy of IR studies and Area Studies. The region has historically been considered within Post-Soviet, or Post-Communist, or Russia and Eurasia studies (Karczmarska and Ortmann 2021) which localize it in Area Studies (Dale, Miklossy and Segert 2016) rather than IR theories which have been built on Western/great powers' experience (Buzan 2018: 391). In turn, IR theories have been "privileged" while Area Studies knowledge has limited theoretical value, and "IR theoretics are less reluctant to cite Area Studies (including critical studies and constructivists) than vice versa" (Kaczmarska 2020) and "knowledge produced in the periphery has to go through the transatlantic core in order to be recognized globally" (Risse, Wemheuer-Vogelaar, and Havemann 2022).

The reasons for this hierarchization are explicitly explained by Alejandro and Mälksoo as related but not limited to the late institutionalization and low internationalization of IR in Eastern Europe that implies late inclusion in IR production; and representation of the Eastern European region as "insignificant" both as an agent of world politics and a "locus of knowledge" (Alejandro 2022: 1001). This representation of the region leads to a situation when Western academic communities speak about others without deep knowledge of what are deemed to be "insignificant" countries and regions. That leads consequently to misperceptions, misunderstandings, and misbeliefs related to regional dynamics. Another reason for the low interest is concentration of the study of Eastern Europe within specific sub-fields and associated with the questions and topics of these sub-fields to the exclusion of others—e.g., Eastern Europe is more represented in international security studies than in IR in general (Mälksoo 2021). Though the discussion on the contribution which the Eastern European region can make to IR studies is not new (see Drulák 2009), an ongoing lack of mutual enrichment between IR theories and Area Studies, separation and hierarchy between them (Kaczmarska, Ortmann 2021) stipulates low probability for the utilization of empirical material provided by Area Studies to IR studies.

Ukraine, being trapped in "epistemological imperialism" (Hendl *et al.* 2023; Sonevytsky 2022), emerges in the scholarly debates due to the Russian invasion of 2022 and its resilient response as well as by way of paying tribute to Ukrainian scholars affected by the war. To secure the long-standing epistemological value the country and the region present for enriching IR theory's development and teaching, we position this discussion as a contribution to integrative pluralism (Dunne: 406) and "pluriversity" that is, in Mbebe's understanding, "a process of knowledge production that is open to epistemic diversity" (Mbembe 2016: 37).

Methodological Approach to IR Syllabi and Curricula Analysis

Relying on the theoretical approaches discussed above, this research into the IR studies curricula and syllabi pursued a two-fold objective. First, it focused on detecting changes predominantly in MA and PhD IR curricula and syllabi of IR theory-related courses brought by/after the Russian invasion. These changes may be represented by a new course or a module or a topic, or a new reading source related to the lessons learnt from the war. Special attention was paid to the inclusion of publications by authors coming from Ukraine. The author focused on MA/PhD programs on IR studies but also examined the syllabi for Introduction to IR courses—courses traditionally delivered to undergraduate students. The latter usually utilize traditional mainstream theories while leaving critical theories and postcolonial theories in particular for masters program courses, but I decided to include them so as to investigate whether the war had given an impetus to re-consider the validity of the mainstream theories through provoking new questions for discussion or relevant readings.

Since this research aims to prove the empirical added value of the war-related material for teaching Postcolonial Studies, another objective set was detecting utilization of Eastern European (post)colonial experience in teaching critical/postcolonial theories in IR as a part of IR theory or broader IR studies. We consider the latter as an appropriate niche where Ukraine's postcolonial experience generalizations along with neocolonial Russia's politics could cover those deficiencies which were revealed in the mainstream theories in explaining the reasons for and nature of the war and actors' behavior. Hence I set out to detect references to Ukraine or other Eastern European countries in topics, assignments, reading sources, discussion questions in the syllabi.

My analysis covered pre-2022 (2015–2022) and post-2022 curricula and syllabi. The year 2015 was selected as the one following Russia's illegal annexation of Crimea and temporary occupation of Eastern Ukrainian territories that could lead to theoretical re-considerations. For this goal, I analyzed such courses as Postcolonial studies, Postcolonial theory, Postcolonial IR theory, and Critical IR theory. A total of 26 universities were selected with 14 from the US and UK and 12 from continental Europe. Thirty-three syllabi and 14 curricula were analyzed (see tables below).

Complementary to these goals, I also paid attention to the utilization of the publications written by the scholars from the non-Western world, namely, the Global South, with the purpose of correlating the trends in decolonizing IR by inclusion of Global South scholars and decolonizing IR by offering publications written by scholars from the Eastern European region.

My main purpose was detecting changes in the syllabi and/or curricula which occurred after Russia launched the full-scale war of aggression. Thus, if no Ukraine/war related content was detected in post-2022 syllabi or the changes directly referred to the war and its consequences, the author skipped searching pre-2022 sources which apparently could not contain any relevant content. In the event that region- (not war-) related content was present in post-2022 sources, the author searched for pre-2022 sources to understand whether changes were brought by the war or occurred earlier. Due to these considerations the author has analyzed 10 pre-2022 and 23 post-2022 syllabi.

For the purposes of this research, the selection of the leading Western schools in IR/political sciences was made based on study portals popular among students such as "Topuniversities" (QS World University Rankings 2023), "Studyportal" (Best IR Schools in the World 2022), and "Shanghai Global Ranking" (Global Ranking of Academic Subjects 2022), which engage from

30 to 150 million viewers annually, as well as *Foreign Policy* journal and *Guardian* IR schools rankings (The Best International Relations Schools in the World 2018; Best UK universities for international relations 2024), in which the rankings of the universities principally overlap. Since IR traditionally remains a predominantly US-UK field, the majority of universities in the rankings belong to the Anglo-American tradition. However, the European IR tradition, having powerful influence over the continent and globally, studies IR in quite a distinct way—hence my decision to include a selection of universities from Germany, France, Italy, and the Netherlands in order to secure fair representation of the so-called Western IR tradition that cannot be narrowed to the Anglo-American one. Two Canadian Universities were also included in the research, again, as IR study and teaching in Canada is very different from the US case (Lipson *et al.* 2007) and as they are attracting an impressive number of students from around the globe.

The main limitation of the research concerns the access to the syllabi and curricula for the requisite consecutive number of years. For a number of universities curricula and syllabi were not available not only for the most recent five years in a row, but sometimes for the current year as well. Sometimes they upload a condensed version of syllabi for open access (without details on questions/assignments for discussion, for example). Still, the author considers that these limitations did not jeopardize detection of general trends as all the universities analyzed provided the latest syllabi designed already after 2022.

Post-2022 Changes in IR Studies: Results of Data Analysis and Discussion of Main Findings

The tables below present the courses on which data was collected, listing program level, year of teaching and presence/absence of Ukraine/Eastern Europe related topics or assignments and questions for discussion, and of Ukrainian scholars' publications in the reading list. The last column shows presence/absence of the respective content on the Global South countries or publications of the scholars representing them in the reading lists.

University	Syllabus	Level	Academic year/semester	EE/UA related content / reading	Non-Western countries content / reading
Bristol University	Theories of International Relations	MA	2021-2022	-	-
Freie Universität Berlin	Introduction to International Relations Theories of IR	BA	2024-2025 2021 2024	-	-
Georgetown University	Introduction to International Relations	MA	Summer 2022	-	-
Harvard University	International Relations Field Seminar	MA	Fall 2022	-	+
	Theories of International Relations	MA	2019	-	+
London School of Economics	International Relations: Theories, Concepts and Debates	MA	2022-2023	-	+
	International Relations: Theories, Concepts and Debates	BA	2021-2022	-	+
Martin Luther Universität Halle-Wittenberg	International Relations	BA	2022	+	
McGill University	International Relations as Postcolonial Relations	MA/ PhD	Fall 2023	-	+
	Theories of International Relations	MA	Fall 2020	-	+
	Theories of International Relations	MA	Winter 2024	-	+
Pennsylvania University	International Relations Theory	PhD	Fall 2023	+	+
Princeton Woodrow Wilson School of Public and Int Affairs	International Politics	MA	2018-2019 2023-2024	- -	+ +
SciencesPo	Theories of International Relations	MA	2021-2022	-	-

	Critical Theories of International Relations. The making of the Modern World Order			2021-2022	-
	Critical Theories of International Relations. The making of the Modern World Order			2023-2024	+
Scuola Normale Superiore	Postcolonialism and IR	PhD, MA	2024	+	
University of Bologna	Theories of International Relations (Advanced)	PhD, MA	Fall 2022	+	-
	Theories of International Relations (Advanced)	PhD, MA	Fall 2021	-	-
University of Glasgow	Post-colonial IR theory	PhD	2023-2024	-	+
	Introduction to International Relations	BA	2024-2025	+	+
	International Relations theories	MA	2023-2024	+	+
University of Oslo	International Politics: Key Debates	MA	Autumn 2024	+	+
	International Politics	MA	Summer 2024 Summer 2021	+	
University of Osnabruck	Introduction to the International Relations	BA	2024	+	
University of London	Postcolonial studies	MA	2023-2024	-	+
University of Toronto	Introduction to International Relations	BA	Summer 2023	-	-
	Postcolonial Debates in International Relations	MA	Winter 2022	-	+
Utrecht University	Postcolonial studies	MA	2024-2025	-	+

Curricula: New courses launched since 2022

Columbia University	Fragmentation of the World: Ukraine and Taiwan as Cases	MA	Fall 2023	+
	Ukraine: Power Politics & Diplomacy	MA	Spring 2024	+
	Ukrainian Foreign Policy: Russia, Europe, and the US		Fall 2022	
	Politics of Identity in Post-Communist Europe		Spring 2024	
Freie Universität Berlin	Russia's attack on Ukraine—geopolitical and geoeconomic perspectives	MA	2023-2024	+
	Russia's War Against Ukraine	MA	2022-2023	+
Humboldt University	Institute for Social Sciences, Faculty of Cultural, Social and Educational Sciences	BA/MA	2023-2024	-
John Hopkins Krieger School of Arts and Sciences	International Studies	BA/MA	2024	-
London School of Economics	Eastern Europe: Domestic Regimes and Foreign Policies	PhD, MA	2022-2023	-
SciencesPo	The Russia-Ukraine War: An International Relations Theory Guide	MA	2023-2024	+
	Comparative Political Economy: Russia, Ukraine and Belarus			
	Politics and society in Russia at a time of war in Ukraine		Spring 2024	
	How the war in Ukraine is changing the EU		Spring 2024	
	First Strategic Lessons of the Russian War in Ukraine		Fall 2024	
St. Andrews University	Theoretical Approaches to International Relations—has Post-Colonialism	MA	2024-2025	-
University of Amsterdam	International Relations (Political Science)	MA	2024-2025	-
University of Cambridge	International Relations	BA	2022-2023	-
Utrecht University	International Relations (minor)	BA	2024-2025	-

The exploration of the curricula and syllabi shows some modest splash of interest in Ukraine's experience and its effect on the teaching of IR—nine out of thirty-three syllabi and six out of fourteen curricula contain changes related to the war and/or its consequences. Newly suggested courses belong mainly to elective ones, which raises a question about their lifespan. Several universities proposed new courses or topics after the invasion of 2022 for their master programs in IR. Columbia University offered a course "Politics of Identity in Post-Communist Europe" (Columbia University 2024) in 2024, inviting a Ukrainian scholar to teach with a focus on relations between politics and identities in post-communist Eastern, Central, and Southern Europe. Free University Berlin launched a new course "Russia's Attack on Ukraine—Geopolitical and Geoeconomic Perspectives" (Freie Universität Berlin 2023–2024) focusing on examination of the causes and consequences of the war from a geopolitical and geoeconomic perspective and the effects for the EU. The University of Bologna included the topic "The Ukrainian War" within the course "Theories of International Relations (Advanced)" (Universita di Bologna 2022–2023) as one of the perspectives on international relations. University of Halle included a topic "Genesis and Consequences of the War in Ukraine" into its IR course (Martin Luther Universität Halle-Wittenberg 2022).

We could argue over the possible reasons for the lack or absence of changes in IR curricula/syllabi, namely, the insufficient time that has elapsed since the start of Russia's full-scale invasion start and the consequent lack of research completed; or the lack of existing publications written by scholars from the region in Anglo-Saxon or Roman languages. However, the first time-related argument is contested by the presence of COVID-related courses already in the summer semester 2021 curricula (Georgetown University 2022; Freie Universität Berlin 2021) although this phenomenon had been intervening into social life for a very short period of time. The second can be contested by a variety of articles which emerged in high-ranking academic journals in 2022–2024—both Scopus and Web of Science indexed—written by representatives of the region (Burlyuk, Misliu 2023; Dudko 2022; Golubev 2023; Kurylo

2023 etc.). An excellent example is the syllabus on Postcolonialism and IR delivered in Scuola Normale Superiore where the topic on the war is supported by a number of sources including those written by Ukrainian scholars (Scuola Normale Superiore 2024).

Empirical material generated by Ukrainian/Eastern European experiences emerge in the curricula and/or syllabi in several capacities. Firstly, as a foundation for reconsideration and theorizing broader topics, which illuminates the perceived limited value that the processes in the region have for theoretical knowledge generation. For example, a number of courses offer the study of the effects the war has for European security and political transformations of the EU (Sciences Po 2024a,b) as well as for nuclear non-proliferation regime perspectives (University of Glasgow 2023-2024a); or how the war reflects US decline (Sciences Po). Secondly, we find a realist-dominated approach to discussing the war that is usually accompanied by Mearsheimer's most famous paper along with others where the authors try to grasp Russia's politics (e.g., "How we Got Putin so Wrong" in University of Oslo 2024). Thirdly, Ukraine/region-generated material is used more like an exotic case-study similarly to how Covid-19 was represented in previous years and most probably will be sidelined after the war ends. In some courses Ukraine becomes an exotic object for explaining theories in a format of events/public lectures, roundtables (Universität Bremen), which prove a temporary transitory interest to be dissolved after the war ends.

Along with the ongoing discourse on decolonizing IR and IR difference, African, Asian, and Latin American cases are present in the curricula as empirical material for gender studies or modernization studies, as well as regional security, foreign policy and development studies—e.g., Indian and Latin American politics as separate courses (Freie Universität Berlin 2021; 2024a,b; Columbia University 2023–2024; University of Glasgow 2023–2024a). While IR theory-related courses at Harvard, John Hopkins University, and St. Andrews University include topics on Postcolonial IR reflecting on African, Chinese, Asian IR (Harvard University 2019; University of St. Andrews 2023–2024; John Hopkins University

2024), Eastern European (post)colonial experience is not suggested for consideration. Where postcolonial studies courses are offered as interdisciplinary minors, they have geographic limits—(South) Africa, the Caribbean, India, South America, Australia as well as highlighting the study of race, gender, class, the violent legacies of slavery along with practices of resistance and national liberation movements which challenged Western thought and brought global IR transformations (Utrecht University 2024; SciencesPo; SciencesPo 2022–2023; Harvard University 2019; University of Glasgow 2023–2024b). While nineteen out of thirty-three collected syllabi contain references either to topics related to the Global South or offer readings by local scholars, the empirical material on Russia's war against Ukraine—which is justly named a war of liberation from Russian (neo)colonial practices—as well as publications of Ukrainian scholars are still awaiting inclusion to the courses within the IR/Postcolonial realm.

Analysis of the reading lists in a number of syllabi on Postcolonial studies/IR reveals the prevalence of traditional works by Fanon, Said, Bhaba, Mbebe, Spivak which reflect on Asian and African colonial experiences (Freie Universität Berlin 2018–2019, Freie Universität Berlin 2022, University of Toronto 2022, McGill University 2023). Seth's, Dunne's and Tickner's papers on pluralism in IR studies (Seth 2021; Dunne 2013; Tickner 2013) nevertheless are not followed by proposal of papers reflecting on Eastern European experiences (Malksoo 2021, 2023; Burlyuk Misliu 2023; Kurylo 2023; Kassymbekova, Chokobaeva 2023; Doyle 2020). Even the fullest reading list on postcolonial IR found in the course syllabus "Postcolonial IR Theories" at the Glasgow School of Social and Political Sciences does not suggest any reading on Eastern European practices (University of Glasgow 2023–2024). This shows that postcolonial approaches are still delivered from the angle of Western colonial practices to the affected countries without any reference to Russia's colonial rule patterns and effects.

Considering the broad presence of Russia-related courses, e.g., foreign and domestic policy of Russia or Russia in world politics at the London School of Economics (2022–2023), Humboldt-

Universität zu Berlin (2024), John Hopkins University (2024), Columbia University (2023–2024), and the offer of alternative reasoning for Russia's subaltern imperial behavior (Morozov) in a Postcolonialism course (Georgetown University 2020) along with quite significant scope of inclusion of publications from Global South scholars into the syllabi, the absence of references to Eastern Europe's epistemic contributions raises a question about the double marginalization of Ukrainian voices. The syllabi, on the other hand, reflect the traditional attention paid to the study of Russia's policies which is apparently needed to comprehend and predict its behavior (a topic beyond the scope of the current study). And on the other hand, they justly include the studies of scholars from Global South in IR/postcolonial studies.

Ignoring Ukrainian voices in those curricula and syllabi can serve as a manifestation of limited or deprived epistemic agency which leads to inter-coloniality. The latter exists together with the inter-imperiality when Ukraine-generated knowledge is marginalized by both Western and Russian academia (Hendl 2023; Doyle 2020; Sonevytsky 2022). When we talk about inter-coloniality of knowledge, we imply silencing by the Western academia of Ukrainian (and other regional) voices and ignoring the significance of Ukraine-generated material on the one hand, and, on the other, rendering insignificance to Ukrainian (neo)colonial experience in relations with Russia as a colonial empire. Even if new IR courses involving Ukraine-related topics emerge, like "Fragmentation of the World: Ukraine and Taiwan as Cases" in Columbia University (Columbia University 2023), they ignore Ukraine as a knowledge-productive source, making it voiceless.

Conclusions

The discussion presented shows the need for encouraging the ongoing decolonization of IR, deprivation of epistemic hegemony and hierarchy of knowledge production followed by enriching IR theorizing in the teaching process as a mean to empower students with diverse epistemological tools. The fact that Russia's war against Ukraine brought about few to no changes in the teaching of IR studies in Western academic institutions reflects the ongoing practices of exclusionary hierarchical constructs centered on the policies and practices of great powers and institutions. Meanwhile, the role of small/medium powers from within areas which have not been traditionally considered as colonized in a classical sense, is still marginalized in IR theories, being rather localised in Area Studies.

This study has shown that Ukraine-generated empirical material and its representation by Ukrainian scholars are either marginalized or included as an object rather than subject of research, underpinning theoretical constructs or performing as material for the study of more tangible and "important" issues like European security or non-proliferation regime perspectives. This inference contributes to the discussion on the "power dynamic of epistemic injustice" when Ukrainians are considered "incapable of producing reliable knowledge" (Hendl 2023).

The meager nature of the post-2022 changes made in the IR studies curricula and syllabi on IR theories and Postcolonial studies, which were at the center of the current research, bring several important inferences. Firstly, they show the unreadiness of Western academia to question the explanatory value of the mainstream IR theories. Secondly, the ongoing process of decolonizing IR, while outlining moderate progress in a broader inclusiveness of scholars from the Global South, whose publications are offered in the syllabi on postcolonialism and even IR theories (as part of non-Western IR theories), still lacks recognition of Eastern European postcolonial experiences and cases, including that of Russia-Ukraine relations. Thirdly, the presence of courses targeting Russia's politics along with Russian scholars in the reading lists without respective Ukrainian components will continue the practices of normalizing Russia's aggression and overlooking the reasons for Ukrainian behavior and responsive practices, while simultaneously silencing Ukrainian voices.

The presence of these three components brings to the surface the need to search for tools for overcoming the existing epistemic inter-coloniality embedded in depriving Ukraine of agency as a knowledge generator and denying its right to possess a decent place in postcolonial studies. Changes that could be expected in the IR/Postcolonial studies syllabi and curricula could include inviting a larger number of Ukrainian scholars to teach and research; and incorporating publications produced by them, especially on Ukraine/Eastern Europe related content and on Russia's neocolonial practices. This acceptance and inclusion to IR studies could relevantly address the deficiencies of the mainstream IR theories with the complementary toolkit offered by postcolonial approaches.

Deeper study of Russian policies and practices in the "near abroad" as (post-/neo-)colonial along with the widely accepted notion of imperial could contribute to IR theories' explanatory potential, placing the East European region in knowledge production and illuminating the role postcolonialism could perform as a helpful bridge in the better understanding of IR, through the employment of concepts such as the power dynamic, colonizer-colonized dichotomy, recognition, identity inferiority, hybridity, representation. Securing the long-standing reference to the country and region to enrich IR theories' development and teaching would correlate with the principles of integrative pluralism (Dunne 2013, 406) and "pluriversity" that in Mbebe's understanding is "a process of knowledge production that is open to epistemic diversity" (Mbebe 2016: 37). Openness to IR studies diversity with integrating EE postcolonial knowledge could help eliminate existing epistemic inequalities and overcome inter-coloniality in Western academia.

References

Acharya, Amitav. (2014) "Global International Relations (IR) and Regional Worlds: A New Agenda for International Studies," *International Studies Quarterly* 58(4): 647–59.

Acharya, Amitav and Buzan, Barry. (2017) "Why is There No Non-Western International Relations Theory? Ten Years On," *International Relations of the Asia-Pacific* 17(3): 341–70.

Adamson, Fiona. (2020) "Pushing the Boundaries: Can We 'Decolonize' Security Studies?" *Journal of Global Security Studies* 5(1): 129–35.

Alejandro, Audrey. (2022) "Do International Relations Scholars Not Care about Central and Eastern Europe or Do They Just Take the Region for Granted?" A conclusion to the special issue, *Journal of International Relations and Development* 25: 1001–1013.

"Best IR Schools in the World 2022." https://www.mastersportal.com/articles/2778/best-international-relations-schools-in-the-world-university-rankings-2022.html.

"Best UK universities for international relations." (2024) https://www.theguardian.com/education/ng-interactive/2023/sep/09/best-uk-universities-for-international-relations-league-table.

Bhabha, Homi K. (1994) *The Location of Culture*. London and New York: Routledge.

Bouchet, Nicolas. (2015) *Democracy Promotion as US Foreign Policy: Bill Clinton and Democratic Enlargement*. London and New York: Routledge.

Burlyuk, Olga and Musliu, Vjosa. (2023) "The Responsibility to Remain Silent? On the Politics of Knowledge Production, Expertise and (Self-)Reflection in Russia's War against Ukraine," *Journal of International Relations and Development* 26: 605–18.

Buzan, Barry. (2018) "How and How Not to Develop IR Theory: Lessons from Core and Periphery," *The Chinese Journal of International Politics* 11(4): 391-414.

Chernetsky, Vitaly. (2003) "Postcolonialism, Russia and Ukraine," *Ulbandus Review* 7: 32–62.

Columbia University. (2021) "Theories of International Relations," Syllabus. https://polisci.columbia.edu/sites/default/files/content/pdfs/JackSyllabus%206801%20Theories%20of%20International%20Relations.pdf.

Columbia University. (2023) "Fragmentation of the World: Ukraine and Taiwan as Cases." https://bulletin.columbia.edu/search/?P=REGN%20U8760

Columbia University. (2023–2024) Political Science. 2023–2024 Year at a glance. https://polisci.columbia.edu/content/2023-24-year-glance.

Columbia University. (2024) "Politics of Identity in Post-Communist Europe," Syllabus. https://bulletin.columbia.edu/search/?P=REGN%20U6520.

Copeland, Dale C. (1996) "Economic Interdependence and War: A Theory of Trade Expectations," *International Security* 20(4): 5–41.

Dale, Gareth, Miklossy, Katalin, and Segert, Dieter (eds). (2016) *The Politics of East European Area Studies*. London and New York: Routledge.

Davis, A., Thakur, V. and Vale, P. (2020) *The Imperial Discipline: Race and the Founding of International Relations*. London: Pluto Press.

Davies, Norman. (2022) "Decolonizing Eastern European Studies: Interview with Professor Norman Davies," Cambridge University Ukrainian Society, 16 June, available at https://www.facebook.com/CUUAsoc/videos/decolonizing-eastern-european-studies-interview-with-professor-norman-davies/1560014551062883/.
Donovan, Victoria. (2023) "Against Academic 'Resourcification': Collaboration as Delinking from Extractivist 'Area Studies' Paradigms," *Canadian Slavonic Papers* 65(2): 163–73.
Doyle, Laura. (2020) *Inter-imperiality: Vying Empires, Gendered Labor, and the Literary Arts of Alliance*. Durham, NC: Duke University Press.
Drulák, Petr. (2009) "Going Native? The Discipline of IR in Central and Eastern Europe," *Przeglad Europejski* 1(27): 10-14.
Dudko, Oksana. (2022) "A Conceptual Limbo of Genocide: Russian Rhetoric, Mass Atrocities in Ukraine, and the Current Definition's Limits," *Canadian Slavonic Papers* 64(2-3): 133–45.
Dunne, T., Hansen, L., Wight, C. (2013) "The End of International Relations Theory?" *European Journal of International Relations* 19(3): 405–25.
Dutkiewicz, Jan and Smolenski, Jan. (2023) "Epistemic Superimposition: The War in Ukraine and the Poverty of Expertise in International Relations Theory," *Journal of International Relations and Development* 26: 619–31.
Fanon, Frantz. (1963) *The Wretched of the Earth*. New York: Grove Press.
"Foreign Policy Concept of the Russian Federation." (2000) Approved by the President of the Russian Federation 28 June 2000, available at https://docs.cntd.ru/document/901764263.
Freie Universität Berlin. (2018–2019) "Introduction into Postcolonial Theory and Critique," https://www.polsoz.fu-berlin.de/polwiss/forschung/international/frieden/lehre/2018_19ws/15364_S/index.html.
Freie Universität Berlin. (2021) "Otto Suhr Institute for Political Science," https://archiv.vv.fu-berlin.de/ss21/en/module/0257b_MA120/.
Freie Universität Berlin. (2022) "Lektürekurs: Frantz Fanon und die postkoloniale Theorie," https://www.fu-berlin.de/vv/de/lv/731190?m=183688&p=183643&pc=74963&sm=682080.
Freie Universität Berlin. (2023–2024) "Russlands Angriff auf die Ukraine – geopolitische und geoökonomische Perspektiven," https://www.fu-berlin.de/vv/en/lv/809069?m=409798&pc=575029&sm=754328.
Freie Universität Berlin. (2024a) "Global IR: Kritische Perspektiven zu 'Internationalen Beziehungen' in Asien," https://www.fu-berlin.de/vv/en/lv/882065?m=409818&pc=575029&sm=814672&id=882065.Freie Universität Berlin. (2024b) "Masterstudiengang Internationale Beziehungen," https://www.fu-berlin.de/vv/de/modul?id=575029&sm=814672.

Gallien, Claire. (2020) "A Decolonial Turn in the Humanities," *Journal of Comparative Poetics* 40: 28–58.
Gat, Azar. (2005) "The Democratic Peace Theory Reframed: The Impact of Modernity," *World Politics* 58(1): 73–100.
Georgetown University. (2020) "Postcolonialism," Syllabus. available at https://giwps.georgetown.edu/wp-content/uploads/2020/10/Postcolonialism.pdf.
Georgetown University. (2022) "Introduction to International Relations," Syllabus. https://static.scs.georgetown.edu/upload/files/syllabi/term_202220/course_GOVT-060/section_21/GOVT060-21.pdf.
"Global Ranking of Academic Subjects." Political Sciences (2022). https://www.shanghairanking.com/rankings/gras/2022/RS0504.
Golubev, Alexey. (2023) "No Natural Colonization: The Early Soviet School of Historical Anti-Colonialism," *Canadian Slavonic Papers* 65(2): 190–204.
Guzzini, S. (2001) "The Significance and Roles of Teaching Theory in International Relations," *Journal of International Relations and Development* 4: 98–117.
Hagström, Linus. (2021) "Great Power Narcissism and Ontological (In)Security: The Narrative Mediation of Greatness and Weakness in International Politics," *International Studies Quarterly* 65(2): 331–42.
Harvard University. (2019) "Theories of International Relations," Syllabus. https://scholar.harvard.edu/files/brianpalmiter/files/POLSCI380.syllabus.spring_2019.pdf.
Hassan, S. and Sajjad, F. (2022) "The Decolonial Turn: New Challenges to International Relations Traditions," *Journal of Contemporary Studies* 11(2): 23–41.
Hendl, Tereza, Burlyuk, Olga, O'Sullivan Mila, Arystanbek, Aizada. (2023) "(En)Countering Epistemic Imperialism: A Critique of 'Westsplaining' and Coloniality in Dominant Debates on Russia's Invasion of Ukraine," *Contemporary Security Policy* 45(2): 171–209.
Hoffman, S. (1977) "An American Social Science: International Relations," *Daedalus* 106(3): 41–60.
Humboldt-Universität zu Berlin. (2024) "Heilige Rus und 'Russische Welt'," https://agnes.hu-berlin.de/lupo/rds?state=verpublish&status=init&vmfile=no&publishid=214755&moduleCall=webInfo&publishConfFile=webInfo&publishSubDir=veranstaltung.
Hutchings, Kimberly (2023) "Doing Epistemic Justice in International Relations: Women and the History of International Thought," *European Journal of International Relations* 29(4): 809–31.
John Hopkins University. (2024) Program in International Studies. https://krieger.jhu.edu/internationalstudies/undergraduate/courses/course-schedule/.

Kaczmarska, Katarzyna. (2020) *Making Global Knowledge in Local Contexts: The Politics of International Relations and Policy Advice in Russia.* London, New York: Routledge.
Kaczmarska, Katarzyna and Ortmann, Stefanie. (2021) "IR Theory and Area Studies: A Plea for Displaced Knowledge about International Politics," *Journal of International Relations and Development* 24: 820–47.
Kassymbekova, Botakoz. (2022) "Empires and Nation-States: The Russian-Ukrainian War and Decolonizing of Eastern European Studies," Deutsch-Ukrainische Historische Kommission, 17 November, available at https://www.youtube.com/watch?v=qL26qQXwjS0.
Kassymbekova, Botakoz, and Chokobaeva, Aminat. (2023) "Expropriation, Assimilation, Elimination: Understanding Soviet Settler Colonialism," *South/South Dialogues.* https://www.southsouthmovement.org/dialogues/expropriation-assimilation-elimination-understanding-soviet-settler-colonialism/.
Kazharski, Aliaksei. (2022) "Explaining the 'Westsplainers': Can a Western Scholar be an Authority on Central and Eastern Europe?," *Forum for Ukrainian Studies*, 19 July, available at: https://ukrainian-studies.ca/2022/07/19/explaining-the-westsplainers-can-a-western-scholar-be-an-authority-on-central-and-eastern-europe/.
Khylko, Olena. (2017) "Security Options for Eastern Europe," *Wschód Europy. Studia Humanistyczno-Społeczne* 3(2): 67–80.
Koplatadze, Tamar. (2019) "Theorising Russian Postcolonial Studies," *Postcolonial Studies* 22(4): 469–89.
Küçük, Mine Nur. (2022) "Postcolonial Approaches in International Relations," in M. Kürşad Özekin and Engin Sune (eds.), *Critical Approaches to International Relations: Philosophical Foundations and Current Debates.* Leiden: Brill, 157–74.
Kurylo, Bohdana. (2023) "The Ukrainian Subject, Hierarchies of Knowledge Production and the Everyday: An Autoethnographic Narrative," *Journal of International Relations and Development* 26: 685–97.
Lipson, Michael, Maliniak, Daniel, Oakes, Amy, Peterson, Susan, Tierney, Michael J. (2007) "Divided Discipline? Comparing Views of US and Canadian IR Scholars," *International Journal* 62(2): 327–43.
London School of Economics. (2022–2023) "International Relations Courses." Master Programme. https://info.lse.ac.uk/current-students/services/assets/documents/Controlled-access-courses-22-23-PDF.pdf.
Makarychev, Andrey and Nizhnikau, Ryhor. (2023) "Normalize and Rationalize: Intellectuals of Statecraft and Russia's War in Ukraine," *Journal of International Relations and Development* 26: 632–42.

Mälksoo, Maria (2021) "Captive Minds: The Function and Agency of Eastern Europe in International Security Studies," *Journal of International Relations and Development* 24: 866–89.

Mälksoo, Maria. (2023) "The Postcolonial Moment in Russia's War Against Ukraine," *Journal of Genocide Research* 25(3–4): 471–81.

Martin Luther Universität Halle-Wittenberg. (2022) "Vorlesung: BA Basismodul Einführung in die Internationalen Beziehungen - (Vorlesung)," https://studip.uni-halle.de/dispatch.php/course/details/?sem_id=078c8f5e3d9ee2801b3e78ed14ac93d4&send_from_searc h=1&send_from_search_page=https%3A%2F%2Fstudip.uni-halle.de %3A443%2Fdispatch.php%3Fkeep_result_set%3D1&set_language= de_DE.

Mbembe, Achille. (2016) "Decolonizing the University: New Directions," *Arts and Humanities in Higher Education* 15(1): 29–45.

McGill University. (2023) "International Relations as Postcolonial Relation," Syllabus. https://www.mcgill.ca/politicalscience/files/politic alscience/poli676_syllabus_f23_final.pdf.

Mearsheimer, John J. (2014) "Why the Ukraine Crisis Is the West's Fault. The Liberal Delusions That Provoked Putin," *Foreign Affairs* 93(5): 77–89.

Moore, David Chioni. (2001) "Is the Post- in Postcolonial the Post- in Post-Soviet? Toward a Global Postcolonial Critique," *PMLA* 116(1): 111–28.

Morozov, Viatcheslav. (2015) *Russia's Postcolonial Identity: A Subaltern Empire in a Eurocentric World*. London: Palgrave Macmillan.

Müller, Martin. (2020) "In Search of the Global East: Thinking between North and South," *Geopolitics* 25(3): 735–55.

Nye, Joseph S. Jr. (2022a) "Eight Lessons from the Ukraine War," *Project Syndicate*, 15 June, https://www.project-syndicate.org/commentary /russia-war-in-ukraine-eight-lessons-by-joseph-s-nye-2022-06.

Nye, Joseph S. Jr. (2022b) "What Caused the Ukraine War?," *Project Syndicate*, 4 October, https://www.project-syndicate.org/commentary/ what-caused-russia-ukraine-war-by-joseph-s-nye-2022-10.

O'Sullivan, Míla and Krulišová, Kateřina. (2023) "Central European Subalterns Speak Security (Too): Towards a Truly Post-Western Feminist Security Studies," *Journal of International Relations and Development* 26: 660–74.

Pavlyshyn, Marko. (1993) "Ukrainian Literature and the Erotics of Postcolonialism: Some Modest Propositions," *Harvard Ukrainian Studies* 17(1/2): 110–26.

Risse, Thomas, Wemheuer-Vogelaar, Wiebke, Havemann, Frank. (2022) "IR Theory and the Core–Periphery Structure of Global IR: Lessons from Citation Analysis," *International Studies Review* 24(3).

Robles, Alfredo C. Jr. (1993) "How 'International' Are International Relations Syllabi?" *Political Science and Politics* 26(3): 526–28.
"QS World University Rankings by Subject 2023: Politics." https://www.topuniversities.com/university-subject-rankings/politics.
Said, Edward W. (1979) *Orientalism*. New York: Vintage Books.
Schultz, Kenneth. (2013) "Domestic Politics and International Relations," in Walter Carlsnaes, Thomas Risse, and Beth A. Simmons (eds.), *Handbook of International Relations*. London: SAGE Publications: 478–502.
Sciences Po. (2022–2023) "Critical Theories of International Relations. The Making of the Modern World Order," https://syllabus.sciencespo.fr/cours/202220/223147.html.
Sciences Po. (2024a) "Comment la guerre d'Ukraine change l'UE," Master Programme. https://syllabus.sciencespo.fr/fr/?mapping/189362
Sciences Po. (2024b) "First Strategic Lessons of the Russian War in Ukraine," Master Programme in International Security, https://syllabus.sciencespo.fr/fr/?mapping/189375#_gl=1*h1o3aw*_gcl_au*MjQ2OTk1ODY5LjE3MTc1MDM5NzU.VVVVVVVVVVVVVVVV.
Sciences Po. (2023) "The Russia-Ukraine War. An International Relations Theory Guide," Syllabus. https://www.sciencespobordeaux.fr/fr/formation/diplome-d-institut-d-etudes-politiques/deuxieme-cycle-parcours-de-masters-cycle2/bordeaux-international-relations-degree-bird-ICOS4UK2/quatrieme-annee-bird-K49N69MV/the-russia-ukraine-war-an-international-relations-theory-guide-LAQNFF1O.html.
Scuola Normale Superiore. (2024) "Postcolonialism and International Relations," Syllabus. https://www.sns.it/en/corsoinsegnamento/postcolonialism-and-international-relations.
Seth, Sanjay (2021) "International Relations: Plural or Postcolonial?" *International Politics Reviews* 9(2): 301–05.
Spivak, Gayatri Chakravorty, Condee, Nancy, Ram, Harsha and Chernetsky, Vitaly. (2006) "Are We Postcolonial? Post-Soviet Space," *PMLA* 121(3): 828–36.
Smith, Steve (1995) 'The Self-Images of a Discipline: A Genealogy of International Relations Theory," in Ken Booth and Steve Smith (eds.) *International Relations Theory Today*. Oxford: Polity Press, 1–37.
Snyder, Timothy. (2022) "The War in Ukraine is a Colonial War," *The New Yorker*, 28 April, https://www.newyorker.com/news/essay/the-war-in-ukraine-is-a-colonial-war.
Sonevytsky, Maria. (2022) "What Is Ukraine? Notes On Epistemic Imperialism," *Topos* 2: 21–30.
Szeptycki, Andrzej. (2011) "Ukraine as A Postcolonial State?" *The Polish Quarterly of International Affairs* 20(1): 5–29.

"The Best International Relations Schools in the World." (2018) https://foreignpolicy.com/2018/02/20/top-fifty-schools-international-relations-foreign-policy/

Tickner, Arlene. (2013) "Core, Periphery and (Neo)Imperialist International Relations," *European Journal of International Relations* 19(3): 627-46.

Tlostanova, Madina V, and Mignolo, Walter G. (2012) *Learning to Unlearn: Decolonial Reflections from Eurasia and the America*. Columbus, OH: Ohio State University Press.

Todorova, Maria. (1997) *Imagining the Balkans*. Oxford: Oxford University Press.

Tolz, Vera and Hutchings, Stephen. (2023) "Truth with a Z: Disinformation, War in Ukraine, and Russia's Contradictory Discourse of Imperial Identity," *Post-Soviet Affairs* 39 (5): 347-65.

Trenin, Dmitriy. (2013) "The Fourth Vector of Vladimir Putin," *Russia in Global Politics*, 30 May, https://globalaffairs.ru/articles/chetvertyj-vektor-vladimira-putina/.

Tucker, K. (2018) "Unraveling Coloniality in International Relations: Knowledge, Relationality, and Strategies for Engagement," *International Political Sociology* 12(3): 215-32.

Universität Bremen. (n/d). "Ukraine. 'Zur Erklärung eines Angriffskrieges," https://www.uni-bremen.de/suchen?q=Kritische+Theorie+syllabus

Universita di Bologna (2022-2023) "Theories of International Relations (Advanced)," Syllabus. https://www.unibo.it/en/teaching/course-unit-catalogue/course-unit/2022/484996.

University of Glasgow. (2023-2024a) "Politics 1B: Introduction to International Relations," https://rl.talis.com/3/glasgow/lists/CFA9C287-3497-A3B9-C6D2-8FF867164F19.html?lang=en-GB.

University of Glasgow (2023-2024b) "Post-Colonial IR theory. Reading List," https://rl.talis.com/3/glasgow/lists/92FDFD55-30D5-BBF2-E092-125C9B1B7767.html?lang=en.

University of St Andrews. (2023-2024) "Theoretical Approaches to International Relations," https://www.st-andrews.ac.uk/subjects/modules/catalogue/?code=IR2005&academic_year=2023%2F4.

University of Toronto. (2022) "Postcolonial Debates in IR," https://politics.utoronto.ca/wp-content/uploads/syllabus/2122_pol486h1s_lo101.pdf.

Utrecht University. (2024) Postcolonial Studies. https://students.uu.nl/en/academics/minors/postcolonial-studies.

Wæver, O. and Tickner, A. (eds.) (2009) *Geocultural Epistemologies. International Relations Scholarship around the World*. London: Routledge.

Walt, Stephen M. (2022) "Liberal Illusions Caused the Ukraine Crisis," *Foreign Policy*, 19 January, https://foreignpolicy.com/2022/01/19/ukraine-russia-nato-crisis-liberal-illusions/.

Waltz, K. (1986) "A Response to My Critics," in Robert O. Keohane (ed.) *Neorealism and its Critics*. New York: Columbia University Press.

Wendt, Alexander. (1992) "Anarchy is what States Make of it: The Social Construction of Power Politics," *International Organization* 46(2): 391–425.

Wilkens, Jan. (2017) "Postcolonialism in International Relations," *Oxford Research Encyclopedia of International Studies*, International Relations Association and Oxford University Press, 20 November.

Wolff, Larry. (1994) *Inventing Eastern Europe. The Map of Civilization on the Mind of the Enlightenment*. Stanford, CA: Stanford University Press.

Zondi, Siphamandla. (2016) "A Decolonial Turn in Diplomatic Theory: Unmasking Epistemic Injustice," *Journal of Contemporary History* 41(1): 18–37.

Teaching International Political Economy in Times of War

Thomas Fetzer

Abstract: For the author of this article, a scholar of international political economy (IPE) specializing in the exploration of the role of ideas, Russia's full-scale invasion of Ukraine in February 2022 came as a wake-up call—a reminder that fundamental questions of war and military security are as relevant for IPE today, as they had been in the past. And, along with this wake-up call, came the need to rethink teaching IPE in times of war.

The article addresses this process of rethinking in two steps. In the first part, it addresses questions related to the politics of knowledge production in contemporary IPE scholarship, which has either neglected questions of war and security, or has shoehorned them into wider theoretical paradigms; this is illustrated with examples drawn from (neo)liberal and neo-Marxist IPE currents.

In the second part, the article proceeds to inquire into the alternative potential for how war and conflict might be systematically brought back into IPE teaching and research. Particular attention is paid to the geoeconomics framework, which, despite various shortcomings, provides key analytical tools and a perspective that favors locally grounded expertise at the expense of sweeping generalization.

For scholars of International Political Economy (IPE) based in Europe, Russia's aggression against Ukraine and the ensuing largest military conflict on the continent since World War II, has posed a fundamental challenge not only to their field of research, but also to their teaching practice. This is so primarily because IPE as a discipline, a few exceptions aside (see e.g. Strange 1994), has had little to say about how its field of studies relates to questions of peace, war, and security during the last decades. This relative neglect is discernible, for example, in mainstream IPE textbooks, some of which have featured a chapter on global security without much linkage to the analysis of the global economy (e.g. Balaam and Dillman 2019), while others hastily added a few snippets on the Russo-Ukrainian war and "weaponized interdependence" only after the full-scale invasion in 2022 (e.g. Oatley 2022). The same picture prevails in the more specialized literature, as evidenced in flagship journals such as the *Review of International Political Economy* (RIPE). In a special issue celebrating RIPE's 30th anniversary, the editors provided a comprehensive list of the core themes covered in the journal's history, ranging from trade, global value chains, international money and finance, to tax governance, labor, health and environment, as well as the international political economy of development—but they made no mention of war, peace, and security (Bair *et al.* 2023).

Perhaps the starkest illustration of IPE's "sanitization" of the discipline from security issues is the recently proliferating scholarship on the interwar crisis of global capitalism, which is informed by a quest to draw analogies and learn historical lessons to address the contemporary globalization predicament. Predominantly steeped in a Polanyian approach to the history of capitalism as a "double movement" between the disembedding and re-embedding of global markets from and into bounded social and territorial compacts, this scholarship addresses the interwar crisis—in retrospective reading from the present—almost exclusively as a crisis of social and economic cohesion (see e.g. Fraser 2014; Burawoy 2015). Yet, the interconnection between the crisis of economic globalization and the broader crisis of the interwar international order had been a crucial preoccupation of key contemporary thinkers—from John Maynard Keynes to the incipient neoliberal circles (see e.g. Mulder 2022).

Against the backdrop of this general neglect of security in the discipline, the question of how to teach IPE in the current times of war poses a major challenge, and the remainder of this article can only provide a few preliminary reflections to this end.[1] It does so in two steps. First, in a perspective drawing from the sociology of knowledge production in IR (see Burlyuk *et al.* 2023), it seeks to demonstrate the pedagogical usefulness of systematic engagement with the shortcomings of several mainstream IPE approaches in making sense of the interrelation between the international economic and security orders, including reflections on how these shortcomings have contributed to misperceptions of the Russo-Ukrainian conflict prior and subsequent to the start of Russia's full-scale invasion in February 2022. This will be explored in relation to liberal and neo-Marxist IPE approaches. In the second part, the article addresses the question of how best to engage with the conceptual tools warranted to ground classroom discussions of IPE in times of war, primarily through the exploration of the concept of weaponized interdependence. The final section concludes.

IPE Knowledge Production and the Interrelation between Economic and Security Orders

A growing and interdisciplinary body of recent work has highlighted how the Russo-Ukrainian war has exposed shortcomings in academic knowledge production in International Relations, particularly in relation to the East European region, where scholars are in the forefront of lively debates about how to overcome the implicit epistemological, ontological, and normative biases of extant Western-dominated writing on the region (see Burlyuk *et al.* 2023). Against this backdrop, an emphasis on the politics of knowledge production is a crucial and pedagogically essential element of teaching IPE in times of war. The Russo-Ukrainian war can be extensively drawn upon to convey to students how assumptions of various disciplinary paradigms, coupled with broader normative beliefs, have translated into specific approaches towards

---

[1] These reflections are based on experiences of teaching IPE courses since the outbreak of Russia's full-scale invasion against Ukraine at Central European University's International Relations department in 2022 and 2023.

the economy-security nexus prior and after the 2022 full-scale invasion, and how this has politically mattered in shaping public debates and policies. In the following, I illustrate this perspective through selected examples of work drawn from the liberal and neo-Marxist IPE paradigms.

(Neo)Liberal Approaches

From a classroom perspective, the Russo-Ukrainian war can be used in multiple ways to highlight key assumptions and policy implications of (neo)liberal IPE approaches, but energy policy is perhaps the most straightforward option. It is easy to highlight the significance of energy policy for the conflict prior and during the war, while linkages to liberal IPE paradigms can be demonstrated in a variety of ways.

A good starting point for class discussion is to ask students to grapple with the magnitude of Europe's dependence on Russian oil and gas prior to February 2022 and, using statistics and/or video material of speeches of key decision-makers, to highlight the implications of this dependence in terms of the limitations placed on EU sanctions against Russia to avoid sudden supply shortages, as well as in terms of the massive contribution European energy payments have been making to finance Russia's war. Moreover, students can be encouraged to think about the costly efforts to diversify European oil and gas supplies away from Russia since 2022, both in relation to domestic economic difficulties and to the turmoil caused on global energy markets (see Siddi 2022).

To link these patterns of European energy policy to liberal IPE, class discussion can then proceed in different ways. One possibility is to take a closer look at the origins of Europe–Russia energy relations during the Cold War, with particular attention to the FRG's new *Ostpolitik* of the 1970s, which coincided with Soviet-German agreements to build a gas pipeline network connecting West Germany with newly discovered Siberian gas fields. While at the time predominantly seen through the lens of East–West security cooperation and détente, *Ostpolitik* bore a strong imprint of liberal IPE approaches in terms of the conceptualization of how domains of "low politics" such as energy cooperation (or social and cultural exchange) might, over time, entail the peaceful transformation of "high politics" antagonisms—reminiscent of liberal debates on the nexus between peace and economic cooperation since Kant's "perpetual peace" (see Russett et al. 1998). This discussion can be further deepened through a linkage with post-Cold War debates on the liberal international order, in particular with regard to the widespread liberal expectations that previously Western institutions such as the World Trade Organization (WTO) could be turned into vehicles to spread liberal economic principles and practices across the globe (see Ikenberry 2018).

Another option is to focus more directly on the development of the European Union's energy policy since the 1990s. Here, following a familiarization with the institutional basics of the European Single Market in the energy sector, students can be invited to engage with case studies of EU-Russia energy relations, for example particular pipeline projects (North Stream) or key pieces of legislation such as the 2019 EU gas directive. Exploring in depth the EU's regulatory policies towards Gazprom, with its emphasis on non-discrimination and competition law rules, can provide particularly compelling evidence of the impact of liberal IPE paradigms (see Goldthau and Sitter 2015). In terms of the broader political framing of EU energy policy it is useful to highlight, on the one hand, the frequent emphasis on how deep economic integration is assumed to shape Russia's opportunity costs in the direction of a trading (rather than invading) state (Rosecrance 1986), while also, on the other hand, paying attention to the EU's self-identification as a liberal international actor that, for the sake of its credible commitment to a liberal world order, ought to refrain from open mercantilist policies (see Goldthau and Sitter 2015).

As highlighted earlier, a pedagogical focus on knowledge production requires that discussion should not be limited to the analysis of policies and institutions, but should place strong emphasis on the contested nature of knowledge production. Again, the field of EU energy policy lends itself very well to this task, as contestation of core (neo)liberal assumptions of the policy, voiced predominantly by scholars and policy experts from Central and

Eastern Europe, goes back to the mid-2000s. Anita Orban's (2008) analysis of Russia's geopolitical approach to European energy relations provides a compelling early case of such CEE critiques; other suitable examples include the work of Ukrainian and Polish scholars like Olena Viter (2006) and Jakub Godzimirski (2019). Engagement with these works helps students understand how liberal notions of the relationship between energy cooperation and peace, while acquiring intellectual hegemony in the post-Cold War period, have been questioned from the Eastern "periphery" of the EU for a long time. In turn, this can then be related back to post-2022 controversies about "what went wrong" in Europe's energy policy where CEE experts' earlier positions have frequently been vindicated.[2]

To highlight the usefulness of a knowledge production approach to teaching IPE in times of war, class discussion can conclude on a forward-looking note that points to the persistent importance of (neo)liberal IPE to address the future of European energy policy. On the one hand, while very few scholars and policy experts still endorse notions of energy policy as "low politics," the knowledge production battles about EU energy policy are now being conducted in terms of concepts of resilience and the question how geopolitics relates to the renewable energy transition (see Vakulchuk *et al.* 2020). On the other hand, it is worth pointing out that energy is just one among other policy challenges facing liberal democracies in the future in terms of determining the parameters of engagement with systemic rivals and competitors—beyond the case of Russia. The take-away for students should be that (neo)liberal IPE will still be a major point of reference in future debates about how liberal democracies are to adjust their strategies and policies in a new geoeconomic international order (Roberts *et al.* 2019).

---

[2] See for example: Janice C. Eberly *et al.*, "How Did Germany Fare Without Russian Gas?," *Brookings*, 26 October 2023, https://www.brookings.edu/articles/how-did-germany-fare-without-russian-gas/.

Neo-Marxist Approaches

Compared to the rather straightforward association of the Russo-Ukrainian war with (neo)liberal IPE, the relevance of neo-Marxist IPE approaches may seem rather questionable. However, this relevance question can be addressed through student engagement with key narratives of anti-war protests and opposition to Western military support for Ukraine, in which, on the Left side of the political spectrum, arguments of the nexus between global capitalism and Western imperialism often loom large. In other words, the relevance of neo-Marxist IPE lies less in its direct impact on policies than in the influence on segments of public opinion in Western Europe and North America. To engage student audiences with neo-Marxist IPE knowledge production in more detail, it is advisable to focus on well-known scholars whose work is widely recognized, while they also appear in broader public debates. This is illustrated here through the examples of David Harvey and Radhika Desai.

Harvey, a bestselling neo-Marxist economic geographer and anthropologist, is perhaps best known to a broader audience through his work on "new imperialism," in which he argues that the United States, the global hegemon of neoliberal capitalism, faces structural economic decline driven by the rise of systemic competitors like China, which is accompanied by the acceleration of domestic social and political tensions, and which entails a drift towards direct political and military expansionism to secure resources and markets for the future (Harvey 2005). Students can directly engage with these arguments through Harvey's brief 2022 text "On recent events in Ukraine" and a follow-up video podcast in which he places the Russo-Ukrainian war into his wider framework of interpretation. In this view, we are dealing with a "capitalist war" through which a challenged US hegemon seeks to reassert its dominance, while getting rid of domestic surplus capital.[3] It is particularly instructive to focus class discussion on questions of

---

[3] Richard Wolff and David Harvey, "Using Marxism to Understand the Ukraine War," *Democracy at Work Youtube channel*, 27 November 2022, https://www.youtube.com/watch?v=NEZP_RzT2Dk.

agency here, which, for Harvey, rests almost exclusively with the West, or, indeed, the United States. Russia's role is reduced to having been victimized by Western "shock therapy" of the 1990s, while Ukraine, fighting an American proxy war, faces the "total neoliberalization" at the hands of Western capital.

Radhika Desai, a key member of the "geopolitical economy" research centre based at the University of Manitoba (Canada), reaches similar conclusions from slightly different theoretical assumptions. Drawing on world systems analysis and state capitalism literatures, Desai likens global capitalism to neo-colonial exploitation of world peripheries, whose resistance finds expression in state-directed development strategies that, in turn, increasingly threaten to overturn Western hegemony (Desai 2013). Within this pattern, Desai portrays Russia as a challenger to Western neo-imperialism and Ukraine as a key battlefield in Russia's resistance against the West's project to undermine state-directed alternative economic development models; Russia itself is explicitly referred to as a non-imperialist power. Even following Russia's full-scale invasion in 2022, Desai has doubled down on her arguments, and her highly controversial public appearance with Putin at the Valdai Club in October 2023 can serve as a useful starting point for a class discussion to explore how neo-Marxist IPE paradigms can shape attitudes towards the Russo-Ukrainian war among segments of academia and public opinion in Western Europe and North America.[4]

To deepen this discussion, as in the case of (neo)liberal IPE, systematic attention needs then to be paid to the contested nature of knowledge production, addressing the controversies triggered by Harvey's and Desai's writings on the Russo-Ukrainian war, not least within left-leaning academic circles themselves. Depending on the author choice, this can focus on slightly different issues: For the Harvey debate, the most straightforward approach would be the engagement with "Westsplaining" critiques (see Hendl et al. 2023) targeting Harvey's abovementioned exclusive emphasis on

---

[4] Karen Pauls, "Professor Stands By Attending Controversial Russian Conference," *CBC News*, 15 October 2023, https://www.cbc.ca/news/canada/manitoba/radhika-desai-valdai-russia-ukraine-1.6995250.

the role of the United States, while denying any meaningful agency to either Russia or Ukraine (see e.g. Hall 2022). Regarding Desai, debate can more specifically focus on engagement with her explicit denial of Russian imperialism, which has been contested even from scholars operating within an overall Marxist approach to imperialism (see Gowans 2023). Again, as with (neo)liberal IPE, this can be connected to a broader reflection on the contestation of spatial hierarchies of knowledge production through the foregrounding of the prominence of intellectuals from Central and Eastern Europe in these debates.

A pedagogically compelling conclusion to such a discussion, in analogy to the earlier elaborated engagement with (neo)liberal IPE, could address the broader significance of neo-Marxist IPE for contemporary academic and policy debates beyond the case of the Russo-Ukrainian war. One key issue in this regard would be the exploration of the ways in which neo-Marxist IPE paradigms shape broader knowledge production patterns of global economic relations through their predominant focus on exploitation of the Global South by the Global North, in particular with regard to legacies of European colonialism. Contextualizing and problematizing these patterns by bringing in recent debates on the neglect of the "Global East" (see Müller 2020) can help students understand at once the continued salience of neo-Marxist IPE approaches, as well as the contested nature of all IPE knowledge production.

Conceptual Tools to Ground IPE in Times of War: The Example of "Weaponized Interdependence"

Beyond engaging with important questions of the politics of knowledge production, the perhaps most crucial challenge to address in teaching IPE in times of war is the question of how to conceptually ground classroom discussions in ways that make it easy to "bring" the Russo-Ukrainian war to the classroom, while, at the same time, allowing for wider analytical contextualization in extant scholarship and ongoing debates about the changing nature of the international economic order. Such conceptual grounding is particularly important in light of the above-mentioned general paucity of IPE engagement with questions of war and security.

While there is of course no one best way to address this challenge, I suggest that the concept of weaponized interdependence (WI) can provide significant support in delivering these tasks of structuring classroom discussions. First proposed by Farrell and Newman (2019), the core idea of this concept is to rethink mainstream assumptions on international economic interdependence mostly derived from liberal IR theory in the wake of Kant's *Perpetual Peace*, namely that economic interdependence raises states' opportunity costs in such a way that they face prohibitive penalties for disrupting interdependence, thus creating a virtuous circle of inter-state cooperation and peace (see Rosecrance 1986). WI analytically foregrounds the opposite dynamic whereby (groups of) states, if they are in a position of control over particular economic nodes and networks, can make strategic use of this interdependence for their own purposes—"to discover and exploit vulnerabilities, compel policy change, and deter unwanted action" (Farrell and Newman 2019: 45). This happens through two main channels conceptualized as "panopticon" and "chokepoint" effects; in the former, controlling states use their network position to extract informational advantages vis-à-vis adversaries, whereas in the latter, they can cut adversaries off from networks altogether (*ibid.*: 46).

Despite its very recent origin, the WI concept has already gained significant traction in the literature, as scholars seek to apply and develop it in a range of geographical and sectoral domains (see e.g. Chang and Yang 2020; Gjesvik 2023). In parallel, a vivid epistemological debate on the analytical limits and possible abuse of the concept has also emerged, which enhances the potential of "weaponized interdependence" to inform classroom debate contexts (see Drezner *et al.* 2021). In the following, these advantages are further explored with particular reference to the potential to bring the Russo-Ukrainian war "into the classroom" and to provide openings into broader debates about international economic order.

"Weaponized Interdependence" and Classroom Discussions on the Russo-Ukrainian War

The WI concept is very well suited to connect abstract reflection on the economy-security nexus with the concrete empirical reality of the Russo-Ukrainian war. The ongoing war not only illustrates the functioning of key mechanisms of WI, here in particular the "chokepoint effect," but can also serve to discuss limitations of applicability, not least regarding assumptions of hierarchical control of economic networks, as well as considerations addressing potential longer-term negative fallout of the strategic use of WI.

On the one hand, this dynamic can be brought into the classroom through the analysis of Russia's use of the energy chokehold, particularly in the gas sector with its pipeline infrastructure and long-term producer-buyer relations (see Grigas 2017). The basic functioning of "chokepoint effects" can be easily highlighted through the reconstruction of the built-up of Russian dominance in European gas markets since the 1990s (see Orban 2008) and of the subsequent leveraging of this dominance. For the latter, a focused case analysis of Russian-Ukrainian gas conflicts since the 2004 "Orange revolution" is particularly well suited, highlighting multiple occasions of gas supply stoppages, as well as stoppage threats as a recurring coercive Russian bargaining strategy, not least against the backdrop of Ukraine's importance as a transit country for Russian gas deliveries to Central and Western Europe.

This analysis of the pre-2022 conflict can then be contrasted with developments following Russia's full-scale invasion, which point to a much more ambiguous picture on the salience of WI. To grasp these dynamics, students can be encouraged to delve into the details of Russian supply disruption efforts in spring and summer of 2022 and the associated expectations to "freeze Europe" in the upcoming winter, and then to explore how and why these strategies failed, as most European countries found alternative supplies, while gas prices slowly returned to 2021 levels. Indeed, class discussion should explicitly address the question whether Russia's use of the energy weapon can be considered as a textbook case of how WI can backfire in the longer-term (see Drezner et al. 2021), given that, by 2024, following the loss of most European markets, Russia's shift towards Eastern customers has been accompanied by a reversal of dependence patterns, particularly reflected in Russia's energy relations with well-diversified China.

On the other hand, the WI concept can be of great pedagogical help to make sense of one of the key elements of Western reactions to Russia's aggression: economic sanctions. Anticipated chokepoint effects of sanctions can be explored at a variety of levels, enabling different groups of students to focus on either "smart" financial sanctions against Russian oligarchs, export embargoes on high-tech and dual use goods, or broader sanctions (e.g. oil bans and oil price caps). This can be coupled with the elaboration of the different channels through which these chokepoint effects are meant to reign in Russia's war effort—from the curtailing of the procurement of military equipment, to the general weakening of Russia's economy, anticipated to translate into either the exhaustion of Russia's fiscal capacity to fund continued warfare and/or the fueling of domestic discontent in Russian society (see Sonnenfeld *et al.* 2022).

At the same time, the debate on limitations of WI strategies allows to shed systematic light on the controversies around the effectiveness of sanctions in the context of the Russo-Ukrainian war (see Schott 2023). Here, students can draw on current media reporting to discuss the ways in which Russia has sought to circumvent chokepoint effects, for example through third-country imports of Western dual-use goods or the partly illicit redirection of oil exports. Broader deterrence effects should also be addressed, as should the question if and how sanctions have entailed unintended "collateral damage" in other parts of the world. Students should be encouraged to assess the question of effectiveness in comparative perspective, taking into account factors such as target country size and different anticipated time horizons (van Bergejik 2022). Scenario exercises can be a useful concluding task, allowing students to grapple with the overall question of the impact of Western sanctions on the further trajectory of the Russo-Ukrainian war.

Weaponized Interdependence and Classroom Discussions on International Economic Order

Beyond allowing to bring in the Russo-Ukrainian war in concrete empirical ways, the WI concept also lends itself well to connect such insights to broader scholarly and policy debates about the changing nature of the international economic order. In the classroom, this can be explored through a more system-centered and/or through a more actor-centered perspective.

In a systems perspective, one of the most interesting questions to be addressed is whether the Russo-Ukrainian war feeds into a broader transformation that some scholars have conceptualized as the shift from a liberal to a geoeconomic order, whereby core liberal principles like the commitment to global market liberalization and multilateral regulatory frameworks are supplanted by more fragmented economic networks associated with geostrategic spheres of influence ("friendshoring"), accompanied by the decline of international law and institutions such as WTO or IMF (Roberts *et al.* 2019).

On the one hand, WI strategies can be considered as a key indicator of such a shift, and the question of their empirical spread—beyond the Russia-Ukraine conflict itself—can be explored through a range of case studies. On the other hand, students can engage with the broader argument of how fears of anticipated WI strategies fuel fragmentation dynamics; wariness of "panopticon effects" can be studied through the analysis of communication infrastructures, for example with regard to satellite technology or submarine cable networks (see Sherman 2021), while fears of "chokepoints" can be addressed through debates on "de-risking" in relation to trade and investment flows (see Farrell and Newman 2023). In-depth case analysis of recent EU-China trade relations can provide particularly compelling material for class discussions. In turn, such discussions can then be related to still more fundamental conceptual and policy questions: Where is the boundary between "de-risking" and Cold War-style "de-coupling"? At what point might the securitization of international economic relations, driven by mutual fears of WI, turn into the opposite dynamic that has long underpinned assumptions of liberal interdependence theories, namely that a shift towards the fragmentation of global economic networks might make states less "invested" in upholding peace and stability?

In a more actor-focused perspective, students can be encouraged to explore the challenges arising from the shift towards a geoeconomic order for liberal democracies. Here, the central question concerns the nature of policy tools to be used—are liberal democracies pursuing WI strategies bound to gradually converge on the "playing style" (Roberts *et al.* 2019: 675) of their systemic adversaries, and, if so, what kind of dilemmas does this pose with regard to the possible compromising of liberal principles themselves? Might liberal democracies end up encroaching, both domestically and internationally, on core liberal values and thus inadvertently further imperil the liberal order they purport to defend?

In the context of the Russo-Ukrainian war, these questions can be addressed in a variety of ways, among which the debate on the freezing and possible seizing of Russian public and private economic assets (see Stephan 2022) provides perhaps the most interesting example. Following the familiarization of students with domestic and international legal frameworks, this theme lends itself well to a formal classroom debate with two groups of students opposing each other, whereby arguments to support asset seizure for the purposes of Ukrainian reconstruction and broader deterrence can be contrasted with skeptical positions focusing on risks in terms of the compromising of property rights and broader principles of legality and due process, as well as on anticipated negative knock-on effects for international investment confidence. As a concluding follow-up, the analytical potential of the WI concept to outline and illustrate the dilemmas of a geoeconomic order for liberal democracies can be reiterated and linked to analogous dilemmas in other domains, for example the challenge of how to engage with autocratic disinformation campaigns, or the weaponization of irregular migration flows. Teaching IPE in times of war can thus be embedded in a framework that helps to raise awareness of the broader predicament of contemporary liberal societies.

Conclusions

As highlighted at the outset, teaching IPE in the current times of war poses major challenges, and this article has only suggested preliminary reflections on some of the ways how this might be done. Whichever way is chosen, broader epistemological and normative difficulties also need to be considered. By way of conclusion, I would like to reflect on two of them, first the problem that the analysis of the Russo-Ukrainian occurs under conditions of rapid changes on the ground, and second, the unavoidable question of the normative positioning when teaching IPE in times of war.

As much as the overall academic and public engagement with the Russo-Ukrainian war, IPE-related debates have also been in considerable flux over the course of the period since February 2022; this is most easily observed in the controversies around the effectiveness of Western sanctions against Russia, which have oscillated between upbeat assessments in how sanctions will cripple the Russian economy and thus severely constrain the aggressors' warfare capacity (see Sonnenfeld *et al.* 2022) and extremely pessimistic views of complete failure. For teaching purposes, such oscillations imply the danger of succumbing to analytical insights whose "half-life" might be very limited. While the contextualization of findings of specific (groups of) authors through a politics of knowledge production approach is always a good tool to hedge such risks, some kind of "mitigation" attempt will frequently also be warranted, for example through conscious efforts to particularly highlight different approaches and conclusions.

The normative challenges are no less important. On the one hand, the assumption of a common normative position in terms of the condemnation of Russia's aggression should be made explicit, and the integration of accounts from Ukrainian students about everyday life in war conditions can help to underpin this common base. On the other hand, especially in classrooms that feature a diverse student body originating from countries of the Global North, Global East, and Global South, views on the causes and consequences of the war, as well as on its importance for global politics, are likely to be different, requiring careful design of classes and teaching material. Concepts with a strong inbuilt normative connotation are better avoided in favour of "neutral" ones, which, as in the case of "weaponized interdependence" are suitable for the analysis of the IPE-security nexus regardless of normative views held by different groups of students. At the same time, classroom discussion should also give students occasion to reflect on their own normative views. As outlined above in relation to (neo)liberal and neo-Marxist writing, the explicit engagement with political implications of different intellectual strands of IPE may be conducive to this end. In sum, students should be encouraged to consider a wartime classroom as being inevitably part of a broader politics of knowledge production, yet also to appreciate that this needs to be done in the spirit of academic and political pluralism.

References

Bair, Jennifer *et al.* (2023) "RIPE 30th Anniversary Special Feature: Looking Back and Looking Forward in IPE," *Review of International Political Economy* 30(1): 1–14.

Balaam, David N. and Dillman, Bradford. (eds.) (2019), *Introduction to International Political Economy*, 7th ed., New York: Routledge.

Burawoy, Michael. (2015) "Facing an Unequal World," *Current Sociology* 63(1): 5–34.

Burlyuk, Olga and Musliu, Vjosa. (eds.) (2023) "The Responsibility to Remain Silent? On the Politics of Knowledge Production, Expertise and (Self-)Reflection in Russia's War against Ukraine," *Journal of International Relations and Development* 26: 605–18.

Chang, Chia-Chien and Yang, Alan H. (2020) "Weaponized Interdependence: China's Economic Statecraft and Social Penetration against Taiwan," *Orbis* 64(2): 312–33.

Desai, Radhika. (2013) *Geopolitical Economy: After US hegemony, Globalization and Empire*, London: Pluto.

Drezner, Daniel W. *et al.* (eds.) (2021) *The Uses and Abuses of Weaponized Interdependence*. Washington: Brookings Institution Press.

Farrell, Henry and Newman, Abraham. (2019) "Weaponized Interdependence: How Global Economic Networks Shape State Coercion," *International Security* 44(1): 42–79.

Farrell, Henry and Newman, Abraham. (2023) "The New Economic Security State: How De-Risking will remake Geopolitics," *Foreign Affairs* 102: 106–17.

Fraser, Nancy. (2014) "Can Society be Commodities All the Way Down? Post-Polanyian Reflections on Capitalist Crisis," *Economy and Society* 43(4): 541–58.

Gjesvik, Lars. (2023) "Private Infrastructure in Weaponized Interdependence," *Review of International Political Economy* 30(2): 722–46.

Godzimirski, Jakub M. (ed.) (2019) *New Political Economy of Energy in Europe: Power to Project, Power to Adapt*. Cham: Palgrave.

Goldthau, Andreas and Sitter, Nikolai. (2015) *A Liberal Actor in a Realist World: The European Union Regulatory State and the Global Political Economy of Energy*. Oxford: Oxford University Press.

Gowans, Stephen. (2023) "What's Wrong with the Argument that Russia Isn't Imperialist? A Critique of Desai et al's 'The Conflict in Ukraine and Contemporary Imperialism,'" *What's Left* blog, 19 January, https://gowans.blog/2023/01/18/whats-wrong-with-the-argument-that-russia-isnt-imperialist-a-critique-of-desai-et-als-the-conflict-in-ukraine-and-contemporary-imperialism/ (accessed 26 April 2024).

Grigas, Anita. (2017) *The New Geopolitics of Natural Gas*. Cambridge, MA: Harvard University Press.

Hall, Derek. (2022) "Russia's Invasion of Ukraine – A Response to David Harvey," *Focal Blog*, 28 February, https://www.focaalblog.com/2022/02/28/derek-hall-russias-invasion-of-ukraine-a-response-to-david-harvey/ (accessed 26 April 2024).

Harvey, David. (2005) *The New Imperialism: Clarendon Lectures in Geography and Environmental Studies*. Oxford: Oxford University Press.

Hendl, Tereza *et al.* (2023) "(En)Countering Epistemic Imperialism: A Critique of 'Westsplaining' and Coloniality in Dominant Debates on Russia's Invasion of Ukraine," *Contemporary Security Policy* 45(2): 171–209.

Ikenberry, John. (2018) "The End of Liberal International Order?," *International Affairs* 94(1): 7–23.

Mueller, Martin. (2020) "In Search of the Global East: Thinking between North and South," *Geopolitics* 25(3): 734–55.
Mulder, Nicholas. (2022) *The Economic Weapon: The Rise of Sanctions as a Tool of Modern War*. New Haven, CT: Yale University Press.
Oatley, Thomas. (ed.) (2022) *International Political Economy*, 7th ed. New York: Routledge.
Orban, Anita. (2008) *Power, Energy, and the New Russian Imperialism*. London: Bloomsbury.
Roberts, Anthea et al. (2019) "Toward a Geoeconomic Order in International Trade and Investment," *Journal of International Economic Law* 22(4): 655–76.
Rosecrance, Richard. (1986) *The Rise of the Trading State: Commerce and Conquest in the Modern World*. London: Basic Books.
Russett, Bruce. (1994) *Grasping the Democratic Peace: Principles for a Post Cold War World*. Princeton, NJ: Princeton University Press.
Schott, Jeffrey. (2023) "Economic Sanctions against Russia: How Effective, How Durable?," *Peterson Institute for International Economics Policy Brief* 23(3).
Sherman, Justin. (2021) *Cyber Defense across the Ocean Floor: The Geopolitics of Submarine Cable Security*. Washington: Atlantic Council.
Siddi, Marco. (2022) "EU-Russia Energy Relations", in Michèle Knodt and Jorg Kemmerzell (eds.), *Handbook of Energy Governance in Europe*. Cham: Springer, 237–61.
Sonnenfeld, Jeffrey et al. (2022) *Business Retreats and Sanctions are Crippling the Russian Economy*. New Haven, CT: Yale School of Management Discussion Paper.
Stephan, Paul. (2022) "Seizing Russian Assets," *Capital Markets Law Journal* 17(3): 276–87.
Strange, Susan (1994) *States and Markets*. 2nd ed., London: Pinter.
Vakulchuk, Roman et al. (2020), "Renewable Energy and Geopolitics: A Review," *Renewable and Sustainable Energy Reviews* 122: 1–12.
Van Bergerijk, Peter. (2022) "Sanctions against the Russian War on Ukraine: Lessons from History and Current Prospects," *Journal of World Trade* 56(4): 571–86.
Viter, Olena et al. (2006) *Ukraine: Post-Revolution Energy Policy and Relations with Russia*. London: GMB Publishing.

From Shock to Adaptation through National Unity and Action: Third-Year Undergraduate Students of Kyiv-Mohyla Academy Reflect on the First Eighty Days of Russia's War against Ukraine

Galyna Solovei

Abstract: *The full-scale Russian invasion of Ukraine interrupted the course I teach to third-year international relations students at the National University of "Kyiv-Mohyla Academy," "Introduction to Peace and Conflict Studies," from 24 February to 9 March 2022. Recognizing that the students had experienced significant trauma from the overwhelming war violence and needed to take care of their mental health, I used Judith Herman's framework, asking students to self-assess their psychological state and coherently describe their experiences of three months of war. I partially adapted the group work model developed by Mooly Lahad to find resilience resources through group interaction in war-torn societies and teacher-student interaction in the university environment. The article contains an analysis of the auto-ethnographic essays of 19-20-year-old Kyiv-Mohyla Academy International Relations students who agreed to publish parts of their essays on the condition of anonymity. Students describe their experiences of the first 80 days of Russia's war against Ukraine. The main themes that emerge in all the essays are: 1) the shock of the outbreak of war; 2) the unity of the Ukrainian nation in fighting; and 3) the suffering from family separation. Parents' efforts to send their children to a safe place at a time when they were in constant danger are described by students as the most traumatic experience that hinders adaptation and has had the greatest impact on their mental health. The resumption of studies* with a return to regular communication with fellows and professors in the safe conditions of mutual trust and emotional support brings students and faculty a sense of belonging and is an additional resource for building resilience.

Keywords: Russia, war, Ukraine, adaptation, volunteering, trauma, recovery.

Introduction

The winter semester of the 2021–22 academic year was interrupted in Ukrainian universities by the full-scale Russian invasion of Ukraine. At six o'clock in the morning on 24 February 2022, the Rector of the Kyiv-Mohyla Academy, Serhiy Kvit, wrote a letter to all faculty, staff, and students of the university informing them that classes were suspended, with a view to allowing them to make decisions directly related to saving their lives and the lives of their families. However, on 9 March, when it became clear that Putin's propaganda slogan about "taking Kyiv in three days" had failed and the attack on the capital had been repelled, online learning resumed at the Kyiv-Mohyla Academy.

One of the courses I teach at the Kyiv-Mohyla Academy in the winter semester is called "Introduction to Peace and Conflict Studies." It provides international relations students with the necessary theoretical and methodological framework to analyze the causes, actors, and levels of international violent conflict, and outlines the known ways to resolve these conflicts, both diplomatically and through peacekeeping missions, sanctions, and peace enforcement.

Undoubtedly, teaching this course as if the Russian war against Ukraine had never happened and as if neither I nor the forty-seven students of the course, if not in the bombing zone, had been displaced then inside Ukraine or abroad, would have been a complete abstraction from reality and a sign of my lack of empathy and ability to respond to circumstances. Our lectures and seminars in the academic year of the outbreak of the war in one way or another touched upon analyzing the behavior of the aggressor country, non-violent and violent resistance to this aggression in the international arena, the need for military confrontation for self-preservation, and the resilience of Ukrainian society. So I offered the students an alternative final assignment in the form of an auto-ethnographic essay about the personal experience of each student facing the war.

In university programs on international security or peace and conflict studies, we focus on actors such as states, international organizations, government and opposition, and organized criminal and terrorist groups. A university professor and her students may often overlook the ordinary person with her experience of living through war. In this study, I build on Christine Silvestre's assertion that understanding the personal experience of war is essential to understanding what war is (Silvestre 2012). I believe that the war can be analyzed not only from the point of view of geopolitics or the struggle for resources but will become more understandable through the personal individual stories.

Auto-ethnography written by students living through the experience of war gives agency to these witnesses of Russian violence, affirming the importance of their testimony, and increasing their personal resilience. As Oded Löwenheim puts it, "Autoethnography enables one to acquire an agentive role in the world by highlighting one's uniqueness and voice. It also aims to create mutual empowerment among people, ordinary individuals, by means of identification, connectivity, and empathy" (Löwenheim 2010: 1023).

Svetlana Alexievich's book *The Unwomanly Face of War: An Oral History* served as a model for this research. Alexievich writes in the preface that the reality around her was full of stories about the war told by village women, but the entire library was full of books about the heroic deeds of the Soviet army written by men (Alexievich 2017). For years, Alexievich collected Soviet women's testimonies about the Second World War, giving a voice to those who were silenced by the Soviet regime, allowing them to heal personal and collective trauma by speaking out. Alexievich had to carefully find each of her interlocutors, build trust between herself and them, and overcome the taboo on the existence and recording of individual stories of the war that differed from the only correct official version approved by the Soviet Communist Party. In the case of the group comprising me as teacher and the students of my course, we all had more than two years of experience of cooperation and trust between us. The situation in which Russia started the war did not allow any authoritarian force to silence Ukrainian voices or silence any part of society. From 2022 to 2024, hundreds of Western journals in fields ranging from psychology to ecology, law, humanities, and social sciences published special issues of Ukrainian Voices, giving Ukrainian scholars and professors a platform to speak out rather than being the object of outside research. With this article, I give a voice to Ukrainian students, as they are an integral part of both Ukrainian society and the teaching and learning process during the war.

While Alexievich's life work overcame the crimes of Soviet authoritarianism by giving a voice to those parts of society whose war stories did not coincide with the official version, Judith Herman, in her book *Trauma and Recovery*, suggests three steps to take to help with traumatic experiences: 1) establish trust and create a safe space; 2) allow the story of the traumatic experience to be told coherently; and 3) restore social ties between group members and the rest of society (Herman 1992). It proved possible to implement this practice through group practical classes for the course "Introduction to Peace and Conflict Studies" in 2021-2022 immediately after the resumption of studies, when students traumatized by the war and scattered around the world easily found "their group" among the fellows and teachers.

In this paper, I also rely on the work of Israeli researcher Mooly Lahad, who, based on many years of research on war-torn societies, identified the basic sources adaptation and resilience resources. The Basic Ph model, which Lahad developed, is suitable for professor–student interaction during the war. The teacher and students can use the resource sources mentioned by Lahad, such as:

1. **B**—Belief & values—faith, beliefs, values, philosophy of life.

2. **A**—Affect—expression of emotions and feelings.

3. **S**—Socialization—social ties, social support, social belonging, communication.

4. **I**—Imagination—imagination, dreams, memories, creativity.

5. **C**—Cognition, thought—mind, cognition, cognitive strategies (Lahad *et al.* 2012).

Only the last element, Physical, or Ph as it is called in Lahad's model, could not be used in my course, since there was no readily available way for me to actively use the body as a resource for resilience given that classes were delivered in an online format.

The purpose of this study is to summarize and analyze the personal experiences of Ukrainian students during the first three months of the war. The students described these experiences in their final auto-ethnographic essays, which became the source of my research data with the students' informed consent. All of the students' essays, written individually, repeated the three themes that I identified inductively after processing them. These themes became the structural elements of this article.

The article is structured as follows. First, I present the method used for data collection and analysis. Second, three main themes appearing in most students' essays are introduced, namely: 1) the shock of the outbreak of the war; 2) sensations of unification of the Ukrainian nation; and: 3) reactions to family separation. I conclude with recommendations for measures that faculty and students should take to adapt to new circumstances.

The answers to the question "How were you personally affected by the war?," which I and the students, through their essays presented in parts in this study, are aimed at trying to respond to, individualize, and emphasize the personal experience of war. This paper complements and illustrates the research on the mental health of Ukrainian students conducted using quantitative methods by psychologists (Javanbakht 2022, Kurapov *et al.* 2022,

Osokina *et al.* 2022, Rogowska and Pavlova 2023). It is worth emphasizing that this study does not aim to analyze the students' mental health from a psychological point of view; rather, it discusses the interaction between a teacher and students who are affected by the war. The ethnographic approach allows us to give students agency in the production of knowledge about the Russian war in Ukraine.

Method

Recognizing that my students and I as a professor are currently experiencing the traumatic events of the war, that I am a person capable of non-judgmental perception and understanding, and that the students trust me, I encouraged them to structure their traumatic experiences into a coherent story, which in itself brings relief through verbalization. In my opinion, teaching is to some extent a participatory research method: we observe the development of our students and correlate our teaching methods depending on their behavior. Participant observation "involves research based on close-up, on-the-ground observation of people and institution in real time and space, in which the investigator embeds herself near (or within) the phenomenon so as to detect how and why agents on the scene act, think and feel the way they do" (Wacquant 2003: 5).

The research was conducted among forty-seven third-year students of international relations at the Kyiv-Mohyla Academy. The students, who come from different parts of Ukraine and were aged 19 or 20, were enrolled in the mandatory course "Introduction to Peace and Conflict Studies" in the 2021–2022 academic year. The main task for the final essay was to produce a free-form description of their personal experience of the first three months of the war. An alternative task was to assess the reaction of Western countries to Russian aggression in Ukraine in the first months of the war. Only seven students from the group decided to complete the alternative task, analyzing the statements and actions of North American and European leaders in January–April 2022. Forty students completed an auto-ethnographic essay, which demonstrates the students' desire to structure their own experiences and make them "visible" and meaningful to the community.

Nineteen of the forty students (3 males and 16 females) gave written authorization to use parts of their essays for publication under a changed name or their real name without identifying their surnames. The main motivation for students to publish parts of their essays is the desire to ensure that this war is not silenced as it happened with the Holodomor of 1932–33 or with the stories of Soviet women in the World War II of 1939–45. Both orally and in writing, students repeated that they preferred being able to tell and record their own story in their own words to analyzing the official versions of the positions of states or governments that had already been formed or would be formed later as a response to the outcome of the war.

Understanding the entire complex of problems that the students of the Kyiv-Mohyla Academy faced in the first months of the war, I decided to replace the final assignment in the course "Introduction to Peace and Conflict Studies," originally an analytical case study, with an auto-ethnographic essay, answering the question "How were you personally affected by the war?" Primarily, my task was to point the way to recovery for my students by empowering them to produce a coherent narrative of their own experiences and the shocking events of the war. After analyzing the content of the students' essays, I realized that first-hand testimonies from the participants of the educational process can provide valuable insight for professors and university administrators both in Ukraine and abroad to pay special attention to the challenges that war-affected Ukrainian students may face.

The Shock of the Outbreak of the War

Abraham Maslow, in his theory of human behavior, tried to explain people's motivation to act in one way or another by the hierarchical nature of human needs. According to his theory, only after satisfying the basic needs for food, sleep, shelter, and security can a person be motivated to satisfy higher needs, such as belonging to a community or self-actualization (Maslow 1943). According to this hierarchy, people who suddenly lose the ability to satisfy the basic need for safety and who face physical destruction cannot satisfy any other higher needs until safety is restored.

Loss of security as a result of war can be a traumatic event if it meets three conditions: 1) it is perceived negatively by people; 2) people lose control over the situation; and 3) they were not prepared, and the event occurs suddenly (Carlson & Dalenberg 2000). However, the power of the traumatic effect and the possibility of post-traumatic growth of individuals affected by war or terrorist attacks will not be the same, according to the authors. Five factors that influence people's reaction to trauma are: 1) biological characteristics; 2) developmental level at the time of the trauma; 3) severity of the stressor; 4) social environment; and 5) previous and subsequent life events (Carlson & Dalenberg 2000).

Students describe their reactions to the outbreak of war and the search for satisfaction of the basic need for at least relative security as follows:

> "24th of February, 5 a.m... explosion ... I woke up and didn't want to believe what was happening... a few minutes later another loud explosion ... I ran to my parents' room ... Did it really happen? Is it reality or a dream? This is definitely not a dream...
>
> In 2 hours, we were already sitting in the car, completely clogged with things, barely fitting, leaving the city. As we drove, we spent every second on the phone, watching the news, and checking every source. We spent 30 hours on the phone, continuing to watch all the news. As soon as we arrived in the Ukrainian Carpathian Mountains, we settled in one room (where the four of us lived for the next few months). For the next few days, we ate almost nothing: we didn't want to. We almost didn't sleep: we didn't want to. We almost didn't get out of bed: we didn't want to. There was complete apathy in every member of the family. But we did not cry. None of us. Why? We were in a state of shock. We did not fully understand reality. Emotions ceased to exist in us"—Liza.
>
> "At first, you feel like a character in a soap opera and childishly hope that it will be over soon, that someone made a mistake in choosing the show on the streaming service and tomorrow you will be able to return to your 'real' life. It is impossible to believe that it was taken away by abstract people you can't even see. The scenery is filled with a hurriedly turned-on news channel, long car jams outside the window, suitcases packed 'just in case,' and a strange atmosphere of tedious prideful tension in the air. On

the same day, rockets began to be fired at my hometown of Kyiv. It was easier to stay within the walls of our dear flat than to go down to the naked basement of a skyscraper building"—Yelisaveta.

"I'm from a small town. All my childhood and youth I wanted to go to the capital and live a better life. But now my soul remains in the half-ruined town that has been under the shots since the beginning of the war. And it is very difficult to realize this. I lived there almost all my life. All victories and troubles are connected with this town"—Olha.

"I remember this feeling of fear and constant anxiety. Sleepless, anxious nights, because every half hour, something explodes so that all the doors, windows, and beds tremble. It was impossible to sleep, so you constantly monitored the news and chatted with friends and relatives. If someone is out of touch for more than an hour, panic begins and you start scrolling through all possible scenarios of what could happen. The worst thing is that it's impossible to stop and distract from what seemed the worst. However, it's only after some time of war that you begin to realize that what you imagined in your head cannot even be compared to the horrible realities of nowadays.

The main worries in the beginning were to stock up on food, sit at home with the lights off, and try to figure out how close the explosions were.

One day bombs were dropped on my village. Two civilian houses were destroyed, and people were killed and injured. It was scary, but we still didn't know if it would happen again and what should we do. A few days later, I woke up with the news that we were bombed again just as my grandfather went to get groceries. Fortunately, the bomb fell into a ditch and my grandfather was only thrown to one side by a shock wave. He escaped with only a burnt jacket and a minor burn on his hand. But for us, it was the last straw, so we decided to get some things and leave the next day"—Sofia.

"We were there [Irpin] for 10 days. Me, my grandparents, my aunt, uncle, 2 cousins and my cat. The first night was the most stressful. There was an annoying and unstoppable thought in my head that something terrible might happen while we were sleeping. I fall asleep just because I couldn't keep my eyes open anymore. The next few days I was running to the basement every time I heard a bang and I had to take sedatives because after dark I started shaking again and again. Every day we heard explosions and shots. One day we even had to go to the bomb shelter in an old post-Soviet camp. On the last day our friend called and said that a convoy of cars would be going out of Irpin the next day and it was our chance to leave with them. Until the very end, we didn't want to leave. Now, recalling everything, knowing about what happened in Bucha and Irpin afterward, I realize how lucky we were.

...soon after we came [to Warsaw], we found out that my aunt's house (where we were for 10 days in Irpin) was under bomb attack and unfortunately now is almost fully destroyed. My grandparents' house also has some damage but thankfully it's not so serious"—Margaryta.

"My husband is a former military man with experience in participating in the anti-terrorist operation in Donbas. My father came to Kyiv to evacuate us and strangers from my university, who asked for help. I remember that morning minute by minute because it was the day when several russian[1] soldiers entered Kyiv using the stolen Ukrainian tanks. One of them went under our windows. We saw them, people who came to kill us all and bring the 'russian world' to Ukraine. The air raid sirens started. I was scared that my father could have died because of the bombing. On the way out of the city, we were stopped by the Ukrainian military: people with guns and tanks behind. They said that the russian tanks were 10 km from us and we couldn't go this way. We left Kyiv using another road. We relocated to Vinnytsia, my hometown. The next day, we bought some military equipment for my husband, and he went to his parents. He was mobilized and now, he is serving in the Armed Forces of Ukraine"—Maryna.

Two of the key factors of influence are common to the study group, namely, the level of development at the time of the trauma (young people aged 19-20) and the severity of the stressor which can be considered as serious as possible. Biological characteristics, social environment, and previous and subsequent life events (in addition to studying at the same university) are individual for each student. All the students say that they lived through the beginning of the war with their families, they made the decision to relocate together and experienced the most stressful moments together, which united family members. The unity of the family at the initial stage of the war and the fact that they endured the first attacks together may indicate that the family was the main resource of

---

1   Since the beginning of the war, the use of the lower case for "Russia" and "Putin" have become common in the Ukrainian media and academic environment. This phenomenon continues to this day. In Ukrainian, "Russian" would normally be spelt with an initial lower-case "r," but we render it as "russian" here in this translation so as to convey this effect.

support and a guarantee of relative security for the individual. Excerpts from the auto-ethnographic essays show that some of the families were ready for relocation, having previously packed their belongings; one of the students' husbands was ready for immediate mobilization to the front. Other students testify to complete surprise and unpreparedness for the outbreak of war, which undoubtedly increases the likelihood of more serious trauma. All the students, even those who survived the occupation in Irpin, say that they cannot complain because they are much more fortunate than others. Having relocated, students begin to feel relatively safe. After a few months of war, the understanding of a critical level of "danger" in which one cannot live anymore is transferred exclusively to the front line and the occupied territories. The rest of Ukraine is perceived as conditionally safe, even under the constant shelling.

Unity of Ukrainians. Volunteering. Working for Ukrainian Victory

Resilience is generally defined as the ability of an individual to "bounce back" after experiencing stress (Wald *et al.* 2006). People can thrive whilst their known world crumbles around them (*Resilience and Trauma—The BASIC Ph Model—Brighton Therapy Partnership*). After the shock reaction, various strategies of adaptation to the changed living conditions come into play. People with higher adaptability, which is an innate quality (biological factor) or a consciously developed skill, can find resources and move on to the post-traumatic growth phase.

The most famous phrase attributed to Charles Darwin, but which he did not record in his books, proclaims that, "It is not the strongest of the species that survive, nor the most intelligent, but the one most responsive to change" (Darwin Correspondence Project n/d). This statement reflects the importance of adaptability in the face of evolutionary challenges. For Ukrainian society, the Russian invasion was just such a challenge, and to survive, Ukrainians demonstrated an unprecedented level of cohesion, unity, and desire to fight the enemy. After three months of war, students described their experiences as follows:

> "You wake up with only one thing in mind—to be valuable to your nation. You crowd-fund for the cars that will soon be destroyed in combat on the frontline, order tourniquets to save the lives of your soldiers; you help people relocate as they are fleeing from the genocide, and you bury yourself in work so as not to feel like a liability"—Tetyana.

> "Of course, we have all come to terms with the war and we do everything to accelerate the onset of our victory. All those who are in safety should help our army, the soldiers who are protecting us every day. My dad and I organized some deliveries of humanitarian aid from Poland. We have a truck, and my father agreed to load the humanitarian aid in Poland that we brought here and handed over to volunteers"—Illya.

> "My family was in Ukraine for the first 10 days of the war. We spent most of those days in the bomb shelter. Despite the danger, these were the most impressive days of my life. I have never seen such cohesion. We helped each other, we tried to make life easier for everyone. The whole yard, all my neighbors in the morning and afternoon were preparing food for our volunteers and the army in a restaurant nearby. Before the war, I had never communicated with my neighbors so sincerely and openly. I had no idea how wonderful my neighbors were. I think the war has shown how much people, in particular the Ukrainian people, united by one problem, can create such great things and create such synergies"—Kateryna.

> "Being a teacher for adults was not easy before the war. Being a teacher for adults while there is war in your country was unbearable. What can we discuss? What can I ask? What if someone has lost something valuable? What if they start crying? What if I say something wrong? And the never-ending list of 'what ifs' that didn't let you be the same person you were before. It felt like I had lost the ability to communicate with people. The boundaries between what's right and what's wrong got blurred and you question every word you say and every move you make. Asking quite a regular 'before' question like 'What's your favorite place to eat out?' made one of my students from Kharkiv burst into tears 'after'... their favorite place was burnt down to ashes. Nevertheless, I realized that I was doing something right. A lot of my students used our lessons to prepare for the interviews for foreign media to spread awareness about what's truly happening in Ukraine. Others asked me to help translate articles and videos to let the world know about our courage. I might not be able to fight holding a gun, but I help Ukrainians to raise their voices and make the whole world hear and understand us"—Olha.

"When the war broke out again, I wanted to be as useful to Ukraine as possible. I was not in shape to be a soldier, I never had substantial experience with volunteering in person, and I could not go abroad to buy thermal imagers and bulletproof vests because I did not even have a driving license. The only thing I knew I could for sure do was writing—and that is how the idea of 'Mediaoffensive' project came to my mind.

I gathered a group of 36 students of international relations and political science, and we started contacting media outlets and newspapers abroad, offering them our help in covering the war in Ukraine. Our goal was simple. We wanted to ensure that foreign readers would get objective, comprehensive, and timely reporting about what was happening in our country. We wrote analytical articles, recorded interviews, told personal stories, contacted experts for exclusive commentary, and more. As of now, we have eleven partners from seven countries in Europe and Northern America. We work with them regularly and on a volunteer basis, and we hope that our contributions raise awareness about the Russian war in Ukraine among foreigners"—Anhelina.

"While coping with aggressive sentiments towards people justifying war crimes and the brutal invasion of my Homeland, I started participating in protests and campaigns concerning awareness-raising in cooperation with the Ukrainian diaspora in Scotland which appeared to be the most natural move since I became a relocated Ukrainian in my 20s. Just as it is always described in modern psychological research, a common goal, and a common enemy bind people together and ease the consequences of the collective trauma respectively. We managed to implement a multi-stage action plan in order to keep reminding local people and media as well that civilians and young children in Ukraine are suffering from an improbable outbreak of violence that should be broadcast everywhere to show some real evidence to those brainwashed. To be honest, it was never an easy goal to reach however we experienced an advantage as representatives of the University community therefore people around us were in favor of receiving our viewpoint. We were protesting in other Scottish towns occasionally and I then accidentally became a coordinator of a Ukrainian society at the University of Glasgow which was established sometime before and regained its potential in 2022 when it was needed at most. In cooperation with the 'Mediaoffensive' initiative that provided us with the required materials for publishing and engaging people to join our efforts, we launched a fundraising campaign for displaced families within Ukraine to support them with necessary supplies and a safe place to stay"—Nivena.

"As soon as I arrived in Germany, I threw myself into volunteering at the main railway station. In the smallest amount of time, with the chaos engulfed because of the nonexistent coordinated and prepared help for

Ukrainians, as mostly everything had been run by the small local volunteer groups and consolers. With my knowledge of Ukrainian, Russian, and English with a little German that I had scratched from the lessons back in my school days, I have found myself useful. There were so many people with lost relatives, so many heartbroken women with children rushing to any available volunteer for help, so many cries of old people who don't have anything left after their long and fruitful life except two bags of clothes and one file with documents. And so many young girls and underage boys without parents, came here because their parents were worried sick if they hadn't fled the country. The first few weeks were the worst ones"—Nguen.

Regarding the involvement of students of this course in volunteer activities and the quality of their studies, it is worth noting three main points. A small number of students found much more meaning in volunteer activities and struggle, which completely diverted their attention and efforts from the educational process. The quality of their academic performance deteriorated, but their mental health was good. A greater share of students managed to combine volunteering, especially at foreign universities, with high academic performance. Here it is worth noting the high positive impact of the openness of partner universities of the Kyiv-Mohyla Academy, which accepted Ukrainian students for semester and year studies after the beginning of the full-scale invasion and strongly supported student initiatives. A large proportion of students began to experience problems with mental health and decreased motivation to study, unable to cope with stress on their own. Undoubtedly, factors that cannot be revealed through autoethnographic essays, such as biological characteristics or preceding events in each student's life before the Russian invasion, contributed to this. However, the student essays do reveal one powerful factor, namely, family separation, which appears to be crucial to the deterioration of resilience and adaptability to the constant stress of war.

Student Desperation over Family Separation

Israeli professor Mooly Lahad, whose goal was to develop methods to increase the resilience of people living in conflict zones, developed a model of coping with stress based on thousands of cases, which he called the *Basic Ph Model*. This model involves a combination of six basic strategies that an individual experiencing the destruction of the familiar world and aggression around him or her should use every day to live a full life (Lahad *et al.* 2012). Below I will describe how I adapted Lahad's model for teaching during the war, without including only the Ph, which is the use of bodily resources to cope with the stress of war and which I felt was impossible to apply in the case of an online course.

B—belief

The belief in this case is not only faith in God, but also unquestioning confidence in the "power" of the students' parents and extended family, who constantly cared for and protected them. Another shared belief of Ukrainian students before the full-scale Russian invasion was the belief in the power of international organizations and the belief in the rule of law, in the ability of the international community to stop Russian aggression. Even in the third month of the war, student essays demonstrate the value of unity among Ukrainians and the belief in Ukraine's victory with the help of international partners.

A—affect

Emotions, such as fear, anger, disgust, and confusion, which an individual can express and find legitimization for in society, facilitate the perception of traumatic experience, do not "drive" it into the trauma of the generation, and make it "felt," "expressed," and "experienced together." Having empathetic people around the students who allowed them to experience emotions and respond to these emotions correctly, without trying to "force happiness," allowed students to increase their resilience.

S—social

This strategy builds on the previous one by emphasizing the strengthening of social ties, such as friendships, hobby clubs, informal connections within the student body, and communication with teachers. An individual's isolation during the stress of war almost negates his or her resilience. In terms of this strategy, the resumption of studies at the Kyiv-Mohyla Academy just two weeks after the start of the invasion played an important positive role in restoring a sense of belonging to the students and faculty.

I—imagination

Creativity and imagination help individuals experiencing constant stress to find strength and express emotions through art, writing, drama, dance, and song. The students' readiness and willingness to write an auto-ethnographic essay in a free creative style instead of analytical research in the midst of war and the free and supportive way of discussing traumatic experiences in the classroom are very positive experiences in my teaching.

C—cognitive

A cognitive strategy for overcoming traumatic experiences involves discussing in a group and thinking about solutions to the problem the individual is struggling with in several ways. Without doubting the high individual cognitive qualities of students, professors, mentors, and teachers working with students from the conflict zone should use more group assignments, where the "wisdom of the group" and the joint search for the best way to solve a problem increases the resilience of each group member.

Most of Lahad's resilience-building strategies emphasize finding support in the group's shared values, empathy for emotions, and joint development of problem-solving strategies. The isolation of an individual, exclusion from the group, and loneliness in the face of the horrors of war make him or her particularly vulnerable to trauma. The main social groups for students are their family, friends, and university communities.

Three types of family separation are highlighted in the student essays: 1) The student goes abroad, and the family remains in Ukraine in "relative safety," which, as noted above, means being at risk of Russian bombing, albeit not on the occupied territory and not on the frontline; 2) Separation of the family in Ukraine, when a student goes to its safest western part, leaving parents in the central, eastern, northern or southern part of Ukraine; 3) Separation from extended multinational family, when Russian relatives are no longer the usual support for students, but become enemies.

Students who, thanks to the support of the Kyiv-Mohyla Academy, their own or their parents' affords, had the opportunity to leave Ukraine to study abroad during the first days of the war, felt much worse than if they had gone to such study as planned. Miriam George distinguishes between anticipatory and acute refugees, noting that acute refugees suffer much more than those migrants who planned their journey (George 2009). Even the previously planned mobility to Germany, which guaranteed the student a safe stay, was perceived by her as very stressful under the conditions of the war because it involved the separation of the family, during which the parents would have to remain in the attacked territory. Similarly, moving to a safer place inside Ukraine, with the condition that their parents would be in danger, caused a lot of stress for the students.

> "The decision to relocate was not an easy one to make, but practically it was much easier for me to embody it than for many other people who had nowhere to go. A few months before the invasion I was accepted for international mobility to the university in Germany. By the end of February, I had a visa, health insurance, and a place to stay, as well as tickets for the flight on the 1st of April. My parents were glad that my residency was figured out, however, I was thinking a lot about whether I should leave or not. I have been waiting for a chance to experience studying and living abroad for a long time, but the ambiguity of circumstances spoke for itself. The 'survivor's guilt' followed me for a long time as I was weighing up rational and irrational reasons to stay or to leave. After all, I agreed with my parents on the reasonability of going rather than staying"—Yuliya.

> "Right now, I'm 2000 kilometers away from my family. They're in Kyiv, I'm in France. When I was saying goodbye to them, a big part of me stayed there. I clenched my fists and gritted my teeth just not to cry in front of them. The moment I left I couldn't stop the tears. My only wish is to see them again, healthy and happy"—Anna.

"When on the morning of the seventh day of the war we were preparing to say our goodbyes, my father went to another room and there he had a panic attack. My mother was reassuring him saying that it was nice that I was leaving because I would be safe. When he came out, for the first time in my life I saw my father crying.

I sat on the couch and finished my breakfast. Mom came over. I joked about something. She looked at me and said that I should not hide my feelings. I said nothing.

Going out into the street to go to the car, I looked at our farm. The pain was sharp. I felt like thousands of eyes were looking at me waiting for me to cry. I wanted to cry so badly that in order not to do this I had to strain every cell of my body.

I hugged my parents. They were crying. I was not. A family friend and I sat in the car. I smiled at my parents through the window. We passed through the gate, drove out into the street, and headed towards the exit from the village.

I thought that now I would finally cry when my parents could not see me, but I did not. Something seemed to break in me, and this breakdown allowed me to feel a saving numbness. What worried me least of all at that moment was my own future fate"—Kateryna.

"My parents called a family council and told me and my boyfriend looking straight into the pupils of our eyes that we should save ourselves and leave alone without them. At first, I didn't believe what they said and denied it. But then my parents convinced us, and we left for Vasylkiv to stay with my boyfriend's dad, to spend the night there and go to western Ukraine the next day. This happened on March 8. While we were driving to Vasylkiv, we were stopped at a military post and the guys from the territorial defense gave me the most beautiful tulip I had ever seen and asked my boyfriend, smiling: 'Are you taking all the pretty girls out of Kyiv?' This way they congratulated me on International Women's Day. As soon as we left the military post, tears streamed down my cheeks, and I couldn't hold back my sobs. Because I was very touched that our defenders, despite the darkness around them, remembered an echo of peaceful life, a holiday I was sure everyone had forgotten about"—Maria.

"Our relatives who have lived in Russia for several decades stopped being our family. We never thought that adults, who we thought were intelligent people, turned out to be zombies without any logical sense. Again 'why?' Maybe because it's easier to be stupid or it's the destiny of Russian civilians, to let someone control their minds and lives"—Anna.

"Once I saw a familiar Russian phone number on the screen, I immediately thought of the aim of the phone call—I expected an offer of help, apologies or mere sympathy. My expectations broke into pieces the exact moment I picked up the phone and heard the question 'How are you doing, khokhols?' [khohols—a derogatory term used by Russians towards Ukrainians to highlight the inferiority of the Ukrainian nation in comparison with the Russian one—GS] in a highly ironic tone. As it turned out, the purpose of the call was mocking the situation my family had got into, blaming Ukrainians for the beginning of the 'military operation' and threatening us with a Russian superior army. While being shocked and extremely emotional, I was not able to control myself under the given circumstances and, obviously, could not tolerate such statements. Quite predictably, our fight further escalated into a scandal—and I decided to never talk to my relatives again. Having heard how disrespectful and ignorant they were towards their own relatives and how desperately they tried to justify Russia's actions, I caught myself thinking that I am unlikely to forgive them"—Valeria.

"Like many other Ukrainians, I had (not sure I can say "have" anymore) many close family members in Russia, unfortunately for us all in Moscow. I spent the first three weeks waiting for a text from them—my little cousin couldn't forget about me, could she? We spent so many years together, kids with only a two-year difference, being proud of how we could understand each other when no one else could. But the day came when this understanding irreversibly cracked—the day when I saw a picture of her smiling at the concert commemorating the anniversary of Crimea's annexation. Covered all in Russian flags, with the letter 'Z' on her chest. This is how I broke all of my connections with anything Russian apart from the language. I am Ukrainian, but I still speak Russian in my family"—Natalia.

Students whose families did not split, either by going abroad together or staying together in a "relatively safe place" in Ukraine, and those students who had separated from the Russian part of their extended family before the full-scale invasion, showed significantly more resilience in their auto-ethnographic essays.

Conclusion

The resumption of studies at the Kyiv-Mohyla Academy on 9 March 2022, just two weeks after the start of the full-scale Russian invasion of Ukraine, has preserved the students' and faculty's sense of belonging to the university community, which has greatly increased our resilience and ability to withstand the stress of war.

The nature of this war, namely its recognition by both Ukrainian and international society as an unprovoked, illegitimate invasion, and not a "special military operation to Ukraine," as Russian propaganda insists, makes it possible not to silence the daily experience of war of Ukrainians, as it was in the Soviet Union, but to speak about it, meeting with understanding among the international community. This speaking out and the understanding of the world community in response removes the stigma of guilt and shame from the victim of aggression for being attacked.

The analysis of auto-ethnographic essays by third-year students of the International Relations program at the Kyiv Mohyla Academy, in which they described their experiences of the first three months of the war, revealed that all students, without exception, experienced the shock of the overwhelming violence with the start of the war. The main factors of this experience, felt by the students as traumatic, were the suddenness of the attack, the inability to control the situation, and the huge scale of violence and destruction. Despite the harshness of the situation, family ties, the unity of the Ukrainian people in resisting the aggressor, involvement in volunteer activities, and a sense of belonging to the university community, acted as pillars that allowed students to increase resilience in critical situations. Meanwhile, separation from their families, and alienation from Russian relatives who fully supported Russia's "special military operation" against Ukraine, therefore, against their own blood relatives, feature as the factors that bring the most suffering to students.

It is worth realizing that factors that affect resilience, such as biological features, events preceding or following the stress in the life of each student, and the severity of losses of each of them, are beyond the control of professors and the university administration. At the same time, professors should be aware that a cohort of students who already have built trust among themselves and with the professor is one of the most important groups from which students can draw resources for resilience. Adapting the resource-oriented model of Mooly Lahad to the university environment professors can use the following tools: 1) emphasizing shared beliefs and common values; 2) providing opportunities to share negative emotions and being able to empathetically respond to them; 3) ensuring that none of the students remains isolated, to promote the creation and maintenance of social connections among students; 4) using imagination and creativity in individual assignments; and 5) using problem-solving teamwork.

References

Alexievich, Svetlana. (2017) *The Unwomanly Face of War: An Oral History of Women in World War II*, trans. Richard Pevear and Larissa Volokhonsky. Penguin Books.

Darwin Correspondence Project. (n/d) *Six Things Darwin Never Said—And One He Did*. Darwin Correspondence Project. https://www.darwinproject.ac.uk/people/about-darwin/six-things-darwin-never-said.

George, Miriam. (2009) "A Theoretical Understanding of Refugee Trauma," *Clinical Social Work Journal* 38(4) (December): 379–87.

Herman, Judith Lewis. (1992) *Trauma and Recovery*. New York: Basic Books.

Javanbakht, Arash. (2022) "Addressing War Trauma in Ukrainian Refugees Before it is Too Late," *European Journal of Psychotraumatology* 13(2) (5 August).

Jong, Joop, ed. (2002) *Trauma, War, and Violence: Public Mental Health in Socio-Cultural Context*. Boston: Kluwer Academic Publishers.

Kurapov, Anton, Pavlenko, Valentyna, Drozdov, Alexander, Bezliudna, Valentyna, Reznik, Alexander, and Isralowitz, Richard. (2022) "Toward an Understanding of the Russian-Ukrainian War Impact on University Students and Personnel," *Journal of Loss and Trauma* (13 June): 1–8.

Lahad, M., Leykin, D., Krkeljic, L., Rogel, R., & Lev, Y. (2012) *BASIC Ph Model of Coping and Resiliency: Theory, Research, and Cross-Cultural Application*. Kingsley Publishers, Jessica.

Löwenheim, Oded. (2010) "The 'I' in IR: An Autoethnographic Account," *Review of International Studies* 36(4) (13 July): 1023–45.

Meadows, Sarah O., Miller, Laura L., and Robson, Sean. (2015) "Understanding Resilience," in *Airman and Family Resilience: Lessons from the Scientific Literature*. RAND Corporation, 9–22.

Osokina, Olga, Silwal, Sanju, Bohdanova, Tatiana, Hodes, Matthew, Sourander, Andre and Skokauskas, Norbert. (2022) "Impact of the Russian Invasion on Mental Health of Adolescents in Ukraine," *Journal of the American Academy of Child & Adolescent Psychiatry* (October).

Rogowska, Aleksandra M., and Pavlova, Iuliia. (2023) "A Path Model of Associations between War-related Exposure to Trauma, Nightmares, Fear, Insomnia, and Posttraumatic Stress among Ukrainian Students during the Russian Invasion," *Psychiatry Research* 328 (October): 115431.

Semerikov, Serhiy O., Vakaliuk, Tetiana A., Mintii, Iryna S. and Didkivska, Svitlana O. (2023) "Challenges facing Distance Learning during Martial Law: Results of a Survey of Ukrainian Students," *Educational Technology Quarterly* (7 October).

Sylvester, Christine. (2013) *War As Experience: Contributions from International Relations and Feminist Analysis*. Taylor & Francis Group.

Wacquant, Loic. (2003) "Ethnografeast: A Progress Report on the Practice and Promise of Ethnography". *Ethnography* 4, № 1: 5–14. https://doi.org/10.1177/1466138103004001001.

Wald, J., Taylor, S., Asmundson, G. J., Jang, K. L., & Stapleton, J. (2006). *Literature Review of Concepts: Psychological Resiliency* (No. DRDC-CR-2006-073). British Columbia University Vancouve

ARTICLES

Narratives about Baikonur: City and Cosmodrome[1]

Kulshat Medeuova and Ulbolsyn Sandybaeva

Abstract: This article examines narratives about the Soviet Baikonur cosmodrome and the cultural landscape around it. Through the analysis of museum exhibitions, artworks, and oral history interviews, the authors explore the complex and contradictory state in which the first cosmodrome now finds itself, as well as the position that space and the space program occupy in the contemporary social imaginary. The article draws upon field research conducted in 2019–2020 at the cosmodrome itself, in the city of Baikonur, and in the surrounding area, covering the peripheries of the Kyzylorda, Zhezkazgan, and Ulytau regions of Kazakhstan.

Baikonur cosmodrome occupies a huge space—its area comprises over six thousand square kilometers. In terms of infrastructure, this is a place which by virtue of its secrecy regime poses certain epistemological challenges when it comes to reconstructing the cultural landscape not only of the valley of Syr Darya river, but also of a large part of central Kazakhstan—the Saryarka region. In this article we discuss first and foremost the space program and outer space[2]—real and imagined—its heroic imagery and its everyday dimensions. In keeping with an inclusive approach, this is a multivocal study—we have studied stories told both by local residents,

---

1   The research for this article was supported by the grant AP14870269 "The Infrastructure of Memory: Revitalization of Kazakhstan's Cultural Landscapes." This article was first published in Russian in *Neprikosnovennyi zapas* 4 (2023), https://magazines.gorky.media/wp-content/uploads/2024/01/6.-medeuova.pdf. It is re-published here in English translation with permission.
2   Translator's note: in the Russian original, the term *kosmos* was used throughout the article, sometimes with reference to the space program, and at other times to refer to "outer space" and/or the "cosmos." In the English translation, we use the relevant specific terms, in the interests of clarity.

and by military personnel who served at Baikonur. In addition, we draw upon museum exhibits (and accounts by museum staff) at former military units, where the history of the cosmodrome's development is presented today. Finally, the works of contemporary artists engaged in re-conceptualizing the phenomenon of the cosmos were also a valuable source for us.

The entire external periphery of the closed zone was drawn in one way or another into everyday life, both in Baikonur the city and at the eponymous cosmodrome. We begin by examining Baikonur as a whole, in its capacity as a closed territory. We then proceed to analyze how Baikonur is represented in museums, in the city and at the cosmodrome's Pad No. 2, Toretam station, and the settlement of Zhosaly, the sites where the history of the cosmodrome's construction began. We also address alternative versions of the early history of the space program in Kazakhstan, recounted to us in the settlement of Baikonyr, which is located 350 kilometers from the cosmodrome, in the district of Ulytau.

The research was conducted from 2019 through 2022. Our fieldwork routes passed through the major regional centers of Kyzylorda, Zhezkazgan, and Karaganda, and further across the periphery of the cosmodrome, onto the cosmodrome itself. Respondents' names and personal data are provided only when permission for this has been provided. Based on their preferences, some respondents are named in the text (and in some cases, where relevant, their religious denomination is indicated), while others are simply designated as "former military serviceperson" or "local resident," without indicating ethnicity or citizenship.

Two versions of the toponym at hand are used in the article: the Kazakh "Baikonyr" and the Russian "Baikonur." This is not simply a matter of different orthography and pronunciation—behind these terms there lies a whole "conspiratorial" Cold War-inflected history. The erection of the cosmodrome (previously a test range) was accompanied by the construction of a settlement near Toretam, a station on the Trans-Aral railway. This settlement, which later became a city (1969), bore the name of Leninsk from 1958. It was only in 1995 that it was re-named Baikonur. But the test range itself was named Baikonur immediately after the launch of Yurii Gagarin's "Vostok" space vessel in 1961; with the aim of disorienting hostile intelligence agencies, at the time of Gagarin's flight, the settlement of Baikonyr in Karagandinskaia (now Ulytauskaia) oblast' was officially named as the launch site. This settlement, which has its own industrial history linked with the early twentieth-century British exploration of brown coal deposits here, is to this day associated with numerous spy stories and conspirological legends, on which more below.

Figure 1. Checkpoint and road sign for the city in Russian and Kazakh languages. Photo by K. Medeuova, 2022.

In the article, we present a range of different narratives and tropes, all of which, we argue, are important for understanding how and in what cultural forms "localization" of space and the space program takes place; what position space and the space program occupy in the contemporary social imaginary; and what influence it exerts over those territories (and their socio-cultural landscapes) directly connected to it.

Cosmic Frameworks

We conducted interviews among various groups, and each of them spoke about Baikonur in their own way. Thus, among the military, even former military, heroic-pathetic intonations are dominant; here we find a narrative that is often very close to the official-media version, involving the reproduction of fragments of a "consensual narrative."[3] Artists draw upon diverse discourses, ranging from the romantic to the critical. The accounts of local residents (not only of Baikonur itself, but also of other settlements located near the cosmodrome) are saturated by nostalgia—and at the same time, by disillusionment, and regret for, in Asif Siddiqi's phrase, an "unrealized future."[4] The theme of ecological anxiety is an important motif in the stories about Baikonur. This concerns first and foremost dangerous chemicals used during rocket launches, in particular, as a fuel component in the "Proton" class rocket-carriers.[5] For example, the major accident in 2007 involving a "Proton-M" rocket, which relies on heptyl fuel, provoked the emergence of the Anti-Heptyl ("Antigeptil") social movement in Kazakhstan.

Another kind of anxiety about the destruction of the cultural landscape is described well in Chinghiz Aitmatov's novel *The Day Lasts More Than a Hundred Years* (1980),[6] in which the main protagonist cannot bury his friend in accordance with Islamic rituals at his native cemetery located on the cosmodrome's territory. A living tradition is broken, but so too access to the tradition's historical-archaeological dimension is complicated: a museum staff member in the settlement of Zhusaly told us that he and his colleagues dream of gaining access to the cosmodrome territory in order to study and describe archaeological objects located there.

---

3   On which see A. Siddiqi, "From Cosmic Enthusiasm to Nostalgia for the Future," in E. Maurer *et al.* (eds.), *Soviet Space Culture: Cosmic Enthusiasm in Socialist Societies* (Palgrave Macmillan, 2011), 283–306.
4   Ibid., 283.
5   See B. Maikanov *et al.*, "The Effect of an Accidental Carrier Rocket Crash on Soil and Vegetation Cover," *Journal of Ecological Engineering* 23, no. 2 (2022): 176–84.
6   *I dol'she veka dlitsia den'*.

The cosmodrome is not only a site for the launching and landing of rockets, but also a kind of frontier with its own distinctive everyday environment. We follow Frederick Jackson Turner here in using the concept of the "frontier" to designate a contact zone for different economic and social systems and cultural peripheries.[7] And, like any borderland zone, this is a special world with diverse actors and diverse carriers of historical and cultural memory.[8]

In contemporary social science, space is called the last/endless frontier; scholars consider its connection with the arms race, and with nostalgia for an "unrealized future." The latter is especially characteristic for post-Soviet states, where, according to Asif Siddiqi, the horizon of the future is closed off by unrealized past projects associated with this future.[9] Reflecting on the interconnection between national identity and space exploration, on narratives engendered by national aspirations and which became the foundation of the space program's history both in the US and in Russia during the "Cold War," Siddiqi speaks of new narratives around those actors that were previously unrepresented in big cosmic history.[10] In addition, there is growing interest today in the cultural dimensions of this history, manifested in art projects.[11] Therefore, for us, the methods used by Kazakh artists for interpreting the cosmos are of special interest.

The ambiguous nature of all forms of "space heritage" engenders diverse discourses and narratives, including colonial, post-colonial, and ecological ones. In the Kazakh case, the history of the Soviet space program is inscribed in distinctive ways into the national narrative of independence and the history of national

---

7   F. Dzh. Terner [F. J. Turner], *Frontir v amerikanskoi istorii* (Moscow: Ves' mir, 2009), 304.
8   See further K. Medeuova and U. Sandybaeva, "Nasledie i frontir: reprezentatsiia kosmosa v muzeiakh Kazakhstana," *Etnograficheskoe obozrenie* 5 (2022): 41–56.
9   Siddiqi, "From Cosmic Enthusiasm."
10 A. Siddiqi, "Competing Technologies, Nation(ist) Narratives, and Universal Claims: Toward a Global History of Space Exploration," *Technology and Culture* 51, no. 2 (2010): 425–43.
11 A. Geppert, "Rethinking the Space Age: Astroculture and Technoscience," *History and Technology* 28, no. 3 (2012): 219–23.

modernization. This narrative was articulated by Nursultan Nazarbaev, who spoke of the symbolic nature of the historical chain of events: in August 1991, the cosmodrome was declared to be the property of Kazakhstan; in October, the first Kazakh flew into space; in December, the Republic of Kazakhstan declared state independence. As Nazarbaev put it, "it turns out that we declared our intention to become a nation state earlier in space than we did on earth."[12] This political message issued by the country's first president has been reflected in Kazakh museums, where the theme of the history of cosmonautics is displayed in galleries devoted to the country's independence, with the main exhibits comprising photographs of Kazakh cosmonauts pictured with Nazarbaev. Hence, we come up against a paradox: on the one hand, space was used as symbolic capital for Kazakhstan; on the other, this capital is displayed in museums in only an indirect and mediated way.

Oftentimes, the cultural landscape of the territory "before the cosmodrome," both in Baikonur museums and Kazakh museums more broadly, is represented as "non-cultural": sparsely populated terrain, effectively desert, as though lacking in any history. In local narratives at various levels, this stereotypical understanding is compensated by the legend of Baikonur as "zher kindigi"— that is, the center, the "belly button" of the whole Earth. We can view this also as localization—as the linking together of the cosmos and local history.[13] The global cosmos is understood by local residents through the legend of Korkyt, who conquered time and death. In almost all versions of the story, Korkyt (Korkut, Korkyt-ata, Khorkhut, Gorkut-ata) is a legendary sage, believed to have come from the steppes located along the Syr Daria river. Escaping death, traveling to all four corners of the earth, the hero returns to the Syr Daria river, which is described as the center of the world, and it is precisely here that he acquires immortality.[14]

---

12 N. Nazarbaev, *Kazakhstanskii put'* (Karaganda: 2006), 307.
13 See L. Messeri, *Placing Outer Space: An Earthly Ethnography of Other Worlds* (Durham, NC: Duke University Press, 2016), 248.
14 S. Kaskabasov, *Kolybel' iskusstva* (Almaty: Oner, 1992), 368.

In the opinion of the Kazakh artist, native of these parts, Rashid Nurekeev, "the only thing we take pride in is the fact that here is the belly button of the Earth, and at Baikonur we link this idea with Korkyt; it's no accident that his grave is there, on the banks of the Syr Daria, and that Baikonur was built precisely at this site."[15]

When a museum-memorial complex was built at Korkyt's burial site, in the 1980s, just 70 kilometers from the cosmodrome, it was planned (and has partially come to function) as an emblematic space in competition with Baikonur, especially for those visiting Baikonur for rocket launches.[16]

A Closed City

The city, the cosmodrome, and Toretam station share complex infrastructural links. The city is surrounded by a concrete wall with barbed wire and two security check points. Similar check points are located at the entrances to the territory of the cosmodrome itself. According to maps of the site, the route across the cosmodrome begins with the numbered pads (*ploshchadki*), which have various purposes, ranging from launchpads to technical and through to memorial ones. The famous Pad 1, known as "Gagarin's Start," leads onto Pad 2, comprising a museum and the Gagarin and Korolev memorial houses. The latter was gifted to Sergei Korolev by the government after the successful launch of the Earth's first artificial satellite. The constructor lived in the house for six years, and in 1975, almost a decade after Korolev's death, the house acquired the status of a memorial museum.

This pad was the site where the first cosmonauts underwent pre-flight training and post-flight recovery. Here too the military created a museum on the base of the infrastructure of military unit No. 25741, whose exposition begins with a room of martial glory. The city Museum of the History of Cosmodrome Baikonur, in contrast, focused on military builders. Here, a room of combat and

---

15 Authors' interview with Rashid Nurekeev, September 2019.
16 See further K. Medeuova, "Zatianuvshaiasia 'sovetskost'" i transformatsii kollektivnoi pamiati: sovetskie i postsovetskie memorial'nye kompleksy v Kazakhstan," *Novoe literaturnoe obozrenie* 1 (2020): 256–74.

labour glory of military builders was opened in 1968 in military unit No. 12253 House of Culture of Builders (later renamed the City Palace of Culture), and later, in 1994, a city museum was created on its foundations.

The museum at the cosmodrome is larger and more extensive than the city museum: here we find an open-air technology exhibit, where special attention is attracted by the "Buran" space ship, which is accessible to visiting members of the public. In both museums we find standard information about the combat path, medals and biographies of generals, builders, and those who have a direct relationship to space—either the cosmonauts themselves, or the builders. In the museum at the pad we find more detailed information about the scientists engaged in the space program. Fragments of space technology, guiding apparatus, cosmonauts' food, dioramas and photographs—in comparison to the major space museums in Moscow, Kaluga, Washington, and New York, all this looks rather meager, but if we compare it to space expositions in Kazakh museums,[17] then it is impressive and informative.

In the case of both museums, we were interested not only in the exhibits, but also in the nature of life in a closed city: to what extent are its residents informed about developments in other regions of the valley of Syr Darya river, the region's main artery? Likewise, we also asked museum staff at the Korkyt-ata memorial complex in Zhosaly what they knew about the city and the cosmodrome. The memorial complex staff are certain of the significance of their memorial museum and of the site itself as special and even sacred—a place where one senses an archetypal cosmic unity, the "center of the world."[18] The staff at the museum at the cosmodrome's Pad No. 2, on the other hand, were unable to explain why a display stand featuring Korkyt was needed in a museum devoted to the space program.[19] For them, Korkyt is only a historical medieval poet who has some kind of significance for Kazakhs; they do not see any link here with the space theme. Meanwhile, for their

---

17 Medeuova and Sandybaeva, "Nasledie i frontir," 41–56.
18 Tour guide 1, Fieldwork materials, October 2021.
19 Tour guide 2, Fieldwork materials, October 2022.

part, museum staff from Zhosaly are unable to access the cosmodrome territory for research.[20]

In the city itself, the area around the abandoned checkpoint is partially in ruins. In response to our question as to whether there were plans to build something new there, or whether what we could see was simply the result of the ongoing demolition of the old barracks, an employee of the city museum said that he was not authorized to answer for the actions of the authorities and that "in general the Kazakh side has lots of fantastic projects—maybe they're building something there, after all they even wanted to build a tourist center at Baikonur, but in the city itself there have long been no major construction projects."[21] In the museum located on the cosmodrome territory, one tour guide, while describing with great enthusiasm Gagarin's summer house, where cosmonauts used to drink tea and where state commissions took important decisions, noted at the same time that the residents of Baikonur have no access to this privileged site, separated off presently by a six-meter fence, but that in her childhood "we used to squeeze through the barbed wire, and the soldiers used to try to catch us."[22]

Life in a city behind a barbed wire fence, undoubtedly, limits the perception of the cultural landscape as a whole. Despite the advantages of centralized supplies and the career opportunities for builders and military personnel, there are few who would like to settle here permanently. Today's Baikonur is a run-down and extremely dilapidated city, where there are few new buildings and future prospects are unclear.[23]

Baikonur cosmodrome passed into the ownership of Kazakhstan after the latter achieved independence in 1991. Under a 1994 agreement, it was leased to Russia, and through a series of agreements in 2004 the lease has been extended until 2050. Consequently, the city and the cosmodrome remain closed to the general public. Admission to the site is heavily regulated and there are complex procedures for applying for permission to visit the city or the museums located at the launchpads. In the 1990s the share of Kazakhs living in the city increased, which led to a change of the

---

20   Tour guide 3, Fieldwork materials, October 2022.
21   Tour guide 4, Fieldwork materials, October 2022.
22   Tour guide 2, Fieldwork materials, October 2022.
23   Authors' interview with former military official, December 2019.

ethnic composition of the population on the whole; a church and a mosque appeared, although the latter is located on the territory beyond the checkpoint, between Baikonur and Toretam. One of our city guides, an ethnic Kazakh, told us how his parents had arrived precisely in this period—they were businesspeople; they did not work for the space industry or the military. His childhood took place in this city; he was accustomed to the sight of city ruins, but, wishing to show us his city in the best light, he carefully avoided buildings where a more or less well preserved façade contrasted sharply with boarded-up windows and doors at the rear.

In Baikonur a city sign with the old name of "Leninsk" has survived; alongside it is an epic mosaic depicting a cosmonaut, which has become a kind of visual brand for the city (Figure 2). An additional sculpture in the shape of a love-heart was erected here too as part of renovations carried out in 2022. We were told that this was done in order to encourage newly-weds to carry out their ritual smashing of champagne bottles not on the cosmonaut (which attracts hundreds of tourists to the cosmodrome for photographs), but on this new construction.

Figure 2. Mosaic and view of the city of Baikonur from the airport and Akai village. Photo by K. Medeuova, 2021.

"Soldiers of Space"

One former military man, now a journalist, an environmental engineer and photographer,[24] believes that the communities of former residents of Baikonur, Priozersk and Sary-Shagan[25] are the most "patriotic" with regard to the places where they served and lived. "After all, there were lots of military towns where life was better, like Plesetsk [Cosmodrome, in Russia's Arkhangel'sk region], where there was no crisis in the nineties, but people remember Baikonur as happiness and joy, and pain in the hearts of those who lived there; these are special towns."[26]

He served at Baikonur in the 1980s and considers this the period of the highest blossoming of the city in the cultural and demographic sense. The socio-economic and age profile of those who came here from different parts of the Soviet Union, he observed, was almost identical:

> ... I myself was young, and the city was unique, amazingly young, at one point they tried to calculate the average age, it turned out to be around 26... There was no special entertainment other than books, cinema, and famous artistes often came touring. In the cultural sense nevertheless life was very rich, but for young officers, who had little free time, on the whole it was difficult to attend all the events.[27]

Speaking of the difficulties linked first and foremost with the adverse epidemiological situation and the harsh climate, he observed that this was compensated by a sense of the importance of the mission they were carrying out as defenders of the fatherland. As for the current security regime at Baikonur, his view was that it doesn't make sense to speak of secrecy in an epoch of satellite intelligence—all the more so since a multitude of international

---

24 K. Medeuova, "Nowhereness: Baikonur," *Cosmic Bulletin* (Institute of the Cosmos) (2022), https://cosmos.art/cosmic-bulletin/2022/nowhereness-baikonur.
25 Priozersk and Sary-Shagan are military towns with test ranges, whose infrastructure is linked with Baikonur, and part of whose territory is currently leased to Russia.
26 Authors' interview with former military official, December 2019.
27 Authors' interview with former military official, December 2019.

projects had been realized through Interkosmos, and NASA delegations had visited the cosmodrome. As he spoke about the cosmodrome, one could sense his nostalgia for the Soviet past. He said that the Soviet Union had been considered a great military power precisely thanks to the space program, and that today the military-industrial complex played an important role in the competition of states.

In his opinion, the slickly promoted image of the US space program, with Elon Musk as figurehead, was incomparable to the Soviet space program, where the ideological priorities were correctly formulated and articulated. At the same time, however, he recognized that skilled marketing was enabling the popularization of space, exemplified by the American, Chinese, and European space agencies:

> What goes on at Baikonur? Ask a Kazakh, and you'll get the answer: they launch something there, basically almost like 20-30 years ago, the same rockets. Of course, the cosmodrome has shrunk now, they used to have all kinds of launchpads for different types of rockets, some of the pads have been abandoned, some have been preserved... The cosmodrome has really shriveled up now...[28]

Our respondent was a former military official who has stayed on to live in Kazakhstan, in Karaganda—a city known today not only for mining but which also positions itself as a "space harbor"[29] and which has its own sites of memory linked to the space program. It is interesting to note that he knows little about the surrounds of Baikonur and had never visited the Korkyt-ata Memorial complex which, like the cosmodrome itself, is administratively located in Kyzylordinskaia oblast'. At the same time, our respondent spoke about Baikonur as the region's cultural center "which at one time even competed with Kyzylorda."

During the Soviet period, when Baikonur had special privileges when it came to supplies and infrastructure, one could talk about "competition" of this kind, but after the collapse of the USSR, Baikonur found itself in a catastrophic situation. Today,

---

28 Authors' interview with former military official, December 2019.
29 "*Kosmicheskaia gavan'*".

leased to Russia and under dual jurisdiction, the city's situation remains complex. Russia invests little in the development of the city's infrastructure, while Kazakhstan, on the contrary, is beginning to develop the city more energetically, at least in the sphere of residential housing construction. Meanwhile, Kyzyzlorda, the region's administrative center, is actively using space symbolism associated with Baikonur and the image of Korkut. Here space represents cultural and symbolic capital that boosts the city's visibility.

Those cities of Kazakhstan with a connection to the space program—Kyzylorda, Karaganda, Zhezkazgan—are often referred to as "space" cities. Our respondent recounted many stories about Karaganda, about encounters with cosmonauts. In the course of his military career and his journalistic and ecological activities he had met around thirty cosmonauts. In his telling, they emerge as very diverse characters—for example, Aleksei Leonov loved jokes, and was a master joke-teller. Many cosmonauts eagerly take up the opportunities to visit schools and interact with school pupils, since space is still their passion, and they want to share this passion:

> One shouldn't attribute some kind of unique elevated qualities to cosmonauts; these are very focused, well-educated, hard-working soldiers of space. These are people who would never behave like you see in the movies, they would never get hysterical, they would never argue with "ground control," they would never disobey orders. Nothing like this ever happens in reality. If you go and wake up this old man tomorrow and tell him: you have to fly tomorrow, then he'll leave everything behind—his dacha, his mansions, if he happened to earn enough for that, he'll spit on his own health—he'll make the flight.[30]

This image of the cosmonaut as "soldier of space" fits neatly with the military discourse whereby service to the motherland, patriotism, and bravery are elevated to priority values.

Undoubtedly, the experience of youth, in the context of the epoch of the Cold War, the rhetoric of the space race, pride in the Soviet Union's achievements—all these elements determine these

---

30 Authors' interview with former military official, December 2019.

narratives. Our resident, who continues to work with space heritage today, now as an ecological activist and photographer, observed that the Kazakhstan authorities were not doing enough to maintain the conversation about space on the previous high level. This case illustrates well Asif Siddiqi's thesis that, as a result of unrealized possibilities, nostalgia for the past is directly linked with "nostalgia for the future."[31]

Competing Narratives: Baikonur vs Baikonyr

The history of Baikonur as cosmodrome is, of course, part of the history of the space race of the Cold War era; as a result, the secrecy regime rendered the cosmodrome effectively "invisible" not only for the republic's population, but for the rest of the world. Different toponyms were used for the site: Leninsk, Taiga, Tashkent, and even Zvezdograd (Star City), in the lead-up to Charles de Gaulle's visit. The American physicist and space engineer, professor of aeronautics Mike Gruntman, who lived in Toretam as a child, has written in detail about how stubbornly the authorities strove to conceal not only the real facts of what went on at the cosmodrome, but even its real geographic coordinates, in place of which the Soviet media used the coordinates for a false cosmodrome purportedly located at Baikonyr settlement. Drawing on archival materials and photographs taken by a US U2 spy-plane in 1957, Gruntman has also shown how, despite these heightened secrecy measures, the true location of the cosmodrome at Toretam station was obvious to the Americans.[32] Toretam was the final railway station on the line used by the military in building the cosmodrome.

From 1961, the toponym Baikonur was used to designate the cosmodrome, and from 1995, it was also used for the military town attached to it. This is the world-famous "Baikonur"—the symbolic center of the whole "space zone." "Baikonyr," on the other hand, is the settlement in Ulytauskaia oblast' with abandoned mines, and

---

31 Siddiqi, "From Cosmic Enthusiasm," 283–306.
32 M. Gruntman, "From Tyuratam Missile Range to Baikonur Cosmodrome," *Acta Astronautica* 155 (2019): 350–66.

the site of the "false cosmodrome." Deeply dilapidated today, it marks the zone where space trash falls.

If the space era begins—in line with the official history—with the launch of sputnik and the first human flight into space precisely from Baikonur cosmodrome near Toretam station, then the alternative history presents us with a different, secret, "real" cosmodrome at Baikonyr in Ulytauskaia oblast'. With the aim of investigating the entangled histories of these cosmodromes, and uncovering local histories of the space program, we set off to visit the town of Zhezkazgan and, later, Baikonyr itself, to talk to local residents—living witnesses of the beginning of the space program in Kazakhstan. What we found is that local residents sincerely believe that their cosmodrome was the first, "real" cosmodrome, whence Gagarin was launched on his flight to space.

However, the only space-related objects in Baikonyr are a small, worn-out banner with a portrait of Gagarin, displayed opposite the construction site for a new mosque, and a street sign featuring a stylized rocket.

Presently the aul is inhabited by families engaged in livestock farming, in contrast to its history as one of the key districts associated with the early stages of industrialization in Kazakhstan. Coal extraction was the main rationale for the construction of the workers' urban-type settlement here, first by the British, and later by the Soviet authorities. In actual fact it probably makes more sense to speak here not about a single settlement but about a locality linked to Baikonyr river or Bulanty. The settlement of Baikonyr itself is divided into two parts, old and new. The old part of the settlement comprises abandoned mines, the ruins of old houses (including the houses of the English who leased this land for coal mining in early twentieth century) and the ruins of barracks and other administrative buildings testifying to the existence of the mine and the Steplag department, which is important for gaining a full picture of the region and its memory.[33] The new part

---

33 Steplag (Stepnoi lager'—Steppe camp) was a camp for political prisoners in the Gulag system, located within the city of Zhezkazgan. In 1954, the Kengir uprising, described by Aleksandr Solzhenitsyn in *Gulag Archipelago*, took

of the settlement is located on elevated territory and resembles a standard Soviet sovkhoz—a pair of perpendicular intersecting streets, an administrative center with a school, office buildings, and a Lenin monument. There are also ruins here—most often these are administrative buildings, such as a hotel, a canteen, offices which are used in various ways by local residents, for example, as a hayloft, since the main economic activity here is livestock farming.

At a meeting with the most authoritative octogenarian aksakal, the respected elder, told us about the history of his line—about his family, who came from the locality where the first cosmodrome was built, and re-settled in Baikonyr, which was then known as Shokpar. In addition, he told us a story about secret events which he and other residents interpreted as the secret history of the Soviet space program.

> The rocket was launched 70 kilometers from here. This is a place called Aksham. This was where the real underground cosmodrome was. This territory was fenced off, if you approached it accidentally from the steppe then you had to turn back. If you happened to end up inside, they would blindfold you and take you away. People who had been there had to sign a statement pledging never to say anything about it to their descendants... Right now we're sitting at the site where Gagarin flew from, but we're not on the map, we're a wasteland.[34]

We were sitting in a circle on Kazakh korpe rugs laid out on the floor in the home of one of the settlement's residents. Other residents also joined in the discussion about the history of Baikonyr's surrounds and whether this had been the site of the first cosmodrome or a false cosmodrome. In the morning, as we walked around the settlement, people said to the resident acting as our guide: "Ah, so these are the people who came from the capitals and who don't believe that we had the real first cosmodrome here."

The aksakal said that, beginning from 1959, more military units had begun to appear in Baikonyr. The residents saw soldiers

---

place here. In the early 1950s, the structure of Steplag included nine camp departments, including Baikonyr. In 1956, Steplag was liquidated.

34 Authors' conversation with local resident, *aksakal*, aged 80, October 2021.

and technical equipment; columns of ten to twenty vehicles would pass by every day—moreover, the vehicles were covered by tarpaulins, and it was forbidden even to look in their direction if one encountered them on the steppe. He also spoke about Okhotpromkhoz, where they processed saiga meat, which airplanes used to come to collect, and about which he had heard various stories. In his re-telling, the first cosmodrome was an underground construction made from concrete blocks either in the form of a cross or a triangle, a form which he linked to the Soviet–US arms race. Later, however, it had been blown up. The main through-line of his account emphasized strongly the notion that this cosmodrome, which everyone believes was fake, was the real one. It was only later, after Gagarin, that cosmonauts began to fly out from near Toretam.

The aksakal also told us an even more intriguing story about a spy caught in their settlement; the spy was working for American intelligence and was secretly transmitting by walkie-talkie information related to the cosmodrome. For the residents, this spy story is a strong argument confirming the existence of the real cosmodrome here. The spy appeared in the guise of a projectionist—a very useful person for the settlement. According to the aksakal, this was a "young person, possibly by ethnicity he was either a Russian or a Latvian, or maybe a German, his name was Misha. It turns out that he wasn't just turning the film spool, he was also handing over some kind of secret information by walkie-talkie.[35]

We were told the same story about the American spy Misha by the village's former akim,[36] a younger man, who had thus had fewer encounters with the military than the aksakal, but had heard stories from his parents and elder brothers. He had heard the story about the spy from his older brother who had interacted directly with Misha—he had drunk spirits with him, believing this to be beneficial. From his viewpoint, this detail was also further evidence of the authenticity of the "false cosmodrome," since spirits were hard to come by in these parts. In his version, Misha had worked here as a projectionist for almost two years. One day, tanks

---

35   Ibid.
36   An *akim* is the head of the local executive authorities.

arrived at the settlement, and the akim's mother used to tell them how she had given tea with kurt (a dried salty cheese) to the soldiers in the tank, and the soldiers had given the local children some badges, but nobody knew why they had come here. After the spy was captured, all the troops left, and, in our respondent's account, everything had then been transferred out of Aksham to Toretam, evidently due to the site's exposure.[37]

For verification of this entertaining story about the spy, another respondent, a history teacher, who accompanied us on our strolls around old and new Baikonyr, took us to the Muslim cemetery to show us the mazar (a grave, with a tomb erected above it), where Misha had hidden, and where he had been captured. However, as we noticed, the date of death indicated on the mazar was the year 1974, that is, the mazar had appeared significantly later than the events described. In response to this observation, our respondent said that it was entirely possible that the events had taken place at a different mazar, perhaps at the old cemetery.

For residents, all these stories represent a kind of symbolic capital: they are like keepers of secret knowledge, prepared to employ all manner of tricks and subterfuge and to seek out material traces of space history so as to preserve this myth about Gagarin's flight from their Baikonyr. One of the residents said to us: "when you arrive in Astana, don't tell them that you didn't believe us, and that we're making everything up, we'll find you some more facts confirming our truth, after all, they declared to the whole world that Gagarin flew not from Leninsk but from Baikonur, and this is the name of our place..."[38]

As the Kazakhstani journalist and writer Murat Uali has observed, "With time the real site of the launch became '*le secret de Polichinelle*' ... the false cosmodrome was in the real Baikonyr, and the real [one] became the false Baikonur."[39]

---

[37] Conversation with local resident, former *akim* of the settlement, aged 55 years, October 2021.

[38] Conversation with local resident, former policeman, now local entrepreneur, aged 50 years, October 2021.

[39] M. Uali, "Prevrashchenie Tiuratama v Baikonur," *Komsomol'skaia pravda* (Kazakhstan), 24 January 2023, https://www.kp.kz/daily/27456/4710563/.

Leninsk really became Baikonur only after the country gained independence. But in Baikonyr, with its rusty, neglected portrait of Gagarin; its entrance sign with a rocket; the layering of different strata of industrial history, from coal to rockets; the obvious social and economic troubles; the stories of the residents, excited by our interest in the region's space history, but constantly complaining that "space" had given them nothing (and that they were not even entitled to ecological compensation payments)—the unresolved problem of social justice was clearly more relevant than nostalgia for the past.

A Shining City

One of our respondents recalled how she arrived with her family from Mongolia for permanent settlement in Kazakhstan in 1991. They were sent to a district of Zhezkazgan, and for some time they spent winters in the Baikonyr settlement. Since they were from Mongolia, the officials had assumed that they would have skills in livestock farming, and they were allocated a large number of sheep. But her family were from the city, and they had no idea how to look after sheep. The children missed the city. "And then one day at Tokbolat summer pastures we saw faraway in the steppe a shining city ... It was all shimmering and it seemed like it was right nearby."[40]

Excited, the children ran towards the city, but it turned out to be a space littered with piles of rocket fragments, multi-colored cables and other technical parts. All this was shimmering in the sun in different colors. Overjoyed, the children climbed all over the fragments, looking for things to play with. When their parents learned about this, they were forbidden from visiting the site. When there were strong winds, our respondent recalled, the fragments would roll like tumbleweed, and ended up near their homes.

---

40 Authors' conversation with woman, aged 45 years, October 2021.

There are many stories connected to these shining piles of metal, and to rocket launches more broadly, and their harmful effect on humans, animals, and the landscape in general. One respondent told us about a tragic story she had heard about the death of a woman who had come with her family from China to Kazakhstan in the 1960s. Growing thirsty while droving cattle, she had drunk some water that had collected in a metal rocket fragment lying out in the steppe, and soon died. There were many such stories about illness caused by contaminated water and soil in the region.

Another respondent from Baikonyr also used the word "city" to describe the huge piles of "space junk" a few kilometers away:

> But now, all this no longer exists, so there's no point looking for anything in the steppe, not even with metal detectors... When I served in the army, the accident at Chernobyl happened. We were sent off as a whole echelon, but they didn't say where to, and there was a check. They checked us, something like an x-ray, and then they asked: "But where did you get the radiation from?" It means the whole region was contaminated then...[41]

Similar stories can be heard in both the Kyzylordinskaia and Karagandinskaia oblasts. The ecological discourse became especially intense after the toxic heptyl fuel spillage caused by the Proton-M rocket-carrier crash. This is yet another side to space history and it is often used in the political field by opponents of the cosmodrome in Kazakhstan.[42]

Religion in the Life of the City and the Cosmodrome

After the Soviet collapse, yet another dimension appeared in the life of the city and the cosmodrome: the religious dimension. Islam is becoming part of the national and local history, and Orthodox rituals now accompany space launches. The theme of space and religion are viewed through various different lenses today. Our

---

[41] Authors' conversation with local resident, former *akim* of the settlement, aged 55 years, October 2021.
[42] S. Glushkova, "Aktivisty 'Antigeptila' prizvali 'ne oskverniat' kazakhskuiu zemliu," *Radio Azattyk*, 19 October 2013, https://rus.azattyq.org/a/astana-m eeting-heptyl-baikonur/25141791.html.

fieldwork at Baikonur and Toretam indicates that religion is becoming an integral part of "space history." According to Aleksandr Nesteruk, cosmology and theology do not so much contradict as supplement one another—the latter lends purpose and eternal meaning to the former.[43] Cathleen S. Lewis has argued that for the duration of the greater part of the history of space flight, the religious aspect of space was primarily Christian.[44] As the International Space Station's partners began to bring in cosmonauts from Islamic countries, they began to encounter new religious problems. Muslim prayer practices require a constant attention to geography and astronomy. One needs to consider, for example, how to pray in conditions of low gravity, how to find Mecca at the space station, and how to schedule prayer times, since Muslims pray facing Mecca five times a day; and if a flight takes place during the month of Ramadan, how to keep the fast, since observing the phases of the Moon is impossible for the lunar calendar, and the appearance of the new Moon at the end of the month of Ramadan heralds the end of the fasting and the beginning of the Eid al-Fitr "Festival of Breaking the Fast." Interestingly, "Guidelines for Performing Islamic Rites *(Ibadah)* at the International Space Station" were produced in 2007.[45]

As Lewis notes, the United States initially recruited only white male Christians for the astronauts program, while Russia recruited mostly ethnic Slavs and, as the space programs diversified, representatives of "well-Russified minorities."[46] These "minorities" include Kazakh cosmonauts: Toktar Aubakirov, Talgat Musabaev, Aidyn Aimbetov. Unlike cosmonauts and tourists from Islamic countries, the Kazakh cosmonauts, educated during the Soviet period, did not practise religious rites, although Musabaev did take a copy of the Quran with him into space.[47]

---

43   A. V. Nesteruk, "The Interplay of Cosmology and Theology in the Constitution of the Human Condition," *Journal of Siberian Federal University. Humanities and Social Sciences* 15 (10) (2022): 1404–44.
44   C. S. Lewis, "Muslims in Space: Observing Religious Rites in a New Environment," *Astropolitics* 11, no. 1–2 (2013): 108–15.
45   Ibid., 114.
46   Ibid., 110.
47   See Nazarbaev, *Kazakhstanskii put'*.

The representation of various religious practices at Baikonur reflects the latter's status as a frontier and a borderland, including in the cultural sense. In 1992 the church of the Holy Great Martyr Georgii Pobedonosets was founded on the territory of the city of Baikonur, and in 1997 the construction of a new building for the church began (completed 2005). The iconostasis for the church was commissioned and funded by the Center for Exploitation of Objects of Ground Cosmic Infrastructure (TsENKI), an enterprise which is part of Roskosmos. The church houses an Our Lady of Kazan icon, gifted by the Patriarch of Moscow and all Rus' Aleksii II; the icon made a flight into space in 2004. The church also houses a certificate confirming that the icon spent time at the ISS.

A mosque was built here in 2011, as noted above, near the checkpoint between Baikonur and Toretam. The Russian side also took part in constructing the mosque, in particular, through donations by Roskosmos structures, city enterprises, and private individuals.[48] For local residents it is important that the mosque bears the name of the eighteenth-century saint Zharimbet-Ata/Zherimbet aulie. This aulie (saint) once dreamed that at this site many years later there would be a large city with houses built on top of one another, and "in it will live many people, whose languages I do not understand, and I see a blinding bright light."[49]

In our conversation with the mosque's imam, he reflected on the cosmodrome as follows:

> Not so many Kazakhs have flown [into space], more Russians, and since the cosmodrome's land is on long-term Russian lease, accordingly, they adhere to Russian customs and traditions for the consecration of space ships and blessing of cosmonauts... Regarding the cosmodrome, I think that we ought not to extend the lease... the attitude from the Soviet epoch is still there, towards us, Kazakhs, as nomads, shepherds, who were taught

---

48 M. Kikimbaev, "Mecheti v postsovetskom Kazakhstane: diskursy, interpretatsii i praktyki reguliatsii," *Central Asia and the Caucasus* 24, no. 4 (2021): 140–54.

49 S. Ansatov, "Zherimbet eulie," *Karmakshy tany*, 28 shilde 2018, https://qarmaqshy-tany.kz/zanalyk/ruhaniyt/4487-zhrmbet-ulie.html.

everything by them, the Russians. Of course, space and space technologies are something we should develop, probably...[50]

According to Nazarbaev's memoirs, the issue of the cosmodrome's lease, which was first raised in the 1994 inter-state agreement "On the Main Principles and Conditions of Use of 'Baikonur' Cosmodrome," was a source of disappointment for many Kazakhstanis and there was a misunderstanding of the term "lease" itself. There was a need for urgent measures to be taken to preserve the cosmodrome, given the difficult economic situation and the out-migration of specialists to Russia, and the next step was the signing of the Lease Agreement, whose preamble underlined the two states' mutual interest in developing space research. Nazarbaev justifies the decision to lease the cosmodrome on the grounds of the imperative to preserve the space complex's intellectual and scientific-technical potential, viewing this as a task at the global level, whose importance transcends that of individual state interests.[51]

The debate about the cosmodrome continues today, but now with an emphasis on the ecological agenda. The imam also takes part in these discussions. On the other hand, the cosmodrome provides employment for the population, and salaries in rubles are much higher than in tenge. Our fieldwork findings indicate that residents of Toretam live on trade, since it is more profitable for residents of Baikonur to buy food and other goods here for tenge, given the strength of the ruble against the Kazakhstan currency. Hotel business is also beginning to develop in the settlement, in response to the Kazakhstani tourists' interest in the cosmodrome. But on the whole, unemployment is a problem.

In this economic situation, the imam says, the role of religion is important. But the existing mosque is much too small for the Kazakhs of Baikonur and Toretam, since it accommodates only 400 people. Speaking about the growing role of religion, the imam had in mind also the growing openness of the religious space in Kazakhstan—here mosques fulfil not only ritual functions, but are

---

50 Authors' conversation with imam, October 2022.
51 See Nazarbaev, *Kazakhstanskii put'*.

also becoming a new public space, a place for collaboration between the state and religious and cultural institutions.[52] This is a place for wide social communication, for discussion of local community problems.

The situation with the Orthodox church is different. Father Sergii (Sergei Bychkov), the abbot of the local church, simultaneously also occupies the office of Roskosmos confessor.[53] Our meeting with Father Sergii took place in the Church of Holy Martyr Georgii Pobedonosets in Baikonur on the eve of a jubilee rocket launch dedicated to the 60th anniversary of Yurii Gagarin's flight into space. The priest came to the meeting after conducting a service praying for completion of the rocket's preparation for flight, wearing a jacket featuring patches reading "Father Sergii" and "Roskosmos Confessor." This service, in his opinion, was important—it was a response to a request for the divine blessing of all those who had worked on the rocket, from the staff of the construction bureaus through to the workers.

Sergei Bychkov, a native of Kyzylorda, served at Baikonur in the 1990s; besides the office of confessor, he also holds the rank of distinguished cosmodrome tester and space technology tester.

Explaining the nuances of this religious procedure to us, he said that there were two types of prayer services. Media coverage often focuses on the pre-flight component—the most visually striking part, when the priest comes out onto the launchpad, blesses the crew and sprinkles holy water on the rocket, naming it "ship of the air" *(vozdushnym korablem)*.

In addition, on launch days there are many meetings in which Father Sergii takes part. He interacts with diverse groups of people, independent of denomination, who come here specially for the launches; moreover, these meetings, in the form of tea drinking, may take place in the church.

---

52 K. Medeuova and M. Kikimbaev, "Muzeefikatsiia mecheti: kazakhstanskii diskurs publichnykh prostranstv," *Vestnik Evraziiskogo natsional'nogo universiteta imeni L. N. Gumileva*, Seriia: Istoricheskie nauki. Filosofiia. Religiovedenie, 140, no. 37 (2022).

53 "NASA vylozhilo v set' foto dukhovnika 'Roskosmosa,'" *RIA Novosti*, 12 March 2019, https://ria.ru/20190312/1551737071.html.

The first crew to receive blessings was Vasilii Tsibleev's crew, this was in 1998, there were only Christians there, that's how it started... By decision of the Roskosmos leadership I became the official Roskosmos confessor... When cosmonauts come here, we always gather, it's become a good tradition. And even when Muslim cosmonauts are going on a flight, they come to the church, and we set the table, we have a little tea drinking session, after all we're a hospitable people, we're Kazakhs... I don't know where the imam comes from, for example, people flew in from the Arab Emirates and they brought their own imam. I bless the Christians, it all gets done in accordance with the tradition that has taken shape... if there was no need to do all of this, then the Lord would not permit me to do it...[54]

The cosmodrome doesn't arouse enthusiasm either in the imam or for local residents of Toretam, for whom the cosmodrome has lost its aura of romanticism, but Father Sergii, on the contrary, represents that group who is inspired by everything taking place at the cosmodrome.

From the Descendants of Extra-Terrestrials to the One-Legged Cosmonaut

In the 1960s, social utopianism and enthusiasm for the space program reached their peak. Space became a powerful metaphor for technological modernization and a bright future. In the United States, NASA (the National Aeronautics and Space Administration) launched its Art Program, offering artists the opportunity to take part in the national space project. Artists were tasked with demonstrating the latest scientific research and achievements in a visual form accessible to broader society. Space art was supposed not only to carry out propaganda functions but also, and first and foremost, to inspire—it was supposed to bring together the worlds of art and science, as stated directly in the Manifesto of the International Association of Astronomical Artists (the IAAA).[55]

---

54 Authors' conversation with Father Sergii, October 2022.
55 K. Boczkowska, *The Impact of American and Russian Cosmism on the Representation of Space Exploration in 20th Century American and Soviet Space Art* (Poznań: Adam Mickiewicz University Press, 2016), 438.

The Soviet Union likewise tasked artists with creating works reflecting the national and global cosmic endeavors. For this purpose several famous artists, including Aleksei Stepanov, were granted permission to visit the cosmodrome. Stepanov's oeuvre comprises the largest collection of space-related art among Kazakhstan artists. His epic canvas "The Man from Planet Earth" (*Chelovek s planety Zemlia*) (1969) became the center of an exhibition of works by Soviet and American artists (1975) devoted to the joint "Soiuz"/"Apollo" flight. Kazakhstani artists from the "sixties" generation also produced works in the same spirit of progressive admiration for cosmos and country. These include such classics as Kamil' Mullashev's triptych "Earth and Time. Kazakhstan" (*Zemlia i vremia. Kazakhstan*) and Amandos Akanaev's "Poem on Immortality" (*Poema o bessmertii*). In the former case, the country is the contemporary Soviet modernist Kazakhstan, while in the latter, it features as a country with a more complex history, with a layering of various tragic events of the twentieth century, against the background of a collage on which is depicted Olzhas Suleimenov, declaiming poetry. In 1961 Suleimenov had dedicated his long poem "Earth, Bow Down to Man!" (*Zemlia, poklonis'cheloveku!*) to Yurii Gagarin. Here the theme of the contradictory nature of the epoch is revealed in the broader sense.

On the eve of the fifth anniversary of the formation of the Soviet Union, exhibitions were staged with standard titles such as "Across the Native Country" or "The Kazakhstani Land"; moreover, with the aim of producing more realistic depictions, artists were encouraged to visit major industrial sites. Even though we are dealing on the whole here with Soviet state-sponsored art, artists displayed highly varied interpretations of contemporary industry and different visions of its future, sometimes involving elements of fantasy. And, of course, the theme of Baikonur cosmodrome in Kazakhstan featured here. Thus, for example, in Yevgenii Sidorkin's "On Kazakhstani Land" series, one of the pieces is devoted to Baikonur. This work is important for gaining a more complete understanding of how artists imagined space and how they represented the Kazakh context.

Sidorkin is famous as a graphic artist whose works are often classified as an example of "brutalist style," of plastic achievements of nomads. As Gul'nara Shalabaeva observes, Sidorkin did not stylize the East; he immersed himself in Kazakh history, and he can be viewed as a continuator of the art of the Eurasian nomads.[56] His work "On Kazakhstan Land. Baikonur" is executed in this style. The painting depicts three figures in space helmets, in circular motion in a state of weightlessness, and connected to one another, as though by an umbilical cord. The cosmonauts are depicted against the background of stone carvings—Balbal stone statues which are found on the steppes of Kazakhstan. In the center of the circle is the head of the ancient goddess Umai, in accordance with the iconography, in a three-horned tiara. She embodies the female principle, the earthly principle, fertility, and she is a solar divinity. But in this image, it is as though Umai were wearing a space suit. The composition combines the ancient history of the nomads and modernity in cosmic space, articulating the idea of the "umbilical cord," the earth's cosmic center located on Kazakhstan land.

After the country acquired independence, the register and repertoire of artistic statements on the cosmic theme has changed: ideological progressivism has given way to irony, and a critical position has become dominant for the new generation of artists.

In his ironic autobiography, 1990s artist Sergei Maslov wrote that he had wanted to become a cosmonaut and that his "favorite, but unwatched film was *2001, A Space Odyssey*."[57] He creates his own "cosmic cycle"—the novel *Star Nomads (Zvezdnye kochevniki)* and the art project *Baikonur-2*. As the art scholar Valeriia Ibraeva writes of Maslov in her introduction to the novel, *"How do you like that, Elon Musk?",* "cosmic motifs were also present in his earlier works ("Fish Were Born for Outer Space" *(Ryby rozhdeny dlia kosmosa)* (1979), "Alien Girl" *(Inoplanetianka)* (1990), "Girl on the Moon" *(Devushka na Lune)* (1997), "Alien Girl, I've Got No Time for You" *(Inoplanetianka, mne do tebia)* (2000), but this time these

---

56   G. Shalabaeva, *Evgenii Sidorkin. Ontologiia khudozhestvennogo metoda* (Almaty: Galereia "Oiu," 2005).
57   *Maslov. Sbornik statei 1996 goda*, ed. Elena Vorob'eva and Viktor Vorob'ev (Almaty: Aspan Gallery, 2021), 80.

were not individual paintings with occasional references to "visitors" from space, but clearly formulated and complete projects."[58]

Baikonur-2 comprises a text, installation, computer collage and sound projection. In the accompanying text Maslov writes that the Kazakhs are the purest and more direct descendants of extra-terrestrial life. They considered their most precious possession to be spaceship-yurts, since at any moment they could transform their yurt home into a rocket and fly away. Later, the Soviet Union and United States had stolen their secrets and created their own spaceships. In Maslov's photo-collages one can see Kazakhs, both men and women, in traditional dress, seated alongside rocket-yurts, or semi-nude women in traditional head-dress, the kimeshek, on a desert surface of a planet landscape alongside a cosmic apparatus, or Kazakh women wearing Soviet-era dress. There is even a photo-collage with references to photographs of Kazakh khans or sultans with a tsarist official or with the emperor himself, but in this case the role of the Russian imperial figures is played a person wearing a cosmonaut's space suit. Kazakhstani artist Kuanysh Bazargaliev in his project "When All People Were Kazakhs" *(Kogda vse liudi byli kazakhskie)*, reflecting on the problem of the loss of Kazakh identity, includes a reference to Maslov's *Baikonur-2* as a scientific work in a post-apocalyptic Kazakhstan.[59]

We are offered a very different image of space by Nurbek Zhardemov's "Kazakh Wedding on Mars" *(Kazakhskaia svad'ba na Marse)*, a large, five-meter-long painting. Zhardemov has said that he never dreamed of space or of becoming a cosmonaut; he always dreamed of becoming an artist. At an international art residency in Cyprus for artists of the Turkic world, he conceived the idea of creating a work about Kazakhstan that would demonstrate the unique nature of the people and the specificity of its cultural space:

> All the artists, and there were many of us there, from Tajikistan, Kyrgyzstan, Azerbaijan, Moldova, from the northern regions of Russia, wanted to depict their own culture, their own traditions, and so I needed to find

---

58 V. Ibraeva, "Kak tebe takoe, Ilon Mask?" in S. Maslov, *Zvezdnye kochevniki* (Almaty: Aspan Gallery, 2021), 94.

59 See D. Kudaibergenova, "Prizraki, mankurty i prochee: 'postkolonial'noe' iskusstvo Tsentral'noi Azii," *Novoe literaturnoe obozrenie* 1 (2020): 175–98.

some kind of special distinctive idea. For example, Tajiks draw pomegranates, they have pomegranates everywhere... But we have something that others don't, and that's Baikonur, that is, outer space, for us this is such an intimate theme... Here I got the urge to draw a Kazakh wedding on the red planet, and for there to be baursaki [Kazakh fried dough] there, horses and camels, lots of people, for there to be a proctor like in the steppe, a kimeshek like a space helmet, and everyone in circular motion like in space... I ended up with this kind of symbiosis, I linked tradition with outer space...[60]

The artist decided that it was precisely through the *toi* (the traditional Kazakh wedding festivities) that one could best show Kazakh customs and traditions, and the very essence of Kazakh culture. Besides this, he wanted to work with the color red, and hence the theme of Mars appeared. Also important here is the fact that the theme of identity and tradition fits perfectly with the cosmic futuristic context with spaceships, travel, and even colonization. The artist perceives the cosmodrome as part of the country's history, lending uniqueness to that history.

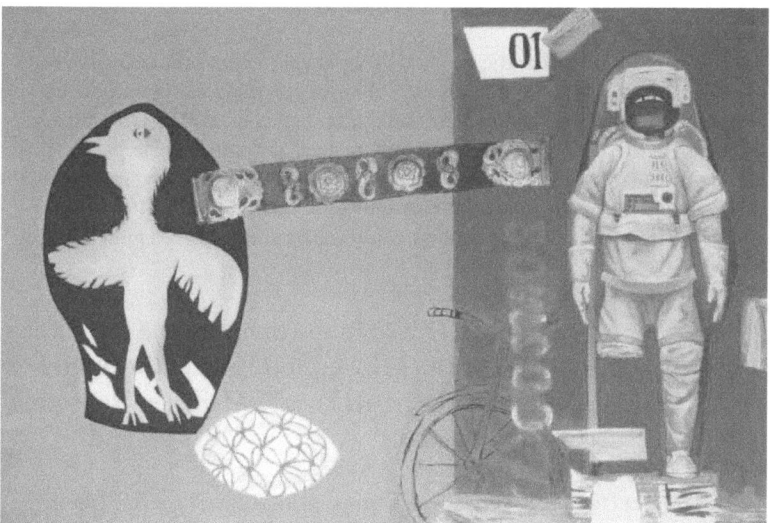

Figure 3. Rashid Nurekeev, "Cosmonaut," 01 series (2017). Reproduced with the artist's permission.

---

60 Authors' conversation with artist Nurbek Zhardemov, October 2022.

In the work of Rashid Nurekeev, space and the space program are presented in a harsher manner, without any romantic play with the national-cultural symbolic context. In a mixed technique collage, in vivid shades of acrylic paint, a cosmonaut is depicted wearing a helmet and all the appropriate trappings, but with an amputated leg (Figure 3). The cosmonaut is leaning on a broken snow shovel, as though on a crutch; next to him are drawn the front wheel and handlebars of an ordinary bicycle, and in the upper part of a cosmic light-blue background in a small white patch the figure 01 stands out in crisp script. The painting of the one-legged cosmonaut occupied a central place in the personal exhibition of this artist, who was born and grew up literally one hundred kilometers from Baikonur, in the district center of Zhosaly,[61] and for whom the space program was not only the television media-reality that is was for the majority of Kazakhstanis. Nurekeev recalls how his grandmother, who had permission to visit this closed territory since her sister lived there, would take him with her on visits:

> I saw ... space probes in the sky, half of the sky would become orange-colored.... but already after the [Soviet] collapse everything was open, and we would walk just like that into the mines, into the hangars, they were huge, there are these gates there, next to them a car looks like a matchbox... I used to see cosmonauts, that happened often, because Zhusaly was like a regional center for people from Baikonur. I knew that parts of a Proton fell not far from my relatives' house... I know guys who gathered gold compounds...[62]

We heard another reference to the theme of the sacred nature of Baikonur as the "earth's belly button," and to the legend of Korkyt, in our interview with the artist Said Atabekov. Reflecting on his project "Baiterek," he said:

> This project is about Baiterek, which turns into a rocket, I got the urge to use it like an advertisement for Astana. The most important cosmodrome is located in our country and this is not simply an ordinary place, this is a

---

61 Previously Dzhusaly, Karmakshi, and Fort No. 2 in the Syr Darya offensive and defensive line.
62 Authors' conversation with artist Rashid Nurekeev, December 2020.

locality which I think is called Zher kindigi (belly button of the earth). I feel these places, where it's as though there are several layers of energetic forces, I feel them, I have an urge to keep walking and walking there....[63]

Like Nurekeev, and like Maslov, Atabekov, when imagining space, turns to national images and especially often to the yurt: "I enter the yurt and I see the cosmos."[64]

Of course, every new generation of artists demonstrates its own vision and interpretation of space. Thus, for many contemporary representatives of Kazakhstan's art space, such as Sergei Maslov, Abrashit Sadykhanov, Said Atabek, Arystanbek Shalbaev, Askhat Akhmed'iarov, Gaisha Madanova, Almagul' Menlibaeva, Anvar Musrepov, Ermina Tauken, Katia Kan—space features both in the capacity of a kind of critical lens, and in the capacity of a metaphor—moreover, an ambivalent metaphor. This may be a reflection on the colonial nature of the cosmodrome's presence in Kazakhstan; it may also be cause for pride and a sense of involvement in broader global processes; or it can be a symbol of the old Soviet order, nostalgia, and traumatic remembering, all at the same time. Of interest in this sense of are the works of Anvar Musrepov, in many of whose motifs the cosmic theme is intertwined with the country's political programs, and with the motifs of nomadism and escapism:

> It seems to me that space was always part of the Soviet period, even though I didn't live in it, it was always part of some kind of political promise: that's why I use the metaphor of escapism, say, in the work "Dzhigitovka" I'm also running in cosmic space, in an ideal space. I'm realizing this political promise, that in some kind of future we were going to live well on Mars, in space... where our state is heading—all these programs, that tomorrow, tomorrow, tomorrow, 2030, and so on; I have a work called 2050, all these narratives... I'm fulfilling this promise, I'm escaping to ... outer space, that's where I am...[65]

---

63 Authors' conversation with artist Said Atabekov, October 2021.
64 *Ibid.*
65 Authors' conversation with artist Anvar Musrepov, December 2022.

In 2019 Anvas Musrepov was curator of "First Contact" (*Pervyi kontakt*), an exhibition of young artists, whose works were permeated by the theme of space and the space program:

> ... But in this exhibition the theme of the space industry, the theme of the testing range, of various technogenic experiments, was examined in a romantic vein, in the sense that, in the awareness that there is a young generation, that's us, I'm arriving at the idea that we are some kind of hybrids, mutants, that the question of identity is always there on the surface. We're already no longer able to reflect in a speculative way on whether we are real Kazakhs or not real ones, shala or not shala, Soviet or post-Soviet; we're some kind of mutants, like a product of some laboratory, where social experiments were carried out, like a re-organizing, a re-crafting of the society of nomads of our culture, through to big experiments like rocket launches, explosions at test ranges, we are the final result ... of a big laboratory... It seems to me that space has always featured, but not in illustrations of space, but rather in some kind of transcendental ... experience...[66]

Thus, Kazakhstani artists imagine space and the space program in different ways—ranging from romantic, technocratic notions through to a de-colonial sensitivity, and it is precisely Nurekeev's one-legged cosmonaut that can be viewed as a symbol of the tension between the current indeterminacy and the narrative of national modernization.

Conclusion

In our view, the above-presented collection of diverse narratives about space in general and about the role of the space programs in the history of Kazakhstan in particular, represents a significant contribution to contemporary social research on space. Despite the obvious fact that the first and largest cosmodrome is located on the territory of Kazakhstan, there are surprisingly few studies on how the local population related and continues to relate to the space project. As authors, we strove to preserve scholarly neutrality and to present a range of diverse voices here.

Among former military personnel, a nostalgic discourse about the great past and unrealized future dominates. The voices

---

66   Ibid.

of local residents, both of Baikonur itself and of the settlements around the cosmodrome, convey a sense of disillusionment: social disadvantage, a lack of future prospects, ecological problems—the cosmodrome clearly does not justify the expectations, even though at first glance it possesses mighty potential for development of the country. On the other hand, the stories connected in one way or another with the cosmodrome—whether the conspirological stories that Baikonur residents tell about spies or the mytho-poetic narrative on the legendary Korkyt and on Baikonur as "belly button of the earth" in the Kyzylordinskii region—these stories comprise a kind of symbolic capital for their narrators. Finally, Soviet and post-Soviet Kazakhstani artists demonstrate various methods for working with the space theme—from romantic admiration to ironic distancing, where intricate stylizations are intertwined with an imagined nomadic cosmology. In conclusion, we can say that in the various registers of Kazakhstani culture one can trace out one and the same motif—the motif of the non-random nature of the choice of site for the cosmodrome: Earth's "belly button," where Korkyt once acquired immortality, has ultimately become a place for overcoming earth's gravity and exiting into the unknown expanses of outer space.

From Decentralization to Warfare Resistance: Building a Cohesive Ukraine[1]

Oleksandra Deineko and Aadne Aasland

Abstract: This article focuses on implementation of the Ukrainian decentralization reform and its impact on social cohesion since the Russian invasion and war. Drawing on quantitative and qualitative data, the authors investigate how the reform has contributed to reinforcing social cohesion under war circumstances. They conceptualize the war factor as a trigger for social cohesion on the national level as a "common threat" (Russian invasion) and "common good" (Ukrainian victory) as well as their intertwining. Previously achieved social capital on the local level made wartime cooperation between the citizenry and the authorities more tangible and coordinated. The authors show how the relative boundaries between state and citizens, relationships, vertical and horizontal social ties have become blurred under military conditions, while rapidly strengthening civil resistance.

Introduction

Russia's fully-fledged military invasion of Ukraine, located in the very heart of Europe, has dramatic humanitarian and social consequences for both the state and the world community. As of 11 July 2022 the Office of the United Nations High Commissioner for Human Rights (OHCHR) had verified a total of 5,024 civilian deaths[2]

---

1 This text has also been published in the volume *Ukraine's Decentralization: Challenges and Implications of the Local Governance Reform after the Euromaidan Revolution*, eds. Andreas Umland and Valentyna Romanova (Stuttgart: *ibidem* Press, 2024).
2 Number of civilian casualties in Ukraine during Russia's invasion verified by OHCHR as of 11 July 2022, https://www.statista.com/statistics/1293492/ukraine-war-casualties/.

and over 6,520 injured. However, these are only the official confirmed verified numbers: the actual figures are much higher, as also confirmed by OHCHR. Moreover, this massive humanitarian catastrophe has involved incessant weapon attacks, massive infrastructural damage, and a severe economic downturn.

In times of such active warfare, society builds on a renewed system of social norms and patterns of behavior, with key emphasis on survival needs. Before the war, people's lives were organized in daily routines with established and clear norms and social practices; the Russian invasion accentuated three main goals for all social actors: to survive, to defend, and to speed up the victory.

These normative goals created the basis for unexpectedly strong military and civil resistance, with mass volunteering, mutual support, high interpersonal and institutional trust, from the first days of the war. There have been accounts of Ukrainians who opened their homes to strangers, now treated as family members;[3] who made their cars available for military purposes[4] and who donated their savings to support the Ukrainian Army.[5] Ukrainian society has shown deep unity against the common threat. Mayors declared their readiness to defend their cities, weapons in hand, standing side by side with the local territorial defense forces.[6]

The way in which people have voluntarily united their efforts and promoted self-initiatives has demonstrated the relevance of the concept of *social cohesion,* as a "sense of togetherness" or a "social glue." With this concept, researchers highlight the vulner-

---

[3] "Valery Shevchuk a resident of Horodyshchensk amalgamated territorial hromada in Volyn sheltered three families in his home," *Suspilne,* 14 May 2022, https://suspilne.media/238946-hotiv-dopomogti-ditam-volinanin-pri histiv-rodinu-z-kiivsini/.

[4] "Dmytro Komarov sold a rare car and handed over a million hryvnias to our defenders", *Ukrainian Reporter,* 12 July 2022, https://ukrreporter.com.ua/war/dmytro-komarov-prodav-ridkisne-avto-i-peredav-nashym-zahysnykam-miljon-gryven.html.

[5] "83-year-old pensioner from Bukovina transferred 100,000 hryvnias and 10,000 dollars to support the Armed Forces", *Suspilne,* 2 March 2022, https://suspilne.media/212995-na-bukovini-83-ricnij-pensioner-pererahuvav-na-pi dtrimku-zsu-100-tisac-griven-ta-10-tisac-dolariv/.

[6] "Klitschko: This is already a bloody war. I have no choice. I will fight!", *Unian,* 25 February 2022, https://www.unian.ua/war/klichko-ce-vzhe-krivava-viy na-v-mene-nemaye-viboru-ya-budu-borotisya-novini-kiyeva-11718019.html.

able, bottom-up and consensually based nature of citizens' attitudes and actions that bind society together "through the action of specific attitudes, behaviors, rules, and institutions, which rely on consensus rather than pure coercion."[7]

Previous studies involving measurements of social cohesion have never considered Ukraine as a socially cohesive society. Among 47 European countries in the European Value Survey, Dickes *et al.* (2008) found that Ukraine was characterized by low levels of behavioral and substantial attitudinal levels of social cohesion.[8] Using the results of the European Social Survey 2012–13 and comparing Ukraine with the other East and Central European countries, Bondarenko *et al.* (2017) found low scores on selected indicators of social cohesion, except for rather high levels of interpersonal trust.[9] However, these measurements were taken before the launch of comprehensive political reforms aimed at promoting democracy and European integration after Ukraine's Revolution of Dignity in 2014.

The decentralization reform is especially important here. Initiated in 2014, it aimed at the formation of a new basic level of local self-government in Ukraine—amalgamated territorial communities (ATC)—to create and maintain a fully-developed living environment for the citizenry, with high-quality, accessible public services and institutions of direct democracy.[10] The pre-history, first achievements and current challenges of the decentralization

---

7   Andry Green Janmaat, Jan Germen, and Christine Han, *Regimes of Social Cohesion* (Centre for Learning and Life Chances in Knowledge Economies and Societies), https://dera.ioe.ac.uk/10486/1/Z.-Regimes-of-Social-Cohesion.pdf, 19.
8   P. Dickes and M. Valentova, "Construction, Validation and Application of the Measurement of Social Cohesion in 47 European Countries and Regions," *Social Indicators Research* 113 (2013): 3.
9   M. Bondarenko, S. Babenko, and O. Borovskiy, "Sotsial'na zhurtovanist' v Ukraini," *Visnyk Kyivskoho natsional'noho universitetu imeni Tarasa Shevchenka, Sotsiologiya* 8 (2017): 58–65.
10 Order of the Cabinet of Ministers of Ukraine "On Approval of the Concept of Reforming Local Self-Government and Territorial Organization of Power in Ukraine," 2014, https://zakon5.rada.gov.ua/laws/show/333-2014-%D1%80.

reform have been analyzed elsewhere;[11] in this article, we emphasize the social specificities and effects of the implementation of this reform in Ukrainian society.

Although not referred to as such in legislative acts, decentralization was planned to become a cohesive reform due to its goal and the procedures involved. The political and geopolitical dimensions of its cohesiveness are highlighted by Romanova and Umland.[12] Researchers have reflected on the socio-political context of decentralization that emerged in opposition to federalization and separatism as a mechanism for strengthening national unity after the Russian annexation of Crimea and the occupation of Donbass in 2014. Shelest and Rabinovych have examined the implications of decentralization for the processes of democratization and European integration of Ukraine, emphasizing its potential as a conflict resolution tool.[13] While the study finds positive as well as negative correlations between decentralization and conflict resolution, one of the authors sees the reform in general as a "vehicle for modernization"[14] aimed at reuniting Ukrainian regions by giving more power and financial opportunities to the new self-government bodies, the amalgamated territorial communities (ATCs, or hromadas). Other scholars have noted how successfully implemented territorial development projects at the ATC level have had significant positive effects on state cohesion.[15] One study of 169 EU regions found the quality of local self-government to be the key factor in the efficiency of the cohesion policy and the usage of EU structural funds.[16]

---

11 See Andreas Umland and Valentyna Romanova (eds.), *Ukraine's Decentralization: Challenges and Implications of the Local Governance Reform after the Euromaidan Revolution* (Stuttgart: ibidem Press, 2024).
12 Valentyna Romanova and Andreas Umland, "Decentralising Ukraine: Geopolitical Implications," *Survival* 61, no. 5 (2019): 99–112.
13 H. Shelest and M. Rabinovych (eds.), *Decentralization, Regional Diversity, and Conflict: The Case of Ukraine* (Palgrave Macmillan, 2020).
14 Olga Oleinekova, "Decentralization Reform: An Effective Vehicle for Modernization and Democratization in Ukraine?" in Shelest and Rabinovych (eds.), *Decentralization, Regional Diversity, and Conflict*, 311–338.
15 Y. A. Zhalilo, O. V. Shevchenko, and V. V. Romanova, *Decentralization of Power: Agenda for the Medium Term* (Kyiv: National Institute for Strategic Studies, 2019).
16 A. Rodriguez-Pose and E. Garcilazo, "Quality of Government and the Returns on Investment: Examining the Impact of Cohesion Expenditure in European

Two further aspects of Ukraine's decentralization reform have contributed to reinforcing social cohesion at the local level. First, according to the nationwide survey "Decentralization and the reform of local self-government: the fifth wave of sociological research results," among those Ukrainians who answered that they were well aware of the decentralization reform, 81% recognized its necessity for Ukraine.[17] Unlike other legislative amendments (e.g., land reform; privatization of state enterprises) which clearly polarized opinions into "pro" and "contra," the decentralization reform has shown a powerful potential for social consolidation of society around a common idea.

Second: the internal aspect of decentralization inputs to social cohesion is connected with the specificities of the amalgamation procedure. It is based on a set of interactions among various local actors, the authorities as well as the citizenry. The amalgamation process involved the initial stage, with public hearings on the decision to merge, adoption of the decision by local councils and then the formation of a working group to draft a decision regarding amalgamation.[18] Viewed from a sociological perspective, the amalgamation procedure activated interactions within and between territorial units, building and strengthening social ties, thus enhancing bridging and bonding social capital[19] among the social actors involved in the future amalgamated *hromada*.

Previous studies have analyzed the social impact of amalgamation specificities on social cohesion in border regions of Ukraine. Within the framework of the ARDU project,[20] we focused on studying the quantitative links between decentralization and

---

Regions," *OECD Regional Development Working Papers* (Paris: OECD Publishing, 2013).

[17] "Decentralization and Reform of Local Self-government: Results of the Fifth Wave of Sociological Research among the Population of Ukraine," 2020, https://decentralization.gov.ua/uploads/library/file/633/2020Report_UKR_ukr.pdf.

[18] Law of Ukraine "About Voluntary Amalgamation of Territorial Hromadas," 2015, https://zakon.rada.gov.ua/laws/show/157-19#Text.

[19] R.D. Putnam, *Bowling Alone: The Collapse and Revival of American Community* (New York: Simon and Schuster, 2000).

[20] Aadne Aasland, Oleksandra Deineko, Olga Filippova, and Sabine Kropp, "Citizens' Perspectives: Reform and Social Cohesion in Ukraine's Border Regions," in *The Accommodation of Regional and Ethno-cultural Diversity in Ukraine*, eds. Aa. Aasland & S. Kropp (Palgrave Macmillan, 2021), 237–72.

social cohesion[21] as well as the qualitative transformations occurring on the local level as results of decentralization in two border regions of Ukraine: Kharkiv and Chernivtsi.[22] Despite the promising shifts evident from the qualitative angle, quantitative data showed scores on social cohesion indices to be quite mixed, with low trust in state institutions but a strong sense of belonging at various levels—local, regional, and national. Amalgamation was found to result in higher levels of participation when compared with non-amalgamated rural communities.[23] We documented a strengthening of social cohesion as a result of the decentralization reform—but it should be noted that data collection for the project was completed by the end of 2020 (fieldwork in 2019; survey in 2020), slightly one year before the Russian invasion of Ukraine.

Bearing in mind the new quality of "sense of togetherness" demonstrated by Ukrainians from the very beginning of the war, we ask:

- how has the decentralization reform contributed to reinforcing social cohesion in Ukrainian society under the war?
- what have been the essential transformations of social cohesion under war circumstances?
- how may the war-factor change the conceptual framework of social cohesion theorizing as developed in peace-time conditions?

---

[21] Aadne Aasland, Olga Filippova, Oleksandra Deineko, and Ruslan Zaporozhchenko, "Decentralization, Social Cohesion and Ethno-cultural Diversity in Ukraine's Border Regions," in *Accommodation of Regional and Ethno-cultural Diversity in Ukraine*, 143–70.

[22] O. O. Deineko, "Social Cohesion in Decentralized Ukraine: From Old Practices to New Order," *Studia Socjologiczne* 1 (240) (2021): 117–38, https://journals.pan.pl/dlibra/publication/136281/edition/119160/content/studia-socjologiczne-2021-social-cohesion-in-decentralized-ukraine-from-old-practices-to-new-order-deineko-oleksandra-no-1?language=en.

[23] Aadne Aasland, Oleksandra Deineko, Olga Filippova, and Sabine Kropp, "Citizens' Perspectives: Reform and Social Cohesion in Ukraine's Border Regions," in *Accommodation of Regional and Ethno-cultural Diversity in Ukraine*, 237–72.

Decentralization, Social Cohesion, and War: Theoretical Framework

Studying social cohesion requires theoretical concretization, given the range of definitions and models of empirical measurement in the scientific discourse. As "social cohesion" is seen as a "quasi-concept" or an ill-defined term,[24] it is always challenging to find and justify an appropriate theoretical framework. It is a relatively new concept in quality-of-life research,[25] but its roots can be traced back to Durkheim's theorizing on social solidarity.[26] Tönnies's concepts of *Gemeinschaft* and *Gesellschaft*[27] illustrated the dialectical changes in social interactions in the context of the early development of capitalism. These (proto)concepts of social cohesion have defined its core identity as an attribute of social interactions and a characteristic of social groups, communities and societies. However, post-modernist globalized modernity represents multiple new challenges to the contemporary "sense of togetherness," which has been held to provoke a decline of social cohesion in today's societies.[28]

Social cohesion is commonly viewed as a feature of society as a whole and is used as a basis for constructing empirical models for cross-cultural measurement.[29] At the meso-social level, social cohesion is studied as a property of territorial communities, such as neighborhoods or local communities.[30] Some researchers employ a broader approach, noting the relevance of studying social

---

24 Jane Jenson, *Mapping Social Cohesion: The State of Canadian Research* (Ottawa: Canadian Policy Research Networks, 1998).
25 H. Noll, "Towards a European System of Social Indicators: Theoretical Framework and System Architecture," *Social Indicators Research* 58 (2000): 1–3.
26 Emile Durkheim, *The Division of Labour in Society*, trans. George Simpson (New York: Free Press, 1933).
27 F. Tonnies, *Community and Association: (Gemeinschaft und Gesellschaft)* (London: Routledge and Kegan Paul, 1955).
28 R. Eckersley, "Whatever Happened to Western Civilization? The Cultural Crisis, 20 Years Later," *The Futurist* (2011): 16–22.
29 J. Delhey, K. Boehnke, G. Dragolov, Z. S. Ignácz, M. Larsen, J. Lorenz, and M. Koch, "Social Cohesion and its Correlates: A Comparison of Western and Asian Societies," *Comparative Sociology* 17, no. 3-4 (2018): 426–55.
30 F. Rajulton, Z. R. Ravanera, and R. Beaujot, "Measuring Social Cohesion: An Experiment Using the Canadian National Survey of Giving, Volunteering, and Participating," *Social Indicators Research* 80, no. 3 (2007): 461–92; and A.

cohesion at all group levels, regardless of their size.[31] This chapter seeks to combine macro- and meso- social levels of social cohesion by a modification of Joseph Chan's methodological framework.[32]

Joseph Chan and colleagues define social cohesion as "a state of affairs concerning both the vertical and the horizontal interactions among members of society as characterized by a set of attitudes and norms that includes trust, a sense of belonging and the willingness to participate and help, as well as their behavioural manifestations."[33] This definition operates with two dimensions (horizontal and vertical) and two components (objective and subjective) of social cohesion. The horizontal dimension concerns horizontal social bonds (relationships among individuals and groups within society); the vertical one identifies relationships between the state and the citizenry. These dimensions are viewed through subjective (state of mind) and objective (behavioral manifestations) components. The following indicators of social cohesion measurement are identified: political participation; trust in public figures; confidence in political and other major social institutions; willingness to cooperate and help; general trust in fellow citizens; social participation and vibrancy of civil society; voluntarism and donations; sense of belonging; and the presence or absence of major inter-group alliances or cleavages.

Chan *et al.* present a fairly static mode of social cohesion; other scholars pay more attention to how social cohesion is (re)produced and maintained in societies. For instance, Green and colleagues recognize the "embeddedness" of social cohesion in historical, political, social, and cultural contexts; and propose a

---

Kearns and R. Forres, "Social Cohesion and Multilevel Urban Governance," *Urban Studies* 37, no. 5–6 (2000): 995–1017.

31 C. Whelan and B. Maître, "Economic Vulnerability, Multidimensional Deprivation and Social Cohesion in an Enlarged European Community," *International Journal of Comparative Sociology* 46, no. 3 (2005): 215–39.

32 Joseph Chan, Ho-Pong To, and Elaine Chan, "Reconsidering Social Cohesion: Developing a Definition and Analytical Framework for Empirical Research," *Social Indicators Research* 75, no. 2 (2006): 273–302.

33 Ibid., 290.

separate category: regimes of social cohesion.[34] They distinguish three regimes of social cohesion: a) liberal regimes (with emphasis on civil society initiatives, tolerance, acceptance of diversity); b) social market regimes (a leading role played by the state, whose institutions ensure welfare and social protection; the importance of common values, a sense of belonging and institutional trust); c) social democratic regimes (similar to social market regimes, but with greater emphasis on equality and social partnership). Drawing on the proposed approach, we see that the decentralization reform in Ukraine employed elements of all three regimes of social cohesion—civil initiatives, welfare from the state to the *hromadas*, equality and social partnership as principles. However, Green *et al.*'s social cohesion conceptualization is insufficiently clear for our purposes. Moreover, it does not offer an understanding of the core that prompts social cohesion building and rebuilding; it also mixes components and factors of social cohesion—for instance, welfare and common values are viewed as factors of social cohesion, whereas civil initiatives are presented as a component.

Martial law as a new normative regime of Ukrainian society prompts reflection on the specificities of social cohesion and its regimes under conditions of war. According to Yarskaya-Smirnova, the emergence of social cohesion may be induced as "adherence to a common good" and "social closure in response to a common threat."[35] Ukraine's decentralization reform has been conceived as a "common good": new financial capacities and procedures of decision-making on the local level contribute to achieving new quality of life and perspectives for local development.

Both "common good" and "common threat" regimes of strengthening social cohesion seem relevant for Ukrainian realities under the war. The classic German sociologist Georg Simmel linked the degree of acuteness of a conflict with the strength of

---

34 A. Green, J. G. Janmaat, and C. Han, *Regimes of Social Cohesion* (Centre for Learning and Life Chances in Knowledge Economies and Societies, UCL London, 2006), https://dera.ioe.ac.uk/10486/1/Z.-Regimes-of-Social-Cohesion.pdf.

35 E. R. Yarskaya-Smirnova and V. N. Yarskaya, "Sotsial'naia splochennost': napravleniia teoreticheskoi diskussii i perspektivy sotsial'noi politiki," *Zhurnal sotsiologii i sotsial'noi antropologii* 17, no. 4 (2014), http://www.jourssa.ru/sites/all/files/volumes/2014_4/Iarskaya_Yarskaya_2014_4.pdf.

internal cohesion of conflicting groups: the more acute the conflict, the more strongly it consolidates these groups internally.[36] Representatives of a certain social group perceive a common external threat, thereby triggering individual and collective actions. If we can say that the core of "common threat" has been articulated and recognized in Ukrainian society since the annexation of Crimea and occupation of Donbas in 2014, the "common good" articulation and recognition has been prompted since 24 February 2022, with the start of the full-scale military invasion. The core of cohesion in categories of "common good" has become "Ukraine's Victory" as a new nation-building idea that can be achieved by individual actions and group interactions. The "common threat" core is based on the invasion by the enemy, and the ongoing warfare.

Data and Methods

This paper draws on research results gathered within the frame of Ukrainian–Norwegian research project "Accommodation of Regional Diversity in Ukraine (ARDU)" research project (2018–2021) and during the full-scale war in Ukraine (March–June 2022). Drawing on the project we present new analyses of the results of a nationwide representative survey conducted by the Dnipro-based opinion poll agency *Operatyvna sotsiolohiia* on behalf of Oslo Metropolitan University in December 2020 (sample size 2100; method used: telephone interviews). The surveyed population was largely representative in terms of geographical distribution across the country, type of settlement, gender, and age. The aim of the survey was to capture social cohesion dimensions at the local level among Ukrainians, based on Chan's methodological approach. Survey results are used in studying perceived effects of the decentralization reform on the work of local government with the help of logistic regressions.

Within the frame of the project, Chan *et al.*'s measurement scheme was modified, with the main emphasis on the local community level defined as the most tangible for studying the impact

---

36 G. Simmel, "The Sociology of Conflict," *American Journal of Sociology* 9, no. 4 (1904): 490–525.

of the decentralization reform. Instead of asking about "people in this country ...", in several questions we modified wording to "people in this local community ..." Further, we changed "relations between local residents and immigrants" to "relations with persons internally displaced from Crimea and Donbas." The "belonging and identity" indicator was enlarged by adding various types of identification (local community, regional, national, and European). Concerning "trust in public figures" and "confidence in political and other major social institutions," we measured the levels of trust in the President, the Parliament of Ukraine, judges, local authorities, NGOs, and the mass media.

To study how decentralization has contributed to enhancing local cooperation, we employed 26 semi-structured interviews in October 2019 with decentralization experts, representatives of civil society, cultural experts, local elected officials and local authorities in the amalgamated *hromadas* of Kharkiv and Chernivtsi regions. The interview guide was developed in collaboration with the project participants, and focused on how the ongoing decentralization reform has affected social cohesion in the newly established amalgamated *hromadas* in two border regions of Ukraine—Kharkiv and Chernivtsi. Concerning local elected officials, representatives from various political parties were selected, to balance possible conformist views among local authorities on the implementation of decentralization.

In the section of this paper addressed to studying resistance under the military invasion of Ukraine, the results of the nationwide survey "War in Ukraine: A Sociological Survey" conducted by the Dnipro-based Ukrainian company *Operatyvna sotsiolohiia* at the request of the Norwegian Institute of Regional and Urban Research (NIBR) among the general population in mid-March 2022 (sample size 3007; method: telephone interviews) have been used. The questionnaire covered issues of relocation and damages, current humanitarian needs, resistance practices, the psychological and emotional state of the populace, and other challenges faced by Ukrainians under conditions of active warfare.[37] We also draw partially on survey data gathered by *Operatyvna sotsiolohiia* (27-

---

[37] O. Deineko, "War in Ukraine: A Sociological Study," *NIBR Working Paper* 102 (April 2022), https://oda.oslomet.no/oda-xmlui/handle/11250/2992091.

30 July 2022) via the Computer Assisted Web Interview (CAWI) method in the mobile application "OperSo." The sample (received questionnaires: 1507) is representative in terms of gender, age, and region of residence.

Because of the lack of sociological surveys conducted in Ukraine during the war we also apply secondary analysis of nationwide survey results gathered by the Sociological Group "Rating" (March–June 2022).

Pre-War Survey Results on Decentralization and Social Cohesion

In the 2020 ARDU survey, i.e. just over a year before the Russian invasion, we asked the respondents, "Since 2015 Ukraine has been undergoing a comprehensive decentralization reform. In your opinion, during this period, has the work of local governments become …", and they were given seven options.[38] This question gives an indication of the success of the decentralization reformed as perceived by ordinary citizens. These options and the results are shown in Figure 1. It testifies that even though a large proportion have not seen big changes, and a considerable proportion is undecided (and one in ten say that they do not know anything about the reform), among those having made up their minds, there are more people tilting towards a positive (32 per cent of respondents) than a negative (20 per cent) assessment. It should be noted that the survey was conducted during a difficult period when the Covid-19 pandemic was at its height and many experienced uncertainties and economic difficulties, thus the assessment was probably more negative than pre-pandemic figures had shown.[39]

---

38   Responses to this question do not necessarily correspond to respondents' attitudes to the reform as such. However, a survey conducted in 2017 showed a relatively high correlation between responses to this question and support to the decentralization reform (r=0.3). See Aa. Aasland and Oleksii Lyska, "Signs of Progress: Local Democracy Developments in Ukrainian Cities," in H. Shelest and M. Rabinovych (eds.), *Decentralization, Regional Diversity, and Conflict: The Case of Ukraine* (Palgrave Macmillan, 2020), 283-310.

39   When the same question was asked in a local democracy survey conducted by Operatyvna sotsiolohiia in the fall of 2017, 11 percent of the responses were negative ("local government work had become slightly worse or worse"), 35 percent said nothing had changed, while 42 per cent said it had become

To better understand which groups of the population were most likely to show satisfaction with the results of the reform at the local level at the time of the survey, we performed logistic regressions with perceived effects of the decentralization reform on the work of local government as the dependent variable. Those answering that this work had become better (including slightly better) were given score 1, those saying nothing had changed or got worse were given score 0 (respondents not knowing about the reform or finding it hard to answer were removed from the analysis). Two models were tested: in the first model we included socio-economic and socio-demographic variables (gender, age, self-reported ethnic identity, educational level, financial situation, geographical location in Ukraine (see map—Figure 2 below), and type of settlement). Descriptive statistics and wording of the questions can be found in Appendix 1.

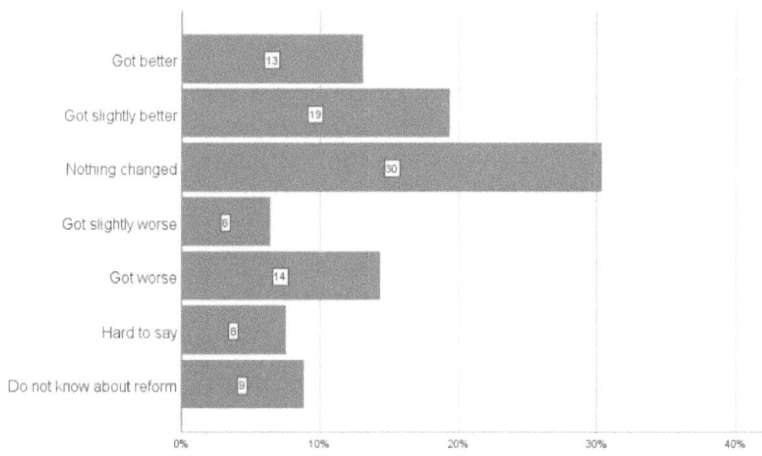

Figure 1. Perceived effects of the decentralization reform on the work of local government, in % (N=2,103, a nationwide sample).

The results are presented in Tables 1 and 2 in the Appendix. Model 1 shows that age, gender and Ukrainian vs other ethnic identity do not have statistically significant effects on the perceived success of the decentralization reform on the work of local

---

slightly better or better (and 11 percent said "do not know"). See also Aasland and Lyska, "Signs of Progress."

government. The largest effect concerns *economic status:* the more financially secure the respondent, the more positive is the assessment of the reform on the work of local government. This might indicate that the better-off segments of the population have benefitted more from the reform than those less well-off. The statistically significant effect of *education* on the dependent variable could indicate that those who know more about the reform (assuming that persons with higher education are more likely to be updated) have a more positive view.

There is a large literature on how people in the various regions of Ukraine differ in their views on Ukrainian politics and reform. For a long time, the concept of "two Ukraines" proposed by Ryabczuk[40] was used by foreign scholars to explain the specificities of political orientations and linguistic preferences of Ukrainians living in the eastern and western parts of the country. Recent studies, conducted after the Revolution of Dignity, have indicated the over-simplification and exaggeration of this approach, however.[41] Moreover, Rabinovych and Shelest (2020) conclude that the occupation of Donbas was "marked by an intense yet 'hybrid' foreign support of separatists, promoting narratives based on the securitization of diversity."[42] Thus, the unproven discourse of diversity became a justification for foreign intervention.

---

40   M. Ryabczuk, "Two Ukraines?," *East European Reporter* 5, no. 4 (1999).
41   J. Fomina, "Language, Identity, Politics: The Myth of Two Ukraines," *Bertelsman Policy Brief* (April 2014), http://aei.pitt.edu/74064/1/Language_Identity_Politics_the_Myth_of_Two_Ukraines.pdf.
42   Shelest and Rabinovych (eds), *Decentralization, Regional Diversity, and Conflict,* 366.

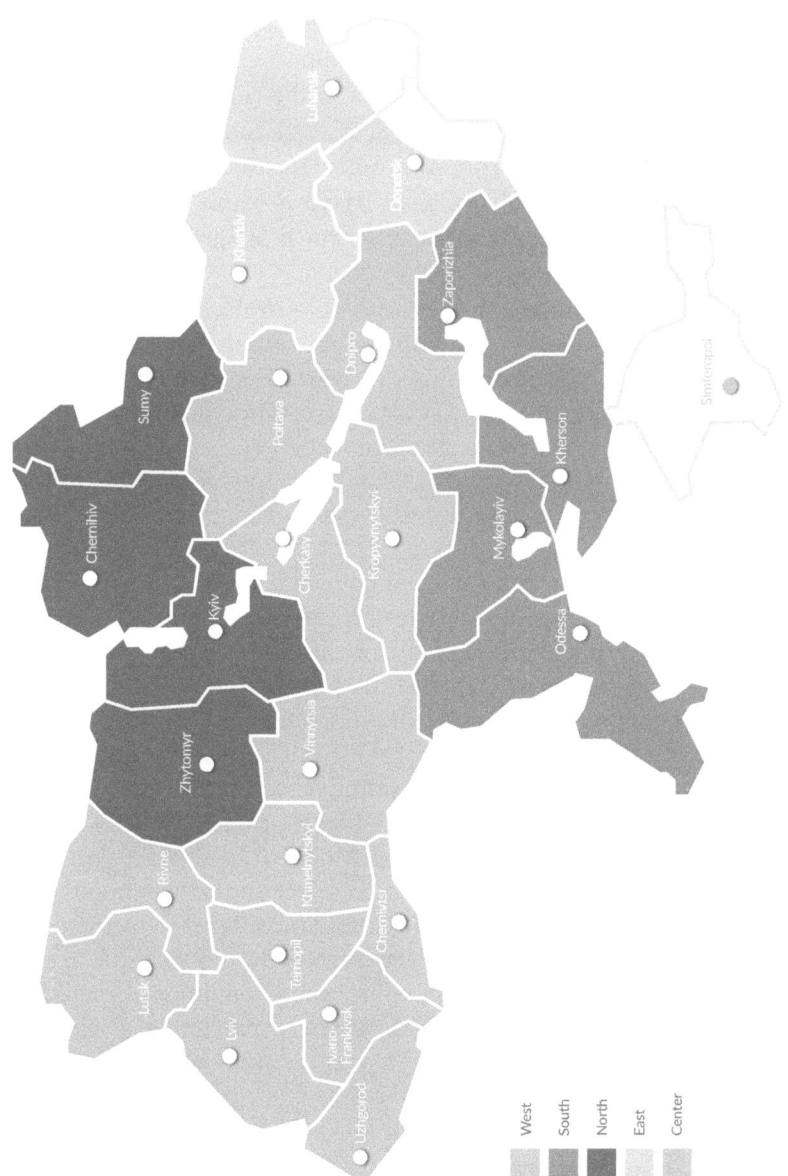

Figure 2. Geographical regions of Ukraine.
Map design: Operatyvna sotsiolohiia, Dnipro

Our data refute Ryabczuk's frame. Concerning assessments of the performance of local government, we find no East–West Ukraine divide. The most positive assessments are given by respondents in the east (see Figure 2), followed by the west, and the south. Less positive are respondents in the central and northern parts of the country. More positive assessments in the east could be explained by the governmental policy focused on rebuilding the controlled territories of Donbas.[43] However, only the differences between the most negative (north) and most positive (east) are statistically significant.

One important aspect of the decentralization reform has been the amalgamation of smaller rural communities into amalgamated territorial communities. However, our findings show that the most positive assessments of local government after decentralization are given by city dwellers, especially those living in *oblast* centers. It seems that the reform has given the resource-endowed urban centers even more resources and more autonomy as to how to spend them.

In line with Chan *et al.*'s framework, in Model 2 we introduced the following social cohesion indicators: trust in institutions and interpersonal trust, organizational participation, sense of belonging to Ukraine and to the local community, organizational membership, local activism, self-declared humanitarian aid and donations, and perceived local disunity (see Appendix for the wording of the questions and descriptive statistics).

As shown in Table 1, the variables that were statistically significant in Model 1 remained so in Model 2. In the latter model, the indicator with clearly the greatest effect on the dependent variable was level of institutional trust: the more trust in institutions (the President, Parliament, local government, media, judicial system), the more likely the respondent was to see improvements in local government after decentralization. Interestingly, also interpersonal trust went together with positive assessment of the performance of local governance, showing the close connection between various dimensions of trust and perceptions of the reform.

---

43 "Derzhavna tsilova prohrama vidnovlennia ta rozbudovy myru v skhidnykh rehionakh Ukrainy" (2020), https://minre.gov.ua/project/derzhavna-cilova-programa-vidnovlennya-ta-rozbudovy-myru-v-shidnyh-regionah-ukrayiny.

Although identifying with the Ukrainian ethnicity was not found to have an effect on perceptions of the decentralization reform, the sense of belonging to Ukraine had a statistically significant and positive effect, as shown in Model 2: the more the respondent identified as a representative of Ukraine, the more likely was that person to give a positive assessment of the reform on the work of local government. Thus, civic rather than ethnic identity correlates with assessment of the reform when controlling for all the other variables in the model. However, we find no similar effect regarding the sense of belonging to the local community.

None of the other independent variables had a statistically significant effect on the dependent one, whether they concerned civic activism (organizational membership or other local activity), help and donations to the needy, or perceived disunity in the local community. Thus, although these indicators are likely to enhance local social cohesion, they do not appear to have affected perceptions of local government performance.

To sum up, the survey results indicate rather positive views on the effect of the decentralization reform on the performance of local authorities, and hence on the prospects for local social cohesion. Furthermore, we see that socio-economic, not socio-demographic, indicators affect satisfaction with the reform; that the reform has yielded benefits to all parts of Ukraine, and that perceptions are not influenced by ethnic affiliations. We also note the importance of institutional trust and sense of belonging (key social cohesion components) as aspects that have positive effects on perceptions of decentralization in Ukraine.

Decentralization and Local Cooperation: Qualitative Angle of Social Cohesion

As noted above, a statistically significant effect on the perceived success of the decentralization reform on the work of local government concerned interpersonal and institutional trust as well as civil identity. In Chan's theoretical framework, all these components are classified as indicators of the subjective dimension of social cohesion—which refers primarily to the level of attitudes and orientations, not actual practices. Whereas regression analysis did not show significant correlations between the objective (practical) dimensions of social cohesion and positive assessments of decentralization, our qualitative interviews with *hromada* representatives and local residents showed otherwise.

Here it should be recalled that the procedure of *hromada* amalgamation has been based on a set of interactions among various local actors, both the authorities and the citizenry. Viewed in sociological terms, the amalgamation procedure in Ukraine has prompted the activation of interactions within and between the territorial units to be merged, building and reinforcing social ties, thus enhances bridging and bonding social capital among the social actors of the future amalgamated *hromada*.

The qualitative data obtained through the ARDU project indicate how the model of cooperation between new *hromada* authorities and local citizens has been improved through greater democratization, mutual responsibility and more active participation of the citizenry. At least at the declarative level, practical transparency has been identified in statements by representatives of the *hromada* authorities in both regions studied:

> People should have an influence on all of us because we are here to work for people. We are "hired workers." Let's say, the people voted for us, so we are accountable to them (ATC starosta, Chernivtsi region).

Local authorities in the ATCs also noted new mechanisms for more active civic participation in *hromadas* compared with pre-amalgamation times. *Hromada* officials have improved the institutional basis for more intensive and fruitful communication and cooperation with the local population:

> And always, any decisions ... we publish all this on the website, and everyone can come, listen, influence (representative of the ATC administration in Kharkiv region).

Participatory budgeting has been introduced in decision-making and participation. Both the local populations and the authorities emphasized the undeniable advantage of decentralization as a means of "being heard." Positive evaluations came also from local critics of the decentralization reform:

In Novovodolazhska ATC, they launched the project of participatory budgeting. Such mechanisms really help to increase local participation in ATC activities (local council deputy, Kharkiv region).

Such attitudes were expressed not only by local officials, but also the citizenry in both studied regions:

All these changes and reforms also provide a chance to feel that something depends on you. That you are a member of a community. Not merely a simple screw—you are a member of this community, you can say something, you can be heard, they can react, you will get results (local activist, Chernivtsi region).

Some interviewees contrasted participatory budgeting with the attitudes of Soviet paternalism, as indicating major changes in the awareness of local residents as regards new practices of active citizenship:

The inertia had become even greater, because for almost 70 years we lived in a structure that said that someone else would think and decide for me. But after seeing the real cases, using participatory budgeting as one example... this showed that people can manage resources, take part in hromada life, identify the most problematic issues and request the necessary funding (representative of ATC administration, Kharkiv region).

Greater funding due to financial decentralization has reinforced the capacity for solving local problems. In return, this has contributed to the intensification of common local practices. Interviewees shared their experiences about donations for solving local issues and self-initiatives that were supported by others in the *hromada*:

There are many people who are not indifferent. For example, the director of ***company. He gave us 400 Crimean pine seedlings. They needed to be watered every day. And I gathered people, distributed the seedlings. And they planted them in school areas, near the churches and across all our hromada... (starosta of ATC, Kharkiv region).

Similar assessments of the impacts of decentralization impacts were expressed even by those participants who were generally critical towards this reform:

The ability to solve local problems has become much more productive. There are more tools for local authorities to solve these issues. The most prosaic tool is money. Earlier, the villages were alone with their problems: but now, having a larger number of these villages in the hromada has made it much easier to solve the problems together (deputy, local council, Kharkiv region).

The latter point relates to the phenomenon of "common good" often noted in research on social cohesion and civil society. Edward Shils links the common good with the behavioral ethos of the civil society—the concept of civility.[44] He sees civility as a component of social cohesion, which helps to transcend class, ethnic, and professional characteristics in conflict situations and work for the common good. Our qualitative research data show that territorial *hromada* amalgamation—accompanied by increases in local budgets, the expansion of the power capacities of local authorities, and stronger social ties among local actors—have contributed to the creation of a "common good" image in the perceptions of local residents. This "common good," seen as new life chances for *hromada* members and with perspectives for enhancing the quality-of-life manifestations of local civil activism, has helped to strengthen social cohesion at the local *hromada* level.

From Decentralization to War: Resistance under the Military Invasion

From the beginning of war, the new images of "common good" and "common threat" came to the fore. The previously underestimated threat of a Russian invasion (only 33% of Ukrainian respondents felt that there was real and serious threat of attack by Russia, according to a representative survey conducted in January 2022 by the sociological group New Image Group)[45] turned real and affected every family. The Russian invasion of Ukraine (as a "common threat") determined the formation of a new "common good" in citizens' perceptions: Ukrainian victory in the war. Both formulas of social cohesion ("common good" and "common threat") were mobilized, empowering each other on the level of citizens' attitudes and practices.

---

44   E. Shils, *The Virtue of Civility: Selected Essays on Liberalism, Tradition, and Civil Society* (Indianapolis, IN: Liberty Fund, 1997).
45   "Are Ukrainians ready for a large-scale war? Results of a sociological research," 27 January 2022, https://uifuture.org/publications/are-ukrainians-ready-for-a-large-scale-war-results-of-a-sociological-research/.

Ukrainian politicians took important steps towards "common good" achievements. President Zelensky's request for political consolidation was supported by representatives of most political parties, uniting their forces to achieve a single common goal: victory for Ukraine. Formerly confrontational political actors changed (at least temporarily) their actions, from criticizing to assisting. Under martial law, the Ukrainian Parliament and government started to work with fewer disputes, rapidly establishing new legal norms: an extremely important action on the part of the political elite to establish the discourse of unity and spread it within Ukrainian society. Indeed, the 1 March survey of the sociological group "Rating" showed that President Zelensky had an absolute level of support, 93%.[46] In comparison, according to survey results on 14–16 December 2021, only 38% of Ukrainians trusted the President while 61% did not.[47] President Zelensky's decision not to escape from Ukraine, but to stay in order to spearhead the national resistance, became a pattern of behavior under the war that resulted in unprecedented levels of trust and support expressed by Ukrainians. Trust levels in state institutions have also increased rapidly: at the end of 2021, only 5% believed that the central authorities successfully managed their commitments;[48] by contrast, in May 2022, 54% of those surveyed supported this statement.[49] We interpret these results as showing that Ukrainians have been keen to show that, despite the multiple weaknesses in state policies and the activities of the authorities, they greatly appreciate the capacities of their country as an independent and sovereign state.

---

46 "Zahalnonatsionalne opytuvannia: Ukraina v umovakh viiny (1 bereznia 2022)," https://ratinggroup.ua/research/ukraine/obschenacionalnyy_opros_ukraina_v_usloviyah_voyny_1_marta_2022.html.
47 "Suspilno-politychni nastroi naselennia (14-16 hrudnia 2021)," https://ratinggroup.ua/research/ukraine/obschestvenno-politicheskie_nastroeniya_naseleniya_14-16_dekabrya_2021.html.
48 "Suspilno-politychni nastroi naselennia (14-16 hrudnia 2021)," https://ratinggroup.ua/research/ukraine/obschestvenno-politicheskie_nastroeniya_naseleniya_14-16_dekabrya_2021.html.
49 "Dvanadtsiate zahalnonatsionalne opytuvannia: Dynamika otsinky obrazu derzhavy (18-19 travnia 2022)," https://ratinggroup.ua/research/ukraine/dvenadcatyy_obschenacionalnyy_opros_dinamika_ocenki_obraza_gosudarstva_18-19_maya_20.

In the course of the war, assessments of Ukrainian state effectiveness have improved significantly in citizens' perceptions. Indeed, 84% of Ukrainians surveyed expressed support to the wartime actions of the local authorities, and a full 98% to the Armed Forces of Ukraine.[50]

From the first days of war, Ukrainians demonstrated unprecedented military and civil resistance to the Russian invasion. Ukrainian media and civil video reports broadcast accounts of how ordinary unarmed civilians halted tanks, prepared and used Molotov cocktails against enemy's capacities to assist the Ukrainian army, and participated in building neighborhood defense systems. People were eager to be engaged in practices of military and civil resistance, standing in extremely long draft-board queues and launching a range of volunteering initiatives. With the beginning of the war, the vast majority of Ukrainians—more than 80%—became volunteers.[51]

According to the results of a nationwide survey conducted by Ukrainian company *Operatyvna sotsiolohiia* at the request of NIBR (13–23 March, N: 3007) Ukrainians wanted to help not only their friends and relatives (38%), but also other people in need (34%). One in every three respondents reported having made monetary donations to support the Ukrainian army and people in need (see Table 3). *Non-formal* volunteering has become much more widespread (as shown by responses to the option "I'm a volunteer (work in volunteer centers; provide financial assistance with things like food)" marked by only 19%), which shows the force of bottom–up self-initiative capacities during the war. According to a survey by the same agency, conducted in July 2022, Ukrainians had not reduced their volunteering activities by the fifth month of war. Moreover, the practice of monetary donations has increased—from 29% in March to 36% in July. Institutional volunteering has become less widespread (from 18.7% to 14.1%) but with no significant changes in helping one's closest surroundings and

---

50 "Zahalnonatsionalne opytuvannia: Ukraina v umovakh viiny (1 bereznia 2022)," https://ratinggroup.ua/research/ukraine/obschenacionalnyy_opros_ukraina_v_usloviyah_voyny_1_marta_2022.html.

51 "Vosme zahalnonatsionalne opytuvannia: Ukraina v umovakh viiny (6 kvitnia 2022)," https://ratinggroup.ua/research/ukraine/vosmoy_obschenacionalny y_opros_ukraina_v_usloviyah_voyny_6_aprelya_2022.html.

other persons in need. Despite war fatigue, people's attitudes demonstrate clear tendencies to mass volunteering and horizontal bonding in Ukrainian society. The latter indicates that the strengthening of social cohesion that has developed seems set to become a longer-term tendency, not merely a short-term effect of the outbreak of the war.

Table 3. Types of volunteering during the war (in %).

Types of volunteering	March 2022 N=3007	July 2022 N= 1507
I help relatives / friends / acquaintances	38	36
I help other people in need	33.5	33.5
I make monetary donations	29.3	36.3
I'm a volunteer (work in volunteer centers; provide financial assistance with things, food)	18.7	14.1
Joined a cyberattack, cyber defense, or online resistance	8.1	5.4
I belong to the Territorial Defense or a volunteer battalion	(no data on security goals)	
I'm in the military		
Other	1.8	0.7
None of the above	15.9	15.6
Difficult to answer	2.3	2.2
I do not wish to answer	1.7	0.2

The recognized necessity of helping others has given rise to new formats of interaction and communications between everyone from complete strangers to close relatives and friends. The flourishing of volunteering practices has led to the formation of new horizontal bonds, enhancing both bridging and bonding social capital. This is particularly evident regarding local levels of cooperation, neighborhoods, districts and *hromadas*, driven by the need to ensure local protection, with visible local support. The recently implemented *hromada* amalgamation has become an important aspect of the decentralization reform, with enhanced trust and stronger social ties among social actors, stimulating local cooperation. War actions occurring throughout the country have made Ukrainians more horizontally bonded, enhancing horizontal social capital. Summing up, the war has significantly reinforced the horizontal dimension of social cohesion (relationships among individuals and groups within society) on both the attitudinal and the practical levels.

With the beginning of the war, significant transformations occurred also within the vertical social cohesion dimension on the local level, concerning relationships between the state and citizens. Importantly, the political and civil efforts of all social actors during the war have been oriented towards achieving the common goal of victory for Ukraine, against the common threat of the Russians invasion. Political actors as well as ordinary citizens have joined the Ukrainian military forces, organized monetary donations, assisted people in need and participated in institutional volunteering.

The special role of city mayors and other local authorities should be noted here. Mayors, as the representatives of the authorities closest to the people, have played a vital role in military and civil resistance, steering the citizenry in conditions of war uncertainty: what to do, how to survive, where to go. During the first days of the war, Vitali Klitschko, *the M*ayor of Kyiv, announced that together with his brother Volodymyr, he would defend Ukraine, weapons in their hands.[52] Vitali Klitschko personally visited the sites of post-shelling destruction, and kept the people informed of the current situation in the city. City Mayor of Kharkiv, Ihor Terekhov, ensured the vital capacities under massive shelling and spent much time in the Kharkiv Metro together with the local people who had sought refuge in large numbers during the first months of the war.[53] Oleksandr Lusenko, City Mayor of Sumi, organized provisions for local territorial defense and personally spread information on the locations of enemy troops.[54] Even under Russian occupation, brave leaders continued to govern their cities under the Ukrainian flag. Ivan Fedorov, the City Mayor of Melitopol, was captured on the 11th day of the city's occupation and was

---

52 "Top 10 most famous mayors during the war," *Glavcom*, 23 May 2022, https://glavcom.ua/country/politics/top-10-meriv-pro-yakih-naybilshe-govoryat-pid-chas-viyni-847039.html.
53 *Ibid.*
54 *Ibid.*

tortured. A further example: at the end of March, another well-known mayor, Vadym Boichenko of Mariupol, who had spearheaded the heroic Mariupol resistance, was forced to leave the city, but was able to maintain control over all information.[55]

Such actions demonstrated by city mayors from the first days of war influenced the general attitudes of the citizenry. Respondents say they are somewhat more satisfied with activities of city mayors and heads of *hromadas* compared with activities of the heads of regional military-civilian administrations whom they do not know well (see Table 4).

Table 4. Satisfaction with activities of mayors/hromada heads, and heads of regional military-civilian administrations (in %, July 2022, N=1507).

Levels of satisfaction	Activities of the heads of regional military-civilian administrations	Activities of city mayors/hromada heads
Fully dissatisfied	5.5%	13.8%
Rather dissatisfied	6.3%	15.4%
Rather satisfied	18.4%	29.5%
Fully satisfied	15.1%	23.9%
I do not know about his/her activity	22.4%	8.6%
I do not know him/her	19.0%	1.8%
Difficult to answer	12.8%	6.6%
I do not want to answer	0.4%	0.4%

These data also indicate the "decentralization trace"—how social bonds formed and maintained during the amalgamation process have contributed to enhancing local awareness and trust during the war. According to the annual monitoring of the *Institute of Sociology, National Academy of Sciences of Ukraine*, 17% of Ukrainians said that fully distrusted the local authorities, 28% partially distrusted and only 2% fully trusted them in 2020. Thus, the

---

55 *Ibid.*

recent war has led to both greater trust in and general satisfaction with local authorities.

The decentralization reform has enhanced institutional trust and prompted new models of cooperation among local actors, thereby contributing to loyal, locally focused practices of Ukrainian mayors during the war. The above-mentioned examples of mayors' resistance show how the relative boundaries between state and citizens, and vertical and horizontal social ties, have become blurred under military conditions, rapidly strengthening civil resistance.

Concluding Discussion

Our study has shown that civic initiatives and the increased institutional and interpersonal trust prompted by the decentralization reform have built social capital among *hromada* members and strengthened civic identity. This has further contributed to the widespread and massive military and civil resistance of Ukrainian society since the beginning of the war. Greater trust in heads of ATCs and city mayors has fostered greater responsibility and local attachment of local leaders, who have proven their leadership skills by personally supporting and participating in military and civil resistance in all parts of Ukraine. Previously built social capital on the local level has made wartime cooperation more tangible and coordinated, as local residents have been able to draw on experience amassed from the amalgamation procedure.

Further, the war has demonstrated the enhancement of social cohesion as regards the "common threat" (Russian invasion) and the "common good" (Ukrainian victory), as well as their intertwining. The previously underestimated threat of a Russian invasion became tangible, leading to the deepening of negative social identity and a discourse of separation ("Ukrainians are not the same as Russians"). The "common good" image has boosted individual and collective practical contributions aimed at speeding up a Ukrainian victory: mass volunteering, mass donations, widespread support to the state power and state institutions.

The specifics of the normative regime during martial law also make clear the importance of reviewing peace-time conceptualizations of how to measure social cohesion. Our case-study could not identify precise distinctions between the various social cohesion indicators offered by Chan et al.'s measurement scheme. For instance, it is not obvious why "help neighbors or friends" should be assigned as an indicator of "voluntarism and donations" (horizontal dimension, objective component) and not as "social participation." There are no criteria for distinguishing such inter-related indicators as "social participation" and "political participation." Instead, all these indicators should be seen as dimensions of the "vibrancy of civil society," which is more in line with Sereda's holistic approach.[56] Drawing on the research results "Region, nation and others: interdisciplinary and transcultural rethinking of Ukraine," Sereda shows the variety of civil activism through the involvement in the state decision-making ("political participation": Chan), participation in NGOs (social participation) and assistance to other people (volunteering; donations). This situation arises due to terminological uncertainty regarding the concept of "civil activism," which is a key element in Chan's empirical model. We see that the interplays of these indicators fail to show *how to make precise distinctions between horizontal and vertical social cohesion dimensions.*

Such distinctions become even more blurred under wartime conditions. Many new "cohesive practices" have appeared since the beginning of the war in Ukraine. For instance, in Chan's framework it is hard to identify the practice of joining the army or territorial defense (should this be considered political or social participation?). The political and civic efforts of all social actors during the war have been oriented towards achieving the common good of Ukrainian victory against the threat posed by the Russian invasion—erasing horizontal and vertical differences.

The examples of mayors' resistance have shown how the relative boundaries between state and citizens' relationships, and the vertical and horizontal social ties postulated in the social sciences, have become blurred under military conditions, rapidly strengthening civil resistance in Ukraine. Political actors and ordinary cit-

---

[56] V. Sereda, *Pereosmysliuiuchy ukrainskyi identyfikatsiinyi prostir: hromadskyi aktyvizm v Ukraini pislia Yevromaidanu. Fenomen Maidanu v ukrainskomu suspilstvi: sotsiolohichni interpretatsii* (Kyiv: Instytut sotsiolohii NAN Ukrainy, 2014), 58–78.

izens alike have joined the Ukrainian military forces, have organized monetary donations, assisted people in need and participated in institutional volunteering.

Thus, peace-time indicators of social cohesion should be re-examined in light of the martial law regime. The latter has made it impossible to rely on voting, participation in demonstrations and signing petitions as indicators of political participation, as they are prohibited in times of martial law. Going beyond the distinction of social cohesion horizontal and vertical dimensions will enable greater room for maneuver.

Appendix

Logistic regression analysis. Dependent variable: Assessment of performance of local government after decentralization reform (1 = improved, 0 = the same or deteriorated). Coefficient, Standard error, Odds ratio, and Significance. (N=1,710)

Table 1. Regression analysis results.

	Model 1			Model 2		
	B	SE	Exp(B)	B	SE	Exp(B)
Female gender (vs. male)	0.02	0.11	1.03	-0.08	0.11	0.92
Age (5 groups)	-0.01	0.04	0.99	-0.01	0.05	0.99
Ukrainian ethnicity (vs any other)	0.11	0.15	1.12	-0.01	0.16	0.99
Educational level (6 categories)	0.14**	0.04	1.15	0.12**	0.05	1.12
Financial situation (5 categories)	0.36**	0.06	1.43	0.28**	0.06	1.32
Type of settlement (vs. rural)						
Oblast center	0.58**	0.22	1.79	0.79**	0.23	2.20
Other city	0.46*	0.23	1.58	0.59*	0.24	1.81
Amalgamated territorial community	0.16	0.23	1.18	0.16	0.24	1.18
Geographical location (vs. West)						
North	-0.39*	0.16	0.68	-0.39*	0.17	1.73
Central	-0.16	0.16	0.86	-0.21	0.16	1.20

East	0.17	0.18	1.19	0.16	0.19	1.23
South	-0.05	0.16	0.95	-0.03	0.17	0.88
Trust in institutions (multiple index)				0.55**	0.07	1.73
Interpersonal trust (scale 1-5)				0.19**	0.04	1.20
Belonging to Ukraine (scale 1-4)				0.21*	0.10	1.23
Local belonging (scale 1-4)				-0.12	0.09	0.88
Organizational membership (vs. not)				-0.11	0.18	0.89
Local activism (scale 1-5)				0.06	0.04	1.07
Donations and help (multiple index)				-0.05	0.06	0.96
Disunity scale (multiple index)				-0.06	0.05	0.94
Constant	-2.352**	0.36	0.10	-4.09**	0.59	0.02
Cox & Snell R squared		0.06			0.12	

**Significant at 0.01 level.

*Significant at 0.05 level.

Table 2. Univariate distribution of variables used in multiple logistic regression analyses.

Socio-economic and socio-demographic variables	N	%
Gender		
Male	933	44.4
Female	1170	55.6
Age, years		
18-24	159	7.6
25-35	412	19.6
36-40	627	29.9
51-59	297	14.2
60+	603	28.7
Missing	5	
Ethnicity		
Ukrainian	1807	85.9
Other/not reported	296	14.1
Education		
Not completed secondary	50	2.4
Completed secondary	288	13.8
Specialised secondary /professional	792	37.9

Higher, not completed	177	8.5
Completed higher	670	32.0
Two or more higher	115	5.5
Missing/Hard to say	11	
Economic status		
Not enough for necessary products	307	15.0
Just enough for necessary products	515	25.1
Purchase of durable goods difficult	728	35.5
Some expensive goods difficult	457	22.3
Can afford anything	45	2.2
Missing/Do not know	51	
Geographical location		
West	443	21.1
North	447	21.3
Central	487	23.2
East	307	14.6
South	419	19.9
Settlement type		
Oblast centre	805	38.4
Other city	580	27.6
ATC	539	25.7
Other rural	174	8.3
Missing	5	

Social cohesion variables	N	Mean (St.Dev)
Trust in institutions index[57][58]		
Mean index score (1=no trust; 5 = fully trust)	2085	2.5 (0.8)
Missing	18	
Interpersonal trust[59]		
Mean score (1=no trust; 5 = fully trust)	2103	2.8 (1.4)
Belonging to Ukraine[60]		
Mean score (1: not at all; 4: fully)	2103	3.7 (0.6)
Belonging to local community[61]		
Mean score (1: not at all; 4: fully)	2103	3.7 (0.6)

---

57 All indices have been tested for internal consistency; Cronbach's Alpha exceeds 0.7.
58 To what extent do you trust the i) president; ii) parliament; iii) local government; iv) NGOs; v) media; vi) judiciary in Ukraine?
59 To what extent do you agree with the statement: It is hard to trust people in my village/town/city. Scale 1= agree completely agree; 5 = disagree completely disagree.
60 To what extent do you feel yourself to be a citizen of Ukraine?
61 To what extent do you feel yourself to be a resident of your city/ town /village?

Local activism[62]		
Mean score (1: very rarely; 5: very often)	2103	2.3 (1.3)
Donations and help index[63]		
Mean index score (1: very rarely; 5: very often)	2072	3.1 (1.0)
Missing	31	
Disunity index[64]		
Mean index score (1: no disunity; 5: very much disunity)	2065	2.3 (1.1)
Missing	38	
	N	%
Organisational participation		
Member of organisation	198	9.4
Not member / not reported	1905	90.6

---

[62] How often do you participate in discussions of problems in your community /(city): signing petitions, public actions / hearings, etc.?

[63] How often do you i) help other people (other than your family) with household chores, work, provide emotional support; ii) do charity work (provide material and financial assistance to those in need)?

[64] Please assess to what extent you agree that there is disunity between different groups in your community: i) between representatives of different ethnic groups; ii) between people speaking different languages; iii) between local residents and internally displaced persons.

Epic Indigenization:
Literature and Nation on the
Soviet-Finnish Borders under Stalinism

Diego Benning Wang

Abstract: *The article discusses the promotion and celebration of the epic poem* The Kalevala *by the Soviet government with a focus on the Stalinist period. By selectively promoting epic poetry and other pre-Bolshevik landmarks of literature, the Soviet regime aimed to achieve politically and ideologically oriented objectives in reinforcing the national identity of Soviet ethno-national territorial entities, indoctrinating the population, universalizing Marxist-Leninist values, and, in some cases, serving the regime's geopolitical ambitions. To better illustrate the Soviet authorities' methodology in celebrating national literary icons and shed light on the pervasiveness of the Soviet policy of literary monumentalization in geopolitically sensitive border regions, the article examines the Soviet approach to* The Kalevala—*an epic poem based on Karelian folklore compiled by the Finnish polymath Elias Lönnrot in the first half of the nineteenth century. By examining the changing ethno-national designation of* The Kalevala *by the Soviet authorities and situating the Soviet government's shifting attitude toward* The Kalevala *in the historical and socio-political context, the article argues that the official approach to* The Kalevala *mirrored not only the shifting priorities of the implementation of the Soviet nationality, language, and cultural policy in a strategically sensitive border region but also the changing geopolitical calculations in the Soviet Union's relations with neighboring Finland.*

In taking recourse to the rich literary and ideational repository of epic literature, the Soviet government managed to achieve an array of objectives in reinforcing the indigenization of non-Russian territories, indoctrinating the population, universalizing Marxist-Leninist values, and serving the regime's geopolitical ambitions. In this paper, I will illustrate the regime-endorsed promotion of the literary icons of Soviet nations in the Stalinist period by examining the Soviet authorities' approach to *The Kalevala*—an epic poem published in the nineteenth century based on Karelian folklore compiled by Finnish scholar Elias Lönnrot.

The Soviet policy of monumentalizing *The Kalevala* as a cultural pillar of Soviet Karelia from the late 1930s onward was rooted in the Soviet ideology and the Soviet nationality policy. In response to concepts of national cultural autonomy in multiethnic state entities developed by Otto Bauer and Austro-Marxists at the turn of the twentieth century, Stalin theorized a territorial, linguistic, economic, and cultural conceptualization of the nation. Following the Bolsheviks' consolidation of power in the early 1920s, this ethno-territorial framing of the modern nation in the context of a contiguous multiethnic state became the official configuration of the Soviet Union, characterized by a *de jure* federal structure and *de facto* one-party rule. In the early 1930s, firmly at the helm of the Soviet Union, Stalin oversaw the consolidation of ethno-nationally delineated Soviet territorial entities with nationalized cultures in regions targeted for Socialist modernization in a totalitarian multiethnic state.[1] The official promotion of elements of national cultures within the class-based Marxist-Leninist framework sat uncomfortably with the Bolsheviks' end goal of achieving Communism. Under the Communist Party's monopoly of power, nations assumed prominence over class in the form of ethnonational territorial entities with institutional and cultural trappings of modern national statehood within a nominally federal state. The cultural components of this peculiar form of national statehood were derived from an emphasis on various salient features of pre-revolutionary traditions subsumed into Socialist values, which can be summarized with the official doctrine on the

---

[1] The promotion of national languages and cultural institutions was crystallized in the policy of indigenization (*korenizatsiia*), which the Soviet government pursued with fervor in the 1920s and early 1930s.

development of national cultures first coined by Stalin—"National in form, Socialist in content." From the early 1930s onward, the titular nation of each Soviet ethnonational territorial entity was allowed to reclaim or reinvent pre-modern national traditions amenable to the Soviet present. The principal mechanism in implementing this policy was the state-led mass-participatory celebration of national literary icons, most notably in lavish country-wide jubilees and festivals. The pivotal message in the state-endorsed monumentalization of national literary icons was the Stalinist notion of the national character centered around the promotion of regime-dictated cultural and literary biographies.[2]

In Soviet Karelia, an ethnonational territorial entity on the borders with Finland, *The Kalevala* was celebrated as the national cultural icon and rhetorical arsenal of the national character of the region's titular population. However, the state-led promotion of *The Kalevala* was inconsistent and marred with competing visions of external and local cultural elites seeking to promote the poem according to their interpretations. *The Kalevala* gave the regime a potent weapon in pursuing its nation-making project in a sparsely populated region sharing a long, porous border with capitalist Finland. The poem encompasses numerous themes that could be integrated into the officially promoted national character of a Soviet nation. On a superficial level, the poem's main heroes embodied humans' struggles against nature. Untamed as its environment may seem, the world depicted in *The Kalevala* is not primitive, thanks to ubiquitous descriptions of its main heroes' assiduous labor and patronage of music. The poem's main heroes are romantic, resilient, and imaginative. When faced with challenges, they manifest a clear preference for tactic and magic over the use of force.

---

2   Stalin's definition of the nation, first iterated in his 1913 treatise "Marxism and the National Question," entails a "historically constituted, stable community of people, formed on the basis of a common language, territory, economic life, and psychological makeup manifested in a common culture." The notion of a collective psychological trait, partially based on nineteenth-century idealist philosophy and developed by early twentieth-century Marxists, is predicated on the socio-psychological dimension of nationalism and the notion of a nation consolidated by shared values inculcated through education and other cultural institutions.

Throughout its celebration of *The Kalevala*, the Soviet regime eagerly appropriated the positivism conveyed in the poem. The value of *The Kalevala* to the Soviet regime weighed far beyond the industriousness and optimism of its main heroes. The strivings for the collective good, among the poem's other purported attributes of a romanticized "primitive communal society" and, more importantly, the ethno-geographic settings, added to the social and geopolitical dividends the Soviet regime exploited. Soviet linguists, Red Finnish émigré politicians, and Soviet Karelian ethnographers developed thoroughgoing studies of the poem in the same ideological framework but with diverging interests in mind.

The Kalevala: Its Finnish Inception and Karelian Settings

The impetus for the publication of *The Kalevala* was rooted in the sociopolitical context of the early nineteenth century, an age known as the Romantic Era. By compiling *The Kalevala* from Karelian runic verses, Lönnrot consciously aimed to reconstruct the Finns' prehistoric past. In Keith Bosley's words, the poem "validated" a national culture that was only fledgling at the time of the poem's creation. As Michael Branch has noted, *The Kalevala* "transformed" the "dying tradition" of runic singing into "a work of literature that was to become a foundation stone of a Finnish national culture and identity."[3]

Like his romantic proto\nationalist contemporaries who canonized the modern literature of various European nations through the creation of epic poems, Lönnrot, through his collection of runes from the pre-industrial peripheries of the Finnic world and his subsequent compilation thereof into an epic poem in literary Finnish, not only documented the folk imaginations of the Finns' pre-Christian past that were slowly disappearing but also, in his own words, derived from his endeavors "benefit for the Finnish language and poetic art" and reaffirmed the belonging of the Finnish culture to a vast northern Eurasian cultural sphere extending from Lapland to eastern Siberia and further, as opposed

---

3   Michael Arthur Branch, "Preface," in *Kalevala: The Land of the Heroes*, trans. W. F. Kirby (London: The Athlone Press, 1985), viii.

to the Germanic cultural milieu in which Finland had long been immersed.⁴ By turning Karelian runes into an epic poem so copious in symbolism and literary finesse, Lönnrot recreated a fascinating pre-historical world and agglomerated a syntax of ethnology, mythology, and poetry based on Karelian traditions, which contributed to *The Kalevala*'s universality and unique status in the modern European literature.⁵

Although *The Kalevala* has long been regarded as Finland's national epic, the runes that make up the poem, particularly its second and final edition, published in 1949, were collected primarily in Karelia, where Lönnrot went on six expeditions.⁶ Karelia, a territory between the White Sea and Finland, as Nick Baron has observed, had been "a divided and disputed borderland" and "dual periphery" long straddled between two "mutually alien and antagonistic" centers.⁷ In the early 1920s, the region was home to a Russian majority, primarily descendants of seventeenth-century Old Believer settlers, and a sizable Karelian minority who spoke three closely related Finnic dialects and professed the Orthodox faith.⁸ Recognizable descriptions of the Karelian landscape and culture are rampant throughout the poem. In the words of a Soviet scholar, *The Kalevala* "brightly and artistically" portrays a world in which "we see the setup of the homestead, kitchen utensils, weaponry, and economic activity of the inhabitants—how they toil on and sow the land, cook, bake bread, brew beer, weave, temper metal,

---

4   Felix J. Oinas, *Studies in Finnic Folklore: Homage to* The Kalevala (Helsinki, Finland: Suomalaisen Kirjallisuuden Seura, 1985), 41.
5   Väinö Kaukonen, "*The Kalevala* as Epic," in *Religion, Myth, and Folklore in the World's Epics:* The Kalevala *and Its Predecessors*, ed. Lauri Honko (Berlin: Mouton de Gruyter, 1990), 176.
6   Helmi Lehmus, "Elias Lennrot—sostavitel' 'Kalevaly'," in *Trudy iubileinoi nauchnoi sessii, posviashchennoi 100-letiiu polnogo izdaniia "Kalevaly"*, ed. Vasilii Bazanov (Karelo-Finskii filial Akademii nauk SSSR, Institut istorii, iazyka i literatury, 1950), 168.
7   Nick Baron, *Soviet Karelia: Politics, Planning and Terror in Stalin's Russia, 1920-1939* (Routledge, 2007), 9.
8   Dmitrii Bubrikh, "K voprosu ob etnicheskoi prinadlezhnosti run 'Kalevaly'," *Trudy iubileinoi nauchnoi sessii, posviashchennoy 100-letiiu polnogo izdaniia "Kalevaly"*, 143-4.

hunt, and fish." Such depictions feel as vivid as the natural landscape of forests, lakes, swamps, hills, cliffs, and biosphere characteristic of Karelia. However, *The Kalevala* is not an ethnographic account. The poem's poeticized reality intends to convey a worldview and express ideals of heroism.[9]

The Kalevala through the Soviet Ideological Prism

Besides the captivating poetic outline of a Soviet territory, *The Kalevala* offered much that could be appropriated into the Soviet cultural and political agenda for Karelia and beyond. The complex plot twist and plenitude of ethnographic elements saturate the poem with allegories that could be easily interpreted through a materialist prism. These allegories can be read as a story about struggles for material wellbeing and communal harmony.[10] Kindred readings of the poem also sounded in ideology-ridden Soviet bureaucratese to disseminate political messages. In Otto Kuusinen's appraisal, *The Kalevala* depicts "a primitive society on the [upper] stage of barbarism." One of the poem's pivotal socioeconomic elements lies in its protagonists' love for labor, respect for knowledge, gift for music, appreciation of beauty, and strivings for "their people's common happiness."[11] In such "primitive communal" settings as Kaleva, social hierarchy and economic stratification are absent. Notwithstanding their supernatural powers, the main heroes possess human emotions and impulses akin to Hellenic deities. Their emotional attachment to their homeland, Kaleva, is transcendent to modern values of patriotism. By extension, the dichotomy between the bright and prosperous Kaleva and the dark and gloomy Pohjola was interpreted as a juxtaposition between the Communist Soviet Union and capitalist Finland. As the leader of Soviet Karelia, Gennadii Kupriianov, declared in 1949, "*The Kalevala* reflects the Karelian people's greatest aspirations

---

9   Vladimir Propp, *Fol'klor i deistvitel'nost'* (Glavnaia redaktsiia vostochnoi literatury izdatel'stva Nauka, 1976), 314–15.
10 Kaukonen, "*The Kalevala* as Epic," 176.
11 Otto Kuusinen, "Epos 'Kalevala' i ego tvortsy," in *Kalevala: Karelo-finskii narodnyi epos*, trans. Leonid Belsky (Petrozavodsk, USSR: Gosudarstvennoe izdatel'stvo Karel'skoi ASSR, 1956), ix.

and ideals in their centuries-old battle with the severe nature and enemy assaults [...] for their people's happiness."[12] The poem's emphasis on labor echoes Marxist conceptions of social progress. The three main protagonists are leaders of their people and creators of their own means of material subsistence. Ilmarinen's skillful mastership and resolve to serve his community perfectly alluded to the Stakhanovite quest for prosperity through labor promoted by the Soviet regime.

The Kalevala's embodiment of labor and prosperity was not only in the main heroes but also in their most remarkable creation—the magical Sampo. Although the poem provides no clear depiction of its shape or mechanism, the products it incessantly churns out are clear and concrete—flour, salt, and gold. Soviet writer Marietta Shahinyan (Shaginian) argued that the poem evolves "around one subject—the struggles for the mysterious Sampo, which symbolizes the people's welfare."[13] The Sampo is not only the trophy of the poem's main heroes' Homeric adventures but also a purveyor of wealth and stability, precisely how the Bolsheviks proclaimed themselves to be. Soviet Karelian writer Yakov Rugoev reckoned that the symbolic significance of Väinämöinen and Ilmarinen's creations—the kantele and the Sampo—concurred with the concepts of the "new Socialist era" of Soviet Karelia.[14] The wealth the Sampo brings to the dark and bleak Pohjola showcases how nature can be reshaped by changes in the means of production, which resonates with Marxist-Leninist notions of modernization. In a joint letter to Stalin during the 1949 Jubilee of *The Kalevala*, Karelian scholars and politicians declared, "In their dreams about a better future and efforts to improve their wellbeing, the people of Karelia created the symbolic image of the Sampo, which embodied their hopes and aspirations. Only the

---

12　Gennadii Kupriianov, *Karelo-Finskaia Sovetskaia Sotsialisticheskaia Respublika* (Gosudarstvennoe izdatel'stvo Politicheskoi literatury, 1949), 4–5.
13　Marietta Shaginian, "Kalevala," in *Kalevala*, trans. Leonid Belsky (Khudozhestvennaia literatura, 1977), 10.
14　Jaakko Rugojev, "Karjalais-Suomalainen Kansaneepos" in *Kalevala. Karjalais-Suomalainen Kansaneepos*, ed. Rugojev (Karjala-Kunstantamo, 1979), 29.

[October] Revolution [...] lifted the Karelian people out of the poverty and sufferings inflicted by the bourgeois serf-holding system and brought them up to the broad path of the building of Socialism" so that "the free and happy Karelo-Finnish people can compose songs about the new Sampo, infusing in them the joy of [Soviet] nations' victory over the loathsome bourgeois-landowning system and the joy of life that the [October] Revolution has brought forth."[15] In an address to Soviet Karelian composers during World War II, Kuusinen directly compared the forging of the Sampo to the achievement of Communism.[16]

Adding to the productive dimension of the materialist theme, the convenient absence of Christianity in *The Kalevala* is also notable.[17] Instead of an institutionalized belief system rife with stories of creation, prophecies, and eschatology, the poem is rooted in a timeless mythical present. It portrays a world whose geography is reminiscent of Karelia and whose folk traditions (beer-brewing, feasting, wedding rituals, sauna, etc.) have continued into modern times.

Furthermore, the poem's overarching theme of peace and harmony emphasizes the importance of political stability for economic prosperity. Soviet Karelian poet Oleg Mishin argued, "The forging of the Sampo is an act of peace."[18] A Soviet scholar argued that the poem's heroes are "first and foremost [craftsmen], and only then warriors;" they are "free people," and their labor is "free labor," as poetry about free labor "makes those of us living centuries after the creation of the runes of *The Kalevala* alive," because in the Soviet Union, "we, the people who live in the epoch of Socialism, understand and are interested in the free world [depicted

---

15 "Pis'mo Tovarishchu I. V. Stalinu ot uchastnikov torzhestvennogo zasedaniia, posviashchennogo 100-letiiu polnogo izdaniia 'Kalevaly'" in *Trudy iubileinoi nauchnoi sessii, posviashchennoi 100-letiiu polnogo izdaniia "Kalevaly"*, v–vi.
16 Olga Savich, "Osnovy natsional'noi kul'turnoi politiki v Karelo-Finskoi SSR v 1940-1945 godakh," *Vestnik Severnogo (Arkticheskogo) federal'nogo universiteta* 2 (2012): 37.
17 The poem's lack of Christian elements likely resulted from Lönnrot's conscious creative efforts; Keith Bosley, introduction to Elias Lönnrot, *The Kalevala*, trans. Keith Bosley (Oxford: Oxford University Press, 1989), xxxiii.
18 Oleg Mishin, *Puteshestvie v "Kalevalu"* (Kareliia, 1988), 120.

in] the runes of *The Kalevala*, which [predated] the suppression of humans by [other] humans that has ended once and for all in our country."[19]

Nevertheless, the monumentalization of *The Kalevala* and the immortalization of its bond to Karelia were based not solely on the poem's materialist and progressivist elements. Geopolitical circumstances also affected *The Kalevala*'s fate during the first four decades of Soviet rule, which saw Karelia's transformation into a pivotal point of a vast network of forced labor camps and its ascension on the Soviet administrative hierarchy from a borderland province to a Soviet member republic tasked with the spread of Communism to Finland. In the meantime, the Finno-centric indigenization policy led by Red Finnish leaders of Soviet Karelia heavily promoted the Finnish language at the expense of vernacular Karelian dialects. After World War II and the subsequent Finno–Soviet rapprochement, Karelia was downgraded into an autonomous republic within Russia. While Finnish gradually faded from public life in Karelia, cultural exchange between Finland and the Soviet Union was frequent and comprehensive in the post-war period. The shifting of Finno-Soviet relations and its implications on Soviet Karelia paralleled the Soviet authorities' and scholars' approach to *The Kalevala*.

The Kalevala as a Finnish Cultural Import, 1933–35

A Soviet scholar remarked during perestroika, "Throughout the past one and a half centuries, *The Kalevala* has existed in different ways—there have been pushes and pulls and periods of more and less pronounced interest in it."[20] In the 1930s, the official Soviet approach to *The Kalevala* and the poem's role in the cultural and political life in Soviet Karelia underwent significant shifts that reflected the changes in Soviet nationality policy and Finno–Soviet relations.

---

19   Elena Lopyreva, "Poema mira i truda," *Trudy iubileinoi nauchnoi sessii, posviashchennoi 100-letiiu polnogo izdaniia "Kalevaly"*, 79.
20   Eino Karhu, *"Kalevala" i nekotorye problemy ee izucheniia* (Karel'skii filial AN SSSR, Institut iazyka, literatury i istorii, 1985), 19.

The first phase of the Soviet official approach lasted from 1933 to the eve of the Winter War in 1939 and was closely associated with the Soviet linguist Dmitrii Bubrikh. Widely considered the founder of Soviet Finno–Ugric studies, Bubrikh was the first Soviet scholar who systematically studied *The Kalevala*. Trained as a linguist before the Revolution, Bubrikh dedicated three decades of his career to studying Finno–Ugric languages. After mastering Finnish, Mordovian, and Udmurt, Bubrikh visited Soviet Karelia for the first time in 1928.[21] He spent the next two decades studying Karelian dialects with the help of academic institutions in Soviet Karelia. Besides his unease with the official policy on linguistics studies and the wavering on the creation of a Karelian literary language, another noteworthy controversy in his career was his writings on *The Kalevala* in the early 1930s.

For more than a decade after Finland achieved independence, *The Kalevala* had rarely been mentioned in the Soviet press by the early 1930s. Little research had been done on the poem in Soviet academia. Bubrikh, the leading Soviet Finno–Ugrist of the time, wrote the first article on *The Kalevala* of the Soviet period, an encyclopedic entry published in 1931, in which he referred to the poem as a Finnish folk epic.[22]

In the first Soviet edition of *The Kalevala*, the words "Finnish folk epic" appeared in bigger font before the book's title. In 1935, as Finland had started preparations for the upcoming centennial of the first edition of *The Kalevala*, Soviet diplomat Ivan Maisky, who had recently spent three years in Finland serving as the Soviet ambassador, precipitated the publication of the first Soviet edition of *The Kalevala*.[23] In his preface to the book, Maisky hailed *The Kalevala* as "the greatest work of Finnish literature" in which he

---

[21] Svetlana Nagurnaia, "Rol' D. V. Bubrikha v sozdanii edinogo karel'skogo iazyka," in *Materialy nauchnoi konferentsii "Bubrikhovskie chteniia: gumanitarnye nauki na Evropeiskom Severe"*, eds. N. G. Zaitseva et al. (Petrozavodsk, Russia: Institut iazyka, literatury i istorii KarNTs RAN, 2015), 260.

[22] Bubrikh, "Kalevala" in *Literaturnaia entsiklopediia. Tom IV*, eds. Anatolii Lunacharskii et al. (Izdatel'stvo Kommunisticheskoi akademii, 1931), 54.

[23] Maisky was still the Soviet ambassador to Finland when he wrote the preface to the book on 22 May 1932. By the time the book went to print, Maiskii had been appointed the Soviet Ambassador to the United Kingdom.

found an "incredibly bright reflection" of "the sullen nature of the Finnish north" with its stunning natural beauty and "the Finnish tribe" that "created" this work "through its millennium-long development." Maisky stated, "Without knowing *The Kalevala*, it would be difficult to understand Finland, its nature, and its people. But in the meantime, it would be difficult to thoroughly understand *The Kalevala* without knowing Finland, its nature, and its people," as *The Kalevala* has "come to embody what could be called the Finnish national character." Maisky opined that it was expedient for the Soviet public to be acquainted with *The Kalevala*, because by getting to know *The Kalevala*, the Soviet public could "gain a fair idea of the character and psychology of a neighboring nation, particularly its peasant masses (*The Kalevala* is chiefly a creation of the Finnish peasantry)."[24] Maisky's Finno-centric position on *The Kalevala* concurred with that of Bubrikh, who was commissioned to write the introduction to the book.

Bubrikh reiterated the prevailing preexisting theories in his introduction to what seemed to be a politically innocuous publication of a foreign work of literature. He provided an overview of *The Kalevala*'s creation and translations, a brief appraisal of the poem's literary values, and a selected bibliography. The bibliography indicates the main theories that Bubrikh put forth in the other two segments. The bibliography encompasses five sources, three in Finnish and two in German. The Finnish sources directly focus on *The Kalevala*. These three sources were written by the same author, Finnish folklorist Kaarle Krohn.[25] Under a methodology that was simultaneously romantic nationalist and historical, Krohn and his followers perceived many linguistic, mythological, geographical, and ethnographic elements in the poem as results of historical contact between Finland and Scandinavia. Krohn's writings on *The Kalevala* remained dominant in Finnish academia when Bubrikh introduced the poem to the Soviet public. Reliance on Krohn led to Bubrikh's replication of the former's theories on the origins of the verses of *The Kalevala* and repudiation of the

---

24 Ivan Maiskii, "Predislovie," in *Finskii narodnyi epos. Kalevala*, trans. Leonid Bel'skii (Academia, 1933), vii–viii.
25 Dmitrii Bubrikh, "Iz istorii 'Kalevaly'," in *Finskii narodnyi epos. Kalevala*, xx.

poem's connection with Soviet Karelia. Like Krohn, Bubrikh seemed more interested in the etymology of the proper names and the specificities of the poem's verses than its plot twists or heroes.

Bubrikh's main arguments concerned *The Kalevala*'s ethnogeographical belonging. He believed that the roots of the poem's verses were Germanic in origin and could be traced to the period of "Finnish Vikings." Runic singing originated in Finland in the feudal period after Finland's conversion to Christianity. *The Kalevala*'s verses and stories "migrated" over time to areas of Eastern Karelia bordering Finland. Runic singing was present only in the westernmost parts of Eastern Karelia and had long become extinct by the early twentieth century. While minimizing the Christian influence on runic poetry, Bubrikh associated the emergence of this poetic genre with the rise of the feudal age and believed that it faded with the rise of bourgeois capitalism in Scandinavia. The preservation of runic poetry in some regions of Eastern Karelia was due to the region's socioeconomic backwardness instead of the spread of Christianity that antagonized pagan practices. More importantly, Bubrikh crystallized his arguments by claiming that the runes of *The Kalevala* were not "something that culturally connected the Finns and the Karelians because it is absolutely evident that their origins are not Finno-Karelian but Finnish."[26] Bubrikh resolutely rejected connections between Soviet Karelia and such a monumental work of literature but instead claimed that *The Kalevala* spread to Eastern Karelia from neighboring Finland. Besides, his perception of the cultural contact that gave rise to *The Kalevala* perpetuated the notion of Karelia as the periphery of Scandinavia, which contradicted the Soviet authorities' vision of Karelia as one of the centers of the Balto-Finnic world extending from Estonia to the Volga. Furthermore, Bubrikh denied the continued existence of rune-singing in Soviet Karelia, which contradicted later claims that such splendid folk traditions were carefully safeguarded under the patronage of the Soviet state.[27]

While rebuking *The Kalevala*'s Karelian genesis, Bukbrikh reprehended contemporary Finnish scholars by connecting his

---

26   Ibid., x–xviii.
27   Viktor Zhirmunsky, *Narodnyi geroicheskii epos* (Goslitizdat, 1962), 369–70.

critique of Finnish Karelophiles with Marxist historical materialist arguments:

> Finnish scholars [,] not without nationalist designs, searched for Finno-Karelian roots in the runes of *The Kalevala* [...] We [Soviet scholars] subject our work to a wholly different worldview. [...] Our interest in the runes of *The Kalevala* stems not only from the fact that they are Finnish but also from the fact that they represent a landmark in the arts of humankind in their given socioeconomic circumstances.²⁸

In addition to denying the Karelian roots of *The Kalevala*, Bubrikh purported to deter Finnish and Soviet scholars from obsessing over the socioeconomic background of the poem. *The Kalevala* was not the collective labor of Karelian peasants but a bourgeois creation of Viking warriors devoid of vital Socialist ideological values. Bubrikh did not extoll the heroic deeds of the heroes of *The Kalevala*, nor did he lavish attention on the symbolism of the Sampo.²⁹ It would be fair to assume that Bubrikh arrived at his conclusions regarding *The Kalevala*'s origins based not on class-oriented antagonism or ideological convictions but on empirical results from the limited body of literature at his disposal. The fact that these arguments were published indicated the authorities' approval. Furthermore, Bubrikh's resistance to the allegedly chauvinist tendencies of Soviet Karelia's Red Finnish leadership in laying claim to *The Kalevala* perfectly conformed to the official doctrines of that period, as the Red Finns of Soviet Karelia had already felt the mounting pressures from Moscow.³⁰

Nevertheless, Bubrikh spoke highly of *The Kalevala*. He suggested that besides offering the Soviet reader a snapshot of Fin-

---

28 Bubrikh, "Iz istorii 'Kalevaly,'" xvii.
29 It should be noted that Bubrikh was no friend to nationalist conceptualizations of Greater Finland popular in neighboring Finland in the interwar period. In fact, he championed the promotion of the vernacular Karelian language in Soviet Karelia when the local Red Finnish leadership propagated the primacy of the Finnish language and culture.
30 Vihavainen, "Natsional'naia politika VKP(b)/KPSS v 1920-e-1950-e gody i sud'by karel'skoi i finskoi natsional'nostei," 22–24.

land's pre-capitalist period, the poem had unique literary and artistic values, most notably in its descriptions of scenery.[31] The official approach to *The Kalevala* would change dramatically shortly after the book's publication.

Karelianizing *The Kalevala*, 1935–39

With the rapid rise of far-right leaders in Europe, Stalin's increasing preoccupations with invasions of its borderland territories, and Moscow's growing suspicions of the Red Finnish leadership of Soviet Karelia, the Soviet authorities started shifting to a new approach to *The Kalevala* in the mid-1930s. Irredentist calls, particularly ones concerning Soviet Karelia by the Academic Karelia Society, a rapidly expanding nationalist organization, persisted in Finland.[32] Stalin's growing paranoia with events unfolding in Finland not only led to efforts to promote the Karelian language in Soviet Karelia but also started the process of "indigenizing" *The Kalevala*. The epic simultaneously fueled Finnish nationalists' expansionist sentiments and became politicized in the Stalinist nation-making enterprise in Soviet Karelia.

The 1935 celebration of the centenary of the first edition of *The Kalevala* heralded the beginning of Soviet efforts to indigenize *The Kalevala*. Small concerts were organized by the regional leadership in the Uhta District, where Lönnrot had collected a substantial volume of runes (mostly after the publication of the first edition of *The Kalevala*). During the modest celebration, the Uhta District was renamed the Kalevala District. The republican press published the first Soviet Finnish-language edition of *The Kalevala* but with a humble print run.[33] Local newspapers published the

---

31   Bubrikh, "Iz istorii 'Kalevaly,'" xix–xx.
32   William R. Trotter, *A Frozen Hell: The Russo-Finnish Winter War of 1939-40* (Chapel Hill, NC: Algonquin Books of Chapel Hill, 2000), 9–10.
33   S. N. Filimonchik, "'Kalevala' v kul'turnoi zhizni sovetskoi Karelii 1930-kh gg.," in *Riabininskie chteniia–2019. Materialy VIII konferentsii po izucheniiu i aktualizatsii traditsionnoi kul'tury Russkogo Severa*, eds. T. G. Ivanova and I. V. Mel'nikov (FITs Karel'skii nauchnyi tsentr RAN, 2019), 190–91.

poem's excerpts throughout the celebration.³⁴ In late 1935, a short article by the Tiflis-born ethnic Armenian ethnographer Evgenii Kagarov published in a narrowly circulated academic journal delivered the first officially endorsed critique of the "migration theory" of *The Kalevala* runes but fell short of identifying the poem as Karelian.³⁵ In early 1937, large-scale festivals started to feature rune-singing performances to showcase the cultural heritage of Soviet Karelians.³⁶ Several scholars presented their works on *The Kalevala* at exhibitions and conferences. One of these scholars was Kagarov.³⁷

Notwithstanding his research focus on the Caucasus, under the Soviet Karelian leadership's endorsement, Kagarov completely overturned the previously dominant theories of the genesis of *The Kalevala* proposed by Bubrikh. Kagarov took a direct jab at Kaarle Krohn, claiming that the runes of *The Kalevala* had been created in the pre-feudal period before the Viking dominance and that *The Kalevala*'s creators were ordinary fishermen, hunters, and bakers rather than court warriors. Furthermore, Kagarov argued that Krohn and his followers deliberately exaggerated the feudal and Christian components in the poem to perpetuate a false narrative of a knightly Finnish national character.³⁸ By dissociating *The Ka-*

---

34 A. V. Belivanova and V. I. Kiiranen, *Bibliograficheskii ukazatel'po traditsionnomu fol'kloru KASSR za sovetskoe vremia (1917 g. – iiun' 1954 g.)* (Karel'skii filial AN SSSR, 1957), 95–96.

35 In his article, Kagarov directly criticized Bubrikh for the latter's uncritical (*bezgovorochno*) acceptance and reiteration of the Germano-centric theories of *The Kalevala* championed by Kaarle Krohn and other "bourgeois" scholars who allegedly fed into the Pan-Finnic irredentism spearhead by Finnish "fascist circles." However, Kagarov's arguments focused primarily on the similarities between the themes in *The Kalevala* and epic tales of non-Germanic peoples. While making a case for the folkloristic universality of the themes in *The Kalevala*, Kagarov did not demonstrate to what extent the poem could be considered native to Karelia; Evgenii Kagarov, "K stoletiiu 'Kalevaly'," in *Sovetskii fol'klor. Sbornik statei i materialov*, eds. Mark Azadovskii et al., no. 2-3 (Moscow: Izdatel'stvo Akademii Nauk SSSR, 1936), 21–30.

36 Filimonchik, "'Kalevala' v kul'turnoi zhizni sovetskoi Karelii 1930-kh gg.," 191.

37 The same article was subsequently reproduced in a union-wide literary journal later in the same year.

38 Evgenii Kagarov, "K stoletiiu 'Kalevaly'," *Karelo-Murmanskii krai* 3 (1935): 3–7.

levala from Finland, Kagarov and his benefactors started contemplating their response to Finnish irredentist claims towards Soviet Karelia.

In addition to dissociating *The Kalevala* from Finland, efforts were made to integrate *The Kalevala* into the incipient Karelian literature that was only fledging under the tutelage of Red Finnish émigré literati. In the mid-1930s, spearheaded by Red Finnish émigré Jalmari Virtanen, a new generation of Soviet Karelian poets started featuring the style and themes of *The Kalevala* in their writings. In 1936–37, Virtanen edited the preexisting Russian translation of *The Kalevala* and created verses using the Kalevala meter developed by Lönnrot.[39]

Apart from altering their views on the origins of *The Kalevala*, Soviet authorities also started looking more deeply into the symbolism of the Sampo in the poem. Although the few scholarly articles published in 1935 barely looked beyond the genesis of the runes of *The Kalevala*, the leader of Soviet Karelia, Edvard Gylling, proclaimed at the fifteenth anniversary of the establishment of Soviet Karelia in 1935 that the Karelian people had "found their Sampo," for which they had long yearned.[40] Two years later, the first scholarly article on the Sampo appeared in the Soviet press, albeit without touching on the magical object's spiritual associations.[41]

No in-depth study of *The Kalevala* was published between 1935 and 1940. The 1935 celebration of the poem's Centenary was considerably less extravagant than the jubilees of the poem that took place in the succeeding decades. Between late 1937 and early

---

39 Tamara Starshova, "'Kalevala' v literaturnom kontekste," *Nauka v Rossii* 4, no. 172 (June–August 2009): 84–90. Virtanen was arrested in February 1938 and perished in a Gulag the following year. After his posthumous rehabilitation, Virtanen was hailed as the first Soviet poet to "open up the Karelian theme and tune his verses according to Karelian traditions"; *Natsional'nye pisateli Karelii: Finskaia emigratsiia i politicheskie repressii 1930-kh godov. Bibliograficheskii ukazatel'*, eds. N. Prushinskaia and E. Takala (Natsional'naia biblioteka Respubliki Kareliia, 2005), 21–23.

40 S. N. Filimonchik, "Prazdnovanie 15-letiia Karel'skoi avtonomii v 1935 godu," in *Riabininskie chteniia–2019. Materialy VIII konferentsii po izucheniiu i aktualizatsii traditsionnoi kul'tury Russkogo Severa*, 171.

41 V. K. Alymov, "Chto takoe 'Sampo'," *Sovetskaia etnografiia* 1 (1937): 155–60.

1940, when the Finnish language was banned in Soviet Karelia, only one article on *The Kalevala* was published in the Soviet Union (in a regional newspaper in Soviet Karelia).[42] Nevertheless, the half-decade preceding the establishment of the Karelo-Finnish Soviet Socialist Republic (KFSSR) heralded a sea change in the official promotion of *The Kalevala* and paved the groundwork for the Soviet authorities' future efforts to entrench the poem's association with Soviet Karelia.

The Kalevala in War and Uneasy Peace, 1940–47

During the sixteen-year existence of KFSSR, the bond between *The Kalevala* and Soviet Karelia strengthened considerably. Moscow and the local leadership's nation-making efforts imbued *The Kalevala* with political messages. It was more intrinsically associated with Soviet Karelia in the public imagination than ever. Like in the preceding years, several central figures played vital roles in shaping the official discourse of the poem during this crucial period.

The first of these key figures is Kagarov. In 1940, the second Soviet Russian-language edition of *The Kalevala* was published. Kagarov, who wrote the introduction, provided the first elaborate, coherent, and mass-circulated reiteration of the now official opinions regarding *The Kalevala*'s ethnogenesis, class orientations, and chronological settings. The geopolitical backdrop and Soviet cultural policy of the time tremendously influenced the ideas Kagarov propagated. In the aftermath of the Winter War, Soviet authorities hastily attempted to restore many of the vestiges of the Soviet Finnish national culture outlawed in the late 1930s.[43] With the founding of KFSSR and the incorporation of newly annexed Finnish territories, the relations between Soviet Finns and Karelians had to be reconstructed from scratch, as the establishment of the

---

42 A. Verminskii, "'Kalevala'—karel'skii narodnyi epos," *Krasnaia Kareliia*, 14 July 1939, 3.
43 Paul M. Austin, "Soviet Karelian: The Language that Failed," *Slavic Review* 51, no. 1 (Spring 1992): 22–33.

new republic in 1940 symbolized the unification of Finns and Karelians.[44] Subsequently, *The Kalevala* was redressed along official ideological lines and refashioned as the rhetorical and literary basis of the Sovietized national character of Soviet Karelia's titular population, a source of localized patriotism, and shared heritage of all the nations inhabiting the poem's greater Soviet homeland.

There are many peculiarities concerning the 1940 Soviet edition of *The Kalevala*. Printed in November 1940, seven months after the establishment of KFSSR, the book appeared more modest than the 1933 edition. It had a smaller print run and no elaborate illustrations. Notwithstanding the book's apparent lack of visual refinement, Kagarov declared in his pithy preface that the present edition aimed at "broader masses of Soviet readers."[45] The book's front-page subheading also declared that *The Kalevala* is now a "Karelo-Finnish folk epic."

Kagarov's introduction put the final stroke in the Soviet authorities' about-face on the question of *The Kalevala*'s belonging. Kagarov affirmed that *The Kalevala* is a collective creation of the toiling masses. In Kagarov's words, even Lönnrot, who supposedly "restored" the poem, came from a humble background amid the poor common folks. However, Kagarov unequivocally denied Lönnrot's creative input. Kagarov highlighted its ethno-geographic origins by dismissing Kaarle Krohn's "bourgeois" theories. By comparing the names of the protagonists of *The Kalevala* with the names of Finnish deities recorded by sixteenth-century Finnish clergyman Mikael Agricola, Kagarov reaffirmed that the origins of the runes of *The Kalevala* lay not in Viking sagas but in Balto-Finnic settings. Subsequently, Kagarov attempted, not very effectively, to demonstrate the poem's connections with Karelia by applying Marx's historical materialist theories and highlighting the poem's pagan elements. Despite fervent accusations hauled at "Finnish chauvinists" and their visions of Finno-Ugric unity, "*The Kalevala* [is] indisputably an epic of the Karlo-Finnish people[.]

---

44 Vihavainen, "Natsional'naia politika VKP(b)/KPSS v 1920-e-1950-e gody i sud'by karel'skoi i finskoi natsional'nostei," 36–38.
45 Kagarov, "Predislovie," *Kalevala. Karelo-Finskii epos*, trans. Leonid Bel'skii (Gosudarstvennoe izdatel'stvo Karelo-Finskoi SSR, 1940), i.

The birthplace of [its] runes is both Karelia and Finland." Notwithstanding his fervent denials of the racial unity between Finns and Soviet Udmurts, Mordovians, and Maris, citing such high-level Soviet leaders as Molotov and Zhdanov, Kagarov affirmed the unity between the Finns and the Karelians and emphasized the necessity of developing the cultures of these "two kindred peoples" in one "brotherly union" through the establishment of KFSSR.

Framing his critique of Finnish nationalists' claims to *The Kalevala* in a Marxist-Leninist framework, Kagarov argued,

> We should confront bourgeois perversions with genuinely scientific Marxist-Leninist interpretations of *The Kalevala* [... and] explain the history of *The Kalevala*'s composition through its conditionality and connection with the socioeconomic structure of its settings. [...] Neither the theory of loans nor the hypothesis of Christian [influence on] Karelian folk poetry nor anti-scientific race theories [can explain] the crystallization of the runes of *The Kalevala*. Only the dialectical materialist method can solve [this] question.[46]

Kagarov also touched on the symbolism of the Sampo. The magical object, as "a source of the happiness and blessings of the people," forms the centerpiece of *The Kalevala*. Besides the Sampo, Kagarov examined the economic relations portrayed in the poem through a Marxist perspective, succinctly analyzed the family relations, marriage practices, and characteristics of matriarchy in the poem. He concluded by declaring that only Soviet power helped the Karelians realize their long-held dreams about the Sampo—an embodiment of happiness and abundance—by transforming the once impoverished Karelia into a prosperous Soviet territory.[47] Such politicized symbolism of the Sampo and its association with Soviet power in Karelia would persist until the demise of the Soviet regime. Amid the wars and upheavals in the early 1940s, the image of the Sampo projected through the Soviet press was quite belligerent.

Another important figure who participated in the reshaping of the official policy on *The Kalevala* during this period was a

---

46   Kagarov, "Kalevala kak pamiatnik mirovoi literatury," ix.
47   *Ibid.*, ix–xli.

young folklorist named Viktor Evseev. Karelian by ethnicity and of peasant background, Evseev was born and raised in Russian Karelia, where he later spent many decades teaching folklore.[48] Evseev had been a Party member since his student years in the 1920s. While he was a graduate student in Leningrad, his credence in Nicholas Marr's Japhetic theory resulted in conflicts with his adviser Bubrikh. After several stints working for Finnish-language propaganda mouthpieces, Evseev dedicated himself to the studies of Karelian folklore and traveled extensively around Karelia, often in expeditions led by Bubrikh. In 1933, Bubrikh claimed that rune-singing had long disappeared from Karelia. When Kagarov asserted in 1940 that rune-singing was not only still existent in Soviet Karelia but also protected through scholarly efforts, he went into detail listing Evseev's recent achievements in collecting Karelian runes.[49] In November 1940, days after the publication of the second Soviet Russian edition of *The Kalevala*, a collection of "Karelo-Finnish runes" edited by Evseev was published in Soviet Karelia.

Through his collection, Evseev managed to provide a coherent and persuasive insight into the ideological significance of the Sampo. The collection, titled *The Sampo*, comprises 112 runic poems unevenly divided into three parts. According to Evseev, the verses were primarily collected from the inhabitants in the southern part of Karelia, particularly from areas less traversed by Lönnrot.[50] The first part consisted of verses recounting stories and figures of *The Kalevala*. The second part consisted of *The Kalevala*-themed runes integrated into historical narratives of the Russo-Swedish struggles over the Karelian Isthmus. The third part consisted of runes exalting Lenin, Stalin, and Stakhanov and runes extolling the Bolshevik victory in the Russian Civil War, the Soviet victory over Japan in Mongolia in 1939, and the escalators in Moscow subway stations.

---

48 A. A. Ivanov, *Pisateli sovetskoi Karelii. Spravochnik* (Gosudarstvennoe izdatel'stvo Karel'skoi ASSR, 1959), 38–39.
49 Kagarov, "Kalevala kak pamiatnik mirovoi literatury," xl–xli.
50 Viktor Evseev, "Karelo-finskie runy" in *Sampo. Sbornik karelo-finskikh run*, ed. V. Evseev (Gosizdat Karelo-Finskoi SSR, 1940), vi.

These politically charged runes fit perfectly into the thematic patterns of the so-called Soviet folklore, a widespread genre of politicized, pro-regime, most lyrical literature based on folk oral literary motifs. Between the late 1920s and the mid-1950s, all Soviet member republics published similar collections of Soviet folklore purportedly collected from their titular populations. As Margaret Schlauch has pointed out, in the 1930s, the Soviet government, through publications like *The Sampo*, asserted to the Soviet public and international community that folklore in the Soviet Union was not only "not a dying art," but was undergoing a "veritable renaissance" and "creatively transforming" into new themes in various genres, despite "prophecies" about the "decline and extinction of epic forms."[51] In his introduction to *The Sampo*, Evseev implied to what extent the runes in his collection were edited or fabricated, reasoning, "Whenever the necessity to merge old and new runes emerged, it was inevitable to make mistakes." It is not unfathomable that these "new runes" were created not by the Karelian folk but by pro-regime elites like Evseev acting under official imperatives.

By establishing a folkloric connection between the image of the Sampo and the Soviet regime's political agendas, Evseev helped to perpetuate the Sampo as a lyricized image of the Sovietized national character of the titular population of KFSSR. In his introduction, Evseev provided a poignant discourse about the quest of the heroes of Kaleva to steal the Sampo from Pohjola. According to Evseev, the Sampo is a means of production that churns out products that could benefit the common folks. While the evil matriarch of Pohjola refuses to relinquish it, the Sampo only benefits one person. In contrast, in trying to steal the Sampo and take it back to their native Kaleva, Väinämöinen, Ilmarinen, and Lemminkäinen try to turn the personal benefit of the Sampo into collective benefit for their community. To place this metaphor in the Soviet context, the goal of the Karelo-Finnish people's struggle for their new Sampo was the triumph of Socialism over the self-serving bourgeois-aristocratic order.

---

51 Margaret Schlauch, "Folklore in the Soviet Union," *Science and Society* 8, no. 3 (Summer 1944): 219.

When the book was published in late 1940 under the looming specter of an all-out war, the image of the Sampo was also embedded in the context of defense and military buildup. In Evseev's words, the core value of the Karelo-Finnish epic lay in "its dream about the magical Sampo, which brings forth the joy of all people" and was now guiding Stalin to the warfront.[52] Many verses in Evseev's collection echoed these sentiments of an imminent war.[53] Shortly after the Soviet victory in World War II, a new collection of Karelian runes of similar themes was published. In his preface to the book, Evseev evoked the Sampo in the context of World War II, during which Karelian Red Army servicemen composed new [runes], in which they expressed confidence that the people's Ilmarinen—the Red Army—"would soon restore the Sampo that had sustained damages wrought by German invaders."[54]

Besides promoting the official discourse of the Sampo, Evseev joined the efforts to "indigenize" *The Kalevala*. Unlike many non-Karelian Soviet scholars, Evseev focused on Kaarle Krohn's theories by emphasizing the influences of Russian *bylinas* on *The Kalevala*.[55] These endeavors aimed to promote ties between the Karelians and Russians and manifested the Karelians' loyalty to the Soviet cause in the post-war years.[56] As is noticeable in Evseev's pseudo-academic enterprises, the end of the war and the Finno-Soviet rapprochement did not halt Soviet efforts to "indigenize" *The Kalevala*. The "indigenization" of *The Kalevala* reached its climax in 1949 when the centennial of the publication of the poem's

---

52   Evseev, "Karelo-finskie runy," v–ix.
53   Here is an example of such a poem: "And when the war comes,/We will defend the Sampo./We will be able to defeat the enemy/And we can fire at him.../We will not surrender the Sampo—/The Sampo of Communism"; *Sampo. Sbornik karelo-finskikh run*, ed. Evseev, 169. This war-related theme likely inspired the 1944 opera *The Sampo* by Soviet composer Leonid Vishkarev; O. A. Bochkareva, *Kompozitory Karelii. Spravochnik* (Ministerstvo Kul'tury KASSR, 1975), 10–11.
54   Evseev, "Predislovie," in *Runy i istoricheskie pesni*, ed. Evseev (Gosudarstvennoe izdatel'stvo KFSSR, 1946), 6.
55   Viktor Evseev, *Istoricheskie osnovy karelo-finskogo eposa. Kniga 1* (Izdatel'stvo Akademii nauk SSSR, 1957), 3–57.
56   Viktor Evseev, "Istoricheskaia druzhba karel i russkikh v otrazhenii pozdnikh versii karelo-finskikh run," *Sovetskaia etnografiia* 2 (1949): 27–34.

second edition was celebrated in the Soviet Union. It would be impossible to discuss the 1949 Jubilee without discussing the role of Otto Kuusinen, the Jubilee's chief organizer and nominal leader of Soviet Karelia throughout the region's existence as a Soviet republic.

The Kalevala and Its Patron Otto Kuusinen, 1949–56

Kuusinen's identity was manifold. The 1953 edition of *The Great Soviet Encyclopedia* describes him as "a prominent figure of the Communist Party and the Soviet state."[57] However, this statement completely overlooks Kuusinen's involvement in literature, particularly the monumentalization of *The Kalevala* in the Soviet Union.

Born and raised in Finland, where he received his doctorate in philosophy and was later elected deputy of the Sejm, Kuusinen defected to Soviet Russia in 1918 after the Reds' defeat in the Finnish Civil War. From the early 1920s to the outbreak of the Winter War in November 1939, Kuusinen served as a leader of the Comintern, where he was involved in Soviet efforts to spread Communism to Finland and Scandinavia. Thanks to his absence in Soviet Karelia, he was spared from the Great Terror that swept away most of the region's Red Finnish leaders. On 1 December 1939, one day after the outbreak of the Winter War, Stalin installed Kuusinen, the most prominent Finn in the Soviet apparatus, as leader of the newly created Finnish Democratic Republic, a Soviet-backed puppet state in Finnish Karelia. After the end of the Winter War and subsequent abolition of the puppet state he headed, Kuusinen was appointed leader of KFSSR and eventually made it to the Politburo. As the leader of the short-lived Soviet member republic from beginning to end, Kuusinen, under both Stalin and Khrushchev, demonstrated the two key qualities that William Trotter ascribes to him—dexterity in Marxist-Leninist discourse

---

57 *Bol'shaia sovetskaia entsiklopediia. Vtoroe izdanie. 24, Kukuruza-Lesnichestvo*, eds. B. A. Vvedenskii *et al.* (Gosudarstvennoe izdatel'stvo "Bol'shaia sovetskaia entsiklopediia," 1953), 149–50.

and ability to ingratiate himself with the central leadership.[58] This was testified by his role in the 1949 Jubilee. His professional knowledge of literary history and intimate familiarity with the contemporary Finnish political and literary scene helped him tremendously.

Kuusinen's contact with Finland might have compelled him to make the Jubilee as extravagant as it was. As early as June 1947, ten months before the Finno–Soviet Treaty, preparations for the Jubilee were already underway in Soviet Karelia.[59] As the Jubilee's chief instigator, Kuusinen headed a Jubilee Committee created in April 1948, which included some of the most distinguished Soviet literary scholars and Finno-Ugrists but conspicuously excluded Bubrikh.[60] Later that year, the KFSSR press started publishing Karelian runes for the Jubilee. According to recently uncovered archival records, Kuusinen deliberately scheduled the Jubilee Gala on the weekend before the actual date of the centenary considering the schedule of similar events in neighboring Finland.[61]

Apart from folk musical concerts, lectures and speeches were given at the meeting, including by Soviet Armenian literary critic Marietta Shahinyan (Shaginyan), who declared:

> Many years have passed since the birth of the ancient runes that sang about the nature of the country of Kaleva [...], which used to be a marshland [but has now] become a granary [after] being drained and turned into fertile arable lands. Next to the old illiterate storyteller Tatyana Perttunen—granddaughter of the famous storyteller who chanted his runes to Lönnrot, we see her granddaughter—a cheerful girl who received higher education thanks to Soviet power. A group of Karelo-Finnish writers traveled at the same time [...] to places where *The Kalevala*'s runes originated,

---

58   William R. Trotter, *A Frozen Hell: The Russo-Finnish Winter War of 1939-40* (Chapel Hill, NC: Algonquin Books of Chapel Hill, 2000), 58.
59   Ekaterina Evseeva, "Bor'ba za 'Kalevalu'," *Internet-zhurnal Litsei*, https://gazeta-licey.ru/culture/75779-borba-za-kalevalu (accessed 19 April 2022).
60   Kirill Chistov, "Vospominaniia o moem pervom direktore," in *D. V. Bubrikh: K 100-letiiu so dnia rozhdeniia. Sbornik statei*, ed. Georgii Kert (Nauka, 1992), 89–97.
61   Ekaterina Evseeva, "Bor'ba za 'Kalevalu'," *Internet-zhurnal Litsei*, 28 February 2019, https://gazeta-licey.ru/culture/75779-borba-za-kalevalu (accessed 19 April 2022).

saw beautiful highways, power stations, wind stations, ambulance stations, [and] schools, all rebuilt from the damages caused by the war [...] Runes are now sung by the new Sampo—the hydroelectric power station. The Karelo-Finnish people's dream about the joy- and prosperity-yielding Sampo has come true. But only in our new system [...] has this been possible [...].[62]

Kuusinen's enterprise aimed at conveying to the Soviet public that *The Kalevala* was not only a work of folk literature but also a repository of progressive ideas. Because of its progressive components, *The Kalevala* belonged to the Soviet people, not the Finnish bourgeoisie, since the fundamental difference between the KFSSR and Finland lay in their political systems.[63]

On 25 February 1949, nine days after the Jubilee Gala in Moscow, celebratory events started in KFSSR. A concert of philharmonic and dance performances followed Kuusinen's inaugural speech.[64] In the next ten days, nearly a dozen distinguished Soviet scholars, including Bubrikh and Evseev, gave speeches on *The Kalevala*, followed by theatrical performances, exhibitions, and conferences on and related to the poem.

During the Jubilee, the local press circulated a booklet to acquaint the local public with *The Kalevala*. It declared that Karelo-Finnish toilers had long yearned for "the completion of the new Sampo" and that Jubilee provided a platform to honor the "poetic genius of the Karelo-Finnish people" and the rune-singers that had kept intact the "faith in the advent of the joyful era" of abundance, happiness, and freedom.[65] Like the 1937 Rustaveli Jubilee in Georgia and the 1939 David of Sassoun Jubilee in Armenia, the 1949 Jubilee of *The Kalevala* seemed like a christening for the newly created KFSSR. Kuusinen set the triumphant tone not only for the celebration but also for the anti-capitalist/anti-Finland

---

62 Marietta Shaginian, *Kalevala (Karelo-finskii epos)* (Izdatel'stvo "Pravda," 1949), 27–28.
63 Vihavainen, "Natsional'naia politika VKP(b)/KPSS v 1920-e-1950-e gody i sud'by karel'skoi i finskoi natsional'nostei," 38–39.
64 *Programma kontserta, posvyashchennogo 100-letiiu "Kalevaly" v Teatre Russkoi dramy 25 fevralia 1949 goda.*
65 Kirill Chistov, *"Kalevala"—velikii epos Karelo-finskogo naroda* (Gosudarstvennoe izdatel'stvo Karelo-Finskoi SSR, 1949), 31–32.

narrative about *The Kalevala* from the Soviet scholars who participated in these events.[66]

At the inaugural session of the celebration, Kuusinen sent his regards to Stalin on behalf of all participants in the meeting by declaring:

> The entire Soviet population is celebrating the Centenary of *The Kalevala* as an extraordinary holiday of the Karelo-Finnish culture [that is] Socialist in content, national in form, as a living testimony that the Socialist system does not extinguish but strengthens and develops the best national traditions [...] In their dreams for a better future [and] strivings to improve their lot, the [Karelo-Finnish people] created an embodiment [of their aspirations]—the Sampo [...] Only the [October] Revolution [...] lifted the repressed Karelian people from the dismal sufferings in the bourgeois serf-owning system and enlisted them to the building of Socialism [...] The free and happy Karelo-Finnish people are [now] composing songs about the new Sampo by infusing into these songs the joy of the triumph [...] over the [bourgeois] system [and] the joy of life that the [October] Revolution has brought [...].[67]

Later at the meeting, Kuusinen made more explicit critiques of his native Finland while delivering another blow at the theories of *The Kalevala*'s genesis once championed by Bubrikh. Kuusinen charged:

> As is well known, almost all folk poems that formed *The Kalevala* were recorded in the territory of our KFSSR [...] In Finland, some bourgeois folklorists undertook desperate attempts to prove that [...] *The Kalevala* was the creation not of the people but of the aristocracy [...] Reactionary folklorists [claimed that] the runes of *The Kalevala* [...] originated in Western Finland [...] and later [somehow] "emigrated" to Russian Karelia.

Kuusinen framed his harshest critique of the contemporary Finnish "reaction" along the lines of the Soviet discourse of *The Kalevala* that he himself was shaping and promoting. He declared,

> Apologists of the reaction are [...] perverting the whole spirit of *The Kalevala* [...] Finnish reactionaries [...] are still trying to disguise the heroes of

---

66   Chistov, "Vospominaniia o moem pervom direktore," 172–73.
67   "Pis'mo tovarishchu I. V. Stalinu ot uchastnikov torzhestvennogo zasedaniia, posviashchennogo 100-letiiu polnogo izdaniia 'Kalevaly'," in *Trudy iubileinoi nauchnoi sessii, posviashchennoi 100-letiiu polnogo izdaniia "Kalevaly"*, v–vi.

The Kalevala under the masks of Western Finnish pirates and interpret the profound humanism of The Kalevala as the barbarian spirit of the Vikings [...] The heroes of The Kalevala personify the [Karelian] people's greatest aspirations and ideals–their yearning for progress and culture. Precisely because of that, the poetry of The Kalevala distinguishes itself through its progressive orientation [and] is so close and dear to our Soviet people.[68]

By hyperbolizing the Karelian roots of a work of literature that had officially been labeled as Finnish only recently, Kuusinen not only attempted to highlight the Soviet state's disingenuous patronage of culture and self-proclaimed commitment to the development of the borderlands but also tried to juxtapose the ideals promoted in Soviet Karelia with those prevalent in capitalist Finland, since Soviet Karelia was intended to be Finland's Socialist antithesis.

This official position regarding The Kalevala undoubtedly had implications for Bubrikh. After being spared from the Great Terror, Bubrikh survived the war and the siege of his home city, Leningrad. This, however, did not spare him from more public humiliation during the 1949 Jubilee, most likely instigated by Kuusinen. Albeit excluded from the Committee, Bubrikh was the first scholar to address the assembly at the Jubilee. He argued that "the problem of the ethnic belonging of the runes should be solved based on modern Marxist ethnogenetic theories."[69] One month before the beginning of the Jubilee, Bubrikh published an atonement of his previous theory of The Kalevala's ethnogenesis in the republican monthly of Soviet Karelia. In his article, titled "About a Gross Mistake of Mine," Bubrikh "renounced" his introduction to the 1933 Soviet edition of The Kalevala by declaring: "I unreservedly admit my mistake. I sternly denounce it. Through research, I have refuted it for a long time."[70] In his speech, Bubrikh rejected

---

68 Otto Kuusinen, "Doklad predsedatelia Prezidiuma Verkhovnogo soveta Karelo-Finskoi SSR O. V. Kuusinena na torzhestvennom zasedanii v Petrozavodske, posviashchennom 100-letiiu polnogo izdaniia 'Kalevaly,' 25 fevralia 1949 g." in *Trudy iubileinoi nauchnoi sessii, posviashchennoy 100-letiiu polnogo izdaniia "Kalevaly,"* 1–4.
69 Chistov, "100-letie polnogo izdaniia Karelo-Finskogo narodnogo eposa 'Kalevala,'" *Sovetskaia etnografiia* 2 (1949): 152.
70 Bubrikh, "Ob odnoi moei gruboi oshibke," *Na rubezhe* 1 (1949): 121–22.

the theory of *The Kalevala*'s Finnish genesis with two linguistic and etymological arguments. Based on apparent etymological connections between the names of *The Kalevala*'s heroes and the deities recorded by Agricola in the sixteenth century, Bubrikh claimed that all the poem's main heroes originated from Karelian mythology. Although Bubrikh might have genuinely reversed his theories based on empirical evidence, pressures from Kuusinen likely forced Bubrikh to publicly denounce his mistakes in the spotlight of the Jubilee sixteen years after he wrote his article. Other scholars who spoke at the Jubilee also dealt blows at Bubrikh.

Soviet folklorist Viktor Zhirmunskii spoke about *The Kalevala*'s ethnogenesis. He claimed that the Jubilee placed before Soviet folklorists the paramount task of reinforcing the "right interpretation" of the poem as opposed to the "false reactionary theories" promoted by "Finnish bourgeois nationalists."[71] He effectively summarized the three arguments that Soviet scholarship was attempting to refute. The corresponding counterarguments were precisely the central ideas promoted by Kuusinen and his comrades:

> (1) *The Kalevala* is a folk epic created by the peasant community in the pre-Christian and pre-feudal period, not by Vikings or aristocratic warriors in the feudal period;
> (2) The stories of *The Kalevala* stem from traditional "Karelo-Finnish" mythology and are free from Christian, Germanic, Scandinavian, and Western Finnish influences; and
> (3) The runes of *The Kalevala* originated in Karelia, not in Western Finland, and never "migrated" westward until they were collected and compiled by Lönnrot.

An expert in Germanic folklore, Zhirmunskii had spent years in wartime evacuation in Tashkent, where he became acquainted with the rich Central Eurasian oral literary traditions. By comparison, the pioneers of the so-called Finnish school that

---

71   Viktor Zhirmunskii, "'Kalevala' i finskaia burzhuaznaia fol'kloristika," in *Trudy iubileinoi nauchnoi sessii, posviashchennoi 100-letiiu polnogo izdaniia "Kalevaly,"* 80.

Zhirmunskii was attacking, Julius and Kaarle Krohn, approached *The Kalevala* primarily through a nineteenth-century Western European scholarly lens. Zhirmunsky resorted to Turkic oral epics known to few European scholars and abandoned the previously dominant Eurocentrism in the studies of heroic epics. In the immense repository of oral epics uncovered by Soviet scholars, it would not have been difficult to find parallels to the characters and stories of *The Kalevala*.

Zhirmunskii's critique of the Finnish academia paled in comparison to the torrid diatribe delivered by Shahinyan, who accused Finnish academia of upholding "fascist positions" and creating "worthless subterfuges" to "pervert and destroy" *The Kalevala*.[72] Other speakers at the Jubilee criticized the Finnish scholarship on *The Kalevala* using similar arguments but without criticizing Bubrikh.[73] They alleged that Finnish pretensions to *The Kalevala* stemmed from bourgeois notions of the superiority of Finnish culture vis-à-vis the culture of their Russian Karelian brethren.[74]

The herculean organizational and scholarly efforts that Kuusinen put into the Jubilee were not simply a political stunt. The Jubilee helped *The Kalevala* reach a broader public in the Soviet Union and enriched the poem through the publication of scholarly articles and new translations into languages of Soviet nations. New editions of the poem were published. Kuusinen himself also rewrote the whole poem in Finnish. Between 1949 and 1956, Kuusinen encouraged Soviet Karelian writers to create "new" poetry based on excerpts of *The Kalevala*, with which many happily complied. These "new" works of poetry were often paraded in the local state-owned press as "folk versions of epic tales," as if their authors had collected their materials from folk settings. Even after the abolition of the KFSSR and his subsequent relocation to Mos-

---

[72] Shaginian, *Kalevala (Karelo-finskii epos)*, 7.
[73] Armas Äikiä, "Velikii poeticheskii pamiatnik karelo-finskogo naroda," in *Trudy iubileinoi nauchnoi sessii, posviashchennoi 100-letiiu polnogo izdaniia "Kalevaly,"* 55.
[74] Josef Sykiäinen, "Poeziia truda v runakh 'Kalevaly'," in *Trudy iubileinoi nauchnoi sessii, posviashchennoi 100-letiiu polnogo izdaniia "Kalevaly,"* 40.

cow, Kuusinen, as a member of the Academy of Sciences, continued his research on *The Kalevala*. As a political leader with a penchant for literature, Kuusinen consolidated the connections of *The Kalevala* to Soviet Karelia both in the official narrative and in the public imagination. Thanks to *The Kalevala*'s recent surge in popularity among the population of Soviet Karelia, state-sponsored artists and performers took over the role of politicians or scholars in promoting the poem in the following decades.

The Kalevala after Its Indigenization, 1956–91

Despite the downgrading of Soviet Karelia in the Soviet administrative hierarchy and the cultural assimilation of the region's Finnic population, *The Kalevala* continued to shape Karelia's cultural profile in the last three and a half decades as an autonomous republic within Soviet Russia. Efforts were made to collect *The Kalevala*-inspired runes from across Soviet regions with significant Finnic populations. Another jubilee of *The Kalevala*—the 150th anniversary of its first edition—was celebrated in 1985, albeit with considerably less fanfare.

The assimilation of *The Kalevala* into the identity of Soviet Karelia also took place in the public sphere. In the 1960s–1970s, many streets, libraries, and cinemas in Soviet Karelia were given names related to *The Kalevala*, its main heroes, and rune-singers who contributed to Lönnrot's compilation of the poem. The most noteworthy events concerning *The Kalevala* in this period concerned art and theater, as many musical and theatrical productions of *The Kalevala* were released and performed in the Soviet Union and Finland.

Thanks to the less repressive political atmosphere in the Soviet Union in this period, some controversies that the authorities had previously suppressed emerged from obscurity. As can be seen in Bubrikh's fate, the officially promoted views of *The Kalevala* were not without controversies. Some of these controversies, however questionable, were never openly challenged. One controversial theory was quietly disseminated by the Soviet press years after the demise of Kuusinen and the theory's proponent.

The controversy first surfaced during the 1949 Jubilee. One of the most revered Soviet folklorists, Vladimir Propp, was invited by Kuusinen to deliver a speech on *The Kalevala*, in which Propp sternly rejected the notion that *The Kalevala* was a folk epic and claimed that it was instead a work of literature by Lönnrot. Propp's affirmation of Lönnrot's authorship of *The Kalevala*, evident as it may seem to many, touched a sensitive nerve of Kuusinen, who ensured that Propp's speech was not to appear in the collection of Jubilee speeches, published in 1950.[75] In the mid-1970s, the text of Propp's speech was published in the Soviet press. Propp stated an obvious fact that could severely discredit Kuusinen's efforts to cement the popular perception of *The Kalevala* as the creation of the Karelian people.

Contrary to the prevailing official notion that Lönnrot "collected and compiled" a folk epic that had come into existence long before his time, Propp argued that *The Kalevala* was an "artificial compendium" created not by the ordinary Karelians but rather by Lönnrot, who, in Propp's opinion, was faithful to neither "the rules and norms of folklore" nor Karelian literary traditions, but instead subjected the collection of folk poetry to the romantic nationalist demands of the nineteenth century. This explained *The Kalevala*'s "immense popularity" following its publication because Lönnrot correctly "surmised the aesthetic demands of the educated readers of his time." Therefore, the publication of *The Kalevala* was not an achievement of the Finnish (or Karelian) people but Lönnrot's success in "showing the whole world that the nation to which he belonged was not an empty geographic understanding, but one that owns a unique, unparalleled, breathtaking treasure of folk creation." *The Kalevala* in Lönnrot's creation came to belong to the people in the sense that "Pushkin was a people's poet" and that every nation is proud of its great national poets and their works.[76]

---

75 Mishin, "'Kalevala' Eliasa Lennrota: Ot fol'klornoi poezii k literaturnoi poeme," in *"Kalevala" v kontekste regional'noi i mirovoi kul'tury*, eds. I. Iu. Vinokurova *et al.* (Karel'skii nauchnyi tsentr RAN, 2010), 24–25.

76 Vladimir Propp, *Fol'klor i deistvitel'nost'* (Glavnaia redaktsiia vostochnoi literatury izdatel'stva, 1976), 304–06.

By labeling Lönnrot as a people's poet and *The Kalevala* as his creation, Propp refuted the legitimacy of monumentalizing *The Kalevala* in Soviet Karelia. If Lönnrot had been a national poet the way Pushkin was a Russian national poet, the ethnonational qualifier of Lönnrot's accolades could have only been Finnish, as opposed to Karelo-Finnish or Karelian, because Lönnrot, a Swedish-speaking Finn, had no Karelian lineage and never lived in Russian Karelia.

Propp was aware of the controversial nature of his views. He suggested that fellow Soviet scholars venture beyond *The Kalevala* and that more attention be directed to the studies of Karelian runes recorded before and after Lönnrot to truly understand and promote the Karelian literary heritage. These suggestions were also informed by Propp's perception of the inaccuracies of the ethnographic elements in *The Kalevala*. The Soviet scholarly opinions supporting Propp's thesis surfaced in the press only in the mid-1980s.[77] However, they often fell short of explicitly crediting Lönnrot as the creator of *The Kalevala*.[78] At the onset of glasnost, Propp's assertion reflected the general trends in Soviet scholarship that were increasingly inclined to view the poem as a work of literature inspired by folklore rather than a genuinely folk creation. Official press releases about *The Kalevala* variously alluded to Lönnrot as the poem's creator who based his work on Karelian runes,[79] the poem's co-author who benefited from considerable input from illiterate Karelian rune-singers,[80] or the person who

---

[77] Sergei Azbelev, "Epopeia i narodnaia tsiklizatsiia epicheskikh pesen," in *"Kalevala"—Pamiatnik mirovoi kul'tury. Materialy nauchnoi konferentsii, posviashchennoi 150-letiiu pervogo izdaniia karelo-finskogo eposa*, ed. E. Karhu (Kareliia, 1986), 82–88.

[78] Viktor Evseev, *Karelo-finskii narodnyi epos, Kniga 1* (Izdatel'skaia firma "Vostochnaia literatura" RAN, 1994), 9. The text is dated 1989. However, Evseev died in 1986. At the very beginning of the text Evseev mentions the 150th anniversary of the first edition of *The Kalevala*.

[79] "K 150-letiiu pervogo izdaniia 'Kalevaly'. Tvorenie narodnogo dukha," *Literaturnaia gazeta* 10 (5024), 6 March 1985, 1.

[80] Iurii Surovtsev, "Dobrye ruki eposa," *Literaturnaia gazeta* 9 (5023), 27 February 1985, 5.

bridged the chasm between ancient Karelian folk creations and modern literary standards.[81]

Conclusion

Post-Soviet Karelia is now Russia's only autonomous republic where Russian is the sole official language. The lack of a titular language is due as much to the ambiguous status of the Karelian language as to the low share of Karelians in the region's population. Nevertheless, reminders of The Kalevala are ubiquitous. An enormous portrait of Väinämöinen adorns Petrozavodsk's main cinema. Crystal-clear water gushes out of a fountain with a portrait of Lönnrot at a park named after The Kalevala in the city's center. Copies of The Kalevala are displayed in every ethnographic museum across the region. In the Kalevala District, where the first anniversary of The Kalevala was held in 1935, a theme park named "The Land of The Kalevala" entices visitors with sculptures of the poem's heroes and a giant windmill dubbed as the Sampo. Even though few inhabitants of post-Soviet Karelia have read The Kalevala, the poem is now inseparable from the region's identity. Ironically, this is a legacy not of Lönnrot but of Kuusinen and his fellow Communist bureaucrats who ingrained The Kalevala in the identity of Soviet Karelia.

---

81 Eino Karhu, "Vkhodnoi bilet v budushchee," *Literaturnaia gazeta* 9 (5023), 27 February 1985, 5.

ABOUT THE GUEST EDITORS

MICHÈLE KNODT is Professor of Political Science, Jean Monnet Chair (ad personam) and Director of the Jean Monnet Centre of Excellence "EU in Global Dialogue" (CEDI), Director of the Jean Monnet Centre of Excellence "EU@School," Co-leader of the DFG Research Training Group "Critical Infrastructures." She serves as Research Area Leader of the Cluster Project "Clean Circles" and PI in the Kopernikus Project "Ariadne—Evidence-Based Assessment for the Design of the German Energy System Transformation" and leader of smaller cooperative and interdisciplinary projects. She has published widely on the EU, is especially interested in energy and climate governance and has received research grants from the German Federal Ministry of Education and Research (BMBF), German Federal Ministry of Economic Affairs and Energy (BMWi), the German Research Council (DFG), the Volkswagen Foundation and the European Commission.

MAKSYM YAKOVLYEV is Head of the Department of International Relations, and Director of School for Policy Analysis at the National University of Kyiv-Mohyla Academy (NaUKMA), where he has also taught in the Department of Political Science, Department of Sociology, Kyiv-Mohyla School of Public Administration, School of Public Health. In autumn 2021 Dr Yakovlyev became member of the Public Council of the Ministry of Foreign Affairs of Ukraine. He completed his BA in social work, MA (with distinctions) from NaUKMA and PhD in politics (2010). He has been a visiting scholar at the University of Oxford, Friedrich-Schiller University of Jena, University of Maastricht, University of Geneva, and taught at Corvinus University in Budapest, Comenius University of Bratislava, University of Helsinki, and Glasgow University. His research focuses on social science concepts, post-socialist social and cultural transformations, Ukrainian identity, the Donbas region, and (post)modern Russian imperialism. After the military invasion of Ukraine, Dr Yakovlyev decided to stay in Kyiv. As an IERES Fellow, he will pursue a research project titled "Challenging the Weltbild of International World Order: Impact of the Russian-Ukrainian War on the Discourses of International Relations and Security."

KATERYNA ZAREMBO (PhD) is an Associate Fellow of the New Europe Center (Ukraine) and a non-resident fellow at Center for East European and International Studies (ZOiS, Germany). Previously, she taught at the Technical University of Darmstadt, Central European University in Vienna, and National University of Kyiv-Mohyla Academy. Her research interests are at the nexus of civil society and security studies. Her articles, focused on Ukraine's civil society role in defence and security as well as Ukraine's European integration, have appeared in, among other outlets, *Cooperation and Conflict, Media, War and Conflict, European Societies, Problems of Post-Communism, European Security*, and the *Kyiv-Mohyla Law and Politics Journal*. Her most recent book *The Ukrainian Sunrise*, dedicated to civil society movements in Ukraine's East before the 2014 Russian invasion, was published by Academic Studies Press in fall 2024.

About the Contributors

AADNE AASLAND is a Research Professor at the Norwegian Institute for Urban and Regional Research (NIBR), OsloMet—Oslo Metropolitan University. He has conducted research on Ukraine since 2008; in projects on decentralisation and local democracy (with the Association of Ukrainian Cities), and on regional diversity (with Karazin Kharkiv National University). Aasland was the project leader of the international ARDU project—The Accommodation of Regional Diversity in Ukraine (2018–2021). Since 2022 Aasland has been the leader of UKRAINETT, a Norwegian network for research on Ukraine.

DIEGO BENNING WANG is a historian of the Caucasus, Armenia, Central Asia, and the Russian North in the modern period. Benning Wang received a PhD in History from Princeton University, an MA in Regional Studies from the Harriman Institute of Russian, Eurasian, and Eastern European Studies at Columbia University, and a BA in Russian and Slavic Studies from New York University.

OLEKSANDRA DEINEKO is a Senior Researcher at the Norwegian Institute for Urban and Regional Research (NIBR), OsloMet—Oslo Metropolitan University (Norway) and an Associate Professor at School Sociology V.N. Karazin Kharkiv National University (Ukraine). She holds a PhD in Sociology (2015). The field of her research is focused on social cohesion, Ukrainian studies, identity, trust, civil activism and migration. Since Russia's full-scale invasion of Ukraine, Oleksandra is studying social transformations occurred in Ukrainian society under the war.

THOMAS FETZER is Associate Professor at Central European University Vienna, Department of International Relations. His current research deals with the role of ideas in the international political economy, with a specific focus on (economic) nationalism, as well as the relationship between international political economy and security studies. Moreover, he is also involved in projects addressing the significance of history and memory politics for International Relations, with particular emphasis on the recent transformations unleashed by the Russo-Ukrainian war.

OLENA KHYLKO, PhD., is a Researcher at the Institute of European Studies and IR, Faculty of Social and Economic Sciences at Comenius University in Bratislava. Previously she worked as Associate Professor at the Institute of International Relations at Taras Shevchenko University of Kyiv. Her research interests include politics and security in the Eastern European region, IR and geopolitics, and postcolonial studies. Dr Khylko has also combined her academic activity with work for Ukrainian and Slovak think tanks where she contributed with research and overseeing initiatives related to Ukraine and Eastern Europe. She is the author of a number of academic articles, a monograph, and policy papers.

IAN MANNERS is a Professor in the Department of Political Science at Lund University. His research is on the European Union's normative power in planetary politics, examining the symbioses between planetary economy, society, ecology, conflict, and polity. He specializes in EU freedom and social solidarity (economy), EU human rights and equality (society), EU sustainable development and climate change (ecology), EU sustainable peace and rule of law (conflict), and EU democracy and good governance (polity). Prior to joining Lund University, he has previously worked at the University of Copenhagen, Roskilde University, the Danish Institute for International Studies, Malmö University, University of Kent, Swansea University, and the University of Bristol.

KULSHAT MEDEUOVA is an Associate Professor in the Department of Philosophy at the L. N. Gumilyov Eurasian National University in Astana. Her research interests include philosophy of culture, philosophical anthropology, philosophy of the city, and memory studies. She is editor of the books *Practices and Memory Places in Kazakhstan* (2019), and *Anthropology of Morality: Discourses and Everyday Practices in Modern Kazakhstan* (2015), and author of chapters on Astana architecture, decolonial approach, and radical memorization in Kazakhstan in the edited volumes, *Kazakhstan in the Labyrinths of Postcolonial Discourse* (2023); *Postcolonial Approaches in Kazakhstan and Beyond* (2024); and *Encountering Toponymic Geopolitics: Place Names as a Political Instrument in the Post-Soviet States* (2022).

ULBOLSYN SANDYBAYEVA is an Associate Professor in the Department of Philosophy at the L. N. Gumilyov Eurasian National University in Astana. Her research interests include social philosophy, memory studies, and cultural studies. She is the author of chapters in the books *Practices and Memory Places in Kazakhstan* (2019), *Processes of Commemoration in the Modern Culture of Kazakhstan* (2019), *Northern Kazakhstan as a Region of Political Repression and Deportations of the Peoples of the USSR* (2017), *Anthropology of Morality: Discourses and Everyday Practices in Modern Kazakhstan* (2015), and of articles on the study of places of memory in Kazakhstan, infrastructure of memory in Kazakhstan, including traumatic memory, museums of Kazakhstan representing space.

GALYNA SOLOVEI is a Doctor of Philosophy and Philosophy of History, and an Associate Professor of the Department of International Relations of the National University "Kyiv-Mohyla Academy." She has been a visiting professor at the University of Amsterdam, the University of Carlos 3, and the University of Comillas in Madrid. She was part of projects to implement courses in violent conflict analysis in the curriculum of the Kyiv-Mohyla Academy (2020–2023) and an academic advisor to the New York Model United Nations Club (2020–2023). She is participating in the "Challenges and Opportunities for EU Heritage Diplomacy in Ukraine" research project studying the identity changes of Ukrainian students since the start of the Russian war in Ukraine.

ibidem.eu